Explore

NELLES

CW00543473

MALDIVES

Authors:
Christian Mietz, Claus-Peter Stoll

An up-to-date travel guide with 148 color photos
and 10 maps

First Edition
1999

Dear Reader: Being up-to-date is the main goal of the Nelles series. Our correspondents help keep us abreast of the latest developments in the travel scene, while our cartographers see to it that maps are also kept completely current. However, as the travel world is constantly changing, we cannot guarantee that all the information contained in our books is always valid. Should you come across a discrepancy, please contact us at: Nelles Verlag, Schleissheimer Str. 371 b, 80935 Munich, Germany, tel. (089) 3571940, fax. (089) 35719430, e-mail: Nelles.Verlag@T-Online.de

Note: Distances and measurements, including temperatures, used in this guide are metric. For conversion information, please see the *Guidelines* section of this book.

LEGEND

	Diving Area		Resort, Hotel		Market
	Nice Beach		International Airport		Administrative Border
Male	Island mentioned in Text		Place of Interest		Main Road
	Reef		Public or Significant Building		Other Road
	Lagoon		Restaurant		
	Shallow Water		Mosque		

MALDIVES
© Nelles Verlag GmbH, D-80935 München
All rights reserved

First Edition 1999
ISBN 3-88618-139-1
Printed in Slovenia

Publisher:	Günter Nelles	**Translation**:	Owen Thomas,
Editor in Chief:	Berthold Schwarz		Anil Kelkar,
Project Editor:	Christian Mietz		Robert Nusbaum
Editor:	Sylvi Zähle	**Cartography**:	Nelles Verlag GmbH
Photo Editor:	K. Bärmann-Thümmel	**Color Separation**:	Priegnitz, München
English Editor:	Anne Midgette	**Printed by**:	Gorenjski Tisk

- T01 -

TABLE OF CONTENTS

FEATURES

GUIDELINES

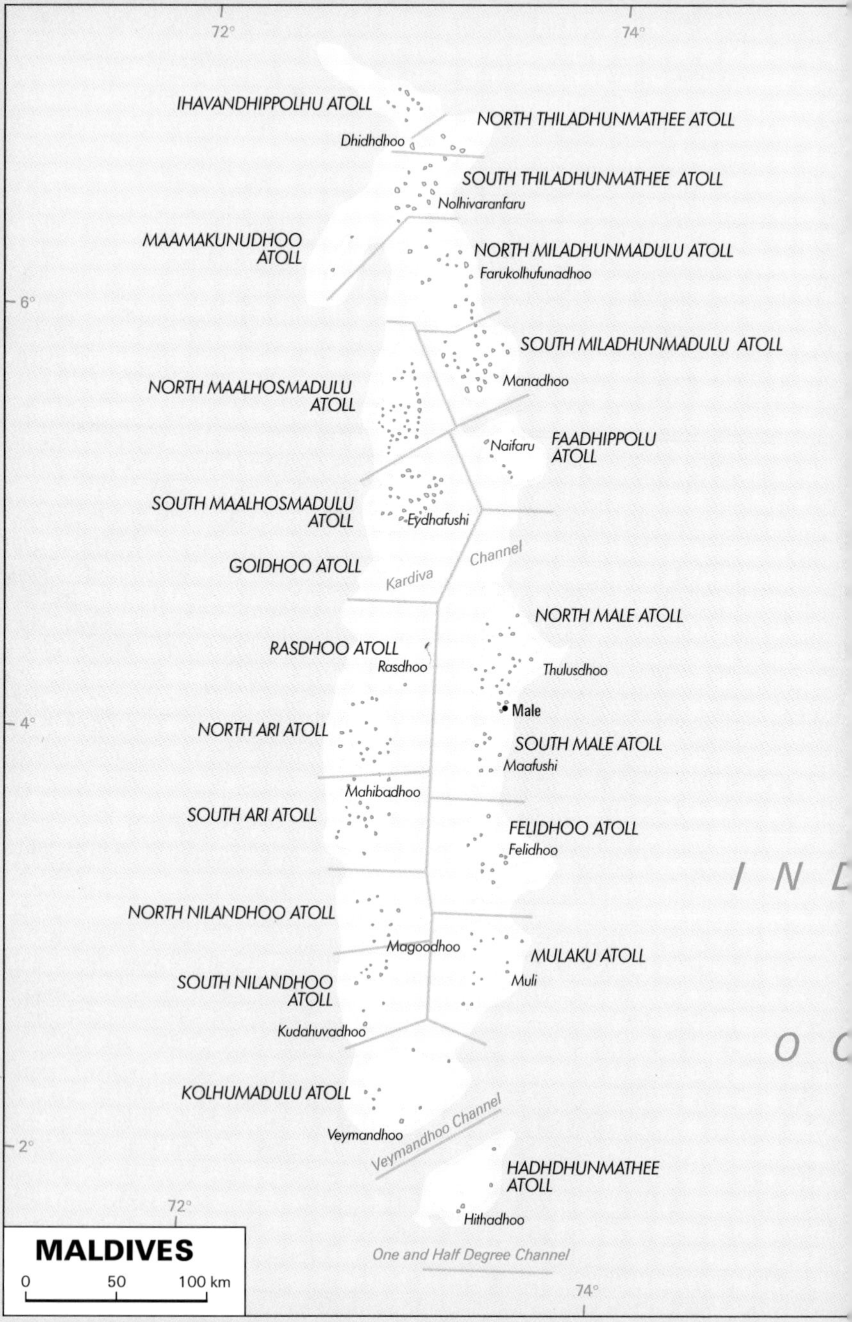

IHAVANDHIPPOLHU ATOLL

NORTH THILADHUNMATHEE ATOLL

Dhidhdhoo

SOUTH THILADHUNMATHEE ATOLL

Nolhivaranfaru

MAAMAKUNUDHOO
ATOLL

NORTH MILADHUNMADULU ATOLL

Farukolhufunadhoo

SOUTH MILADHUNMADULU ATOLL

Manadhoo

NORTH MAALHOSMADULU
ATOLL

Naifaru

FAADHIPPOLU
ATOLL

SOUTH MAALHOSMADULU
ATOLL

Eydhafushi

GOIDHOO ATOLL

Channel

Kardiva

NORTH MALE ATOLL

RASDHOO ATOLL

Rasdhoo

Thulusdhoo

Male

NORTH ARI ATOLL

SOUTH MALE ATOLL

Maafushi

SOUTH ARI ATOLL

Mahibadhoo

FELIDHOO ATOLL

Felidhoo

I N D

NORTH NILANDHOO ATOLL

Magoodhoo

MULAKU ATOLL

Muli

SOUTH NILANDHOO
ATOLL

Kudahuvadhoo

O C

KOLHUMADULU ATOLL

Veymandhoo

Veymandhoo Channel

HADHDHUNMATHEE
ATOLL

Hithadhoo

One and Half Degree Channel

MALDIVES

| 0 | 50 | 100 km |

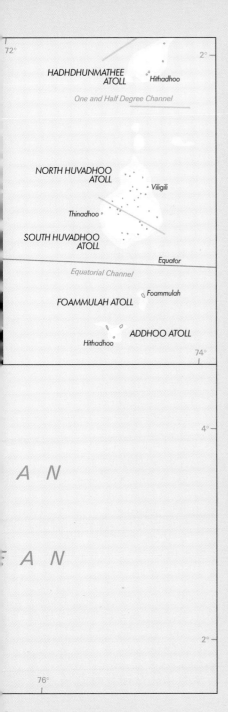

GEOGRAPHY AND GEOLOGY OF MALDIVES

The earthly paradise of the Maldives archipelago, coral islands which work like a magnet to draw snorkelers, divers and sunbathers, lie adrift in the Indian Ocean, to the southwest of the Indian subcontinent. From the northernmost Maldive island, it's 670 kilometers to the coast of Sri Lanka, to the east, and 480 kilometers to Cape Comorin, the southern tip of India. The Chagos Archipelago, a British territory, lies 550 kilometers to the south of the southernmost of the Maldives.

The island republic measures some 820 kilometers from north to south, 130 kilometers from east to west; it extends, in short, over an area of about 100,000 square kilometers. However, the vast majority of this area is water. In 1997, only 0.3% of it was actually inhabited: 200 islands, that is, with a total surface area of 298 square kilometers. The actual available land of this island nation, which supports some 256,000 Maldivians, is therefore equivalent to the little Mediterranean island of Malta, where about 368,000 people live on 316 square kilometers.

Maldives lies between the latitudes of 7° 6' 30" N and 0° 41' 48" S; their longitude is between 72° 32' 30" and 73° 45' 54" W. These coordinates indicate that they extend for 823 kilometers in a north-south, 130 kilometers in an east-west direction.

According to the official tally, there are 1,190 islands in Maldives; but it must be noted that the government defines any land protruding from the water an "island" as long as it sports some degree of

Preceding pages: Gorgeous beaches, blue lagoons and the fascinating world underwater make Maldives a vacation paradise. Left: Like glowing emeralds, the Maldive islands lie gently on the blue velvet of the Indian Ocean.

vegetation, be it grass, shrubs or palm trees. Sand bars don't counted as "islands" in the official literature. This is probably wise, since the islands change considerably according to season, depending on the direction of the monsoon at any given moment; new sand bars are always springing up, while old ones vanish. Because of this fact, various sources quote the number of Maldive islands as being anywhere from 1,120 to 2,000, depending on whether or not sand bars are included.

Maldives seems to function as a kind of playground for the mighty oceanic forces that can create and destroy islands seemingly at will. In the Shaviyani Atoll, for example, a 1955 storm created no fewer than three new islands. As if to balance this out, the relatively large island of Feydhoo Finolhu in the Male Atoll would have been completely washed away in 1960 if it hadn't been saved through human intervention. Kalhuhuraa, an island in the South Male Atoll which sported coconut palms as recently as 100 years ago, has ceased to exist. In the North Male Atoll, Viligilimathidhahuraa is an example of one island formed from two, as sand deposits over time created an evidently permanent union. Other islands have split up, such as the inhabited island Huraa in the North Male Atoll, "left" by the island Kuda Huraa, which is now doing well for itself as a resort. The resort islands Lankanfinolhu (Paradise Island) and Hudhuveli were once joined together, as well.

Creation Stories

The Maldives islands are a unique manifestation, rising from the deep blue waters of the Indian Ocean like mysterious, shining jewels.

There are two theories about how this unusual atoll world came to be: the early hypothesis of Charles Darwin, which is more than 150 years old, and the more re-

cent theory of scientist Hans Hass. The islands of Maldives sit atop the crest of what was once a chain of powerful volcanoes, the remains of which extend south of the Indian subcontinent through the Laccadive Islands down to the Chagos Archipelago and the island of Diego Garcia at its tip. In the course of the earth's history, these mountains gradually sank deeper an deeper beneath the ocean; today, only their tops rise from the depths of 3,000 to 4,000 meters.

Darwin, who never actually visited Maldives, developed his theory based on the abovementioned facts. As the mountains slowly sank millions of years ago, he claimed, coral settled in the shallower, warm water around them. If the coral's growth took place at a rate comparable to the speed at which the volcanos sank, the result would be a reef that gradually expanded as the mountaintops sank. Fi-

Above, right: Charles Darwin (right) and Hans Hass developed the generally accepted theory of the atolls' origins.

nally, all that remained was a large collection of extensive ring reefs surrounding smooth expanses of lagoon. Darwin's tectonic sinking theory seemed confirmed when Exxon's seismic measurements near the island of Bandos established the presence of volcanic stone beneath a layer of limestone 2,100 meters thick.

Hans Hass's theory emphasized a particular aspect of atoll formation. According to him, coral grows toward the light, and therefore keeps developing outward, like the rings of trees. As the reef grows, conditions grow worse and worse for the coral at the middle of the formation, until the polyps in this area finally die out. Because of the tides, water builds up in the center, creating strong pressure underground. Erosion, currents, tides, and the effects of weather then combine to expand this inner area at a rate corresponding to the rate of growth of the reef's outer edge. When the outer reef can no longer withstand the onslaught of heavy storms and waves, it breaks, creating channels that carry fresh sea water and foodstuffs to the inner area of the reef, providing the conditions for the growth of new coral within the lagoon, which creates new atoll systems in its turn. Hass's theory thus also explains the presence of the small *faros* (small, round reef formations) within the larger reefs. According to the theory, the islands also formed through deposits of sand and gravel within the lagoon; these formed small sand bars which gradually firmed up until the first plants were able to take root.

However the islands developed, changes in the level of the ocean during the last Ice Age, 15,000 years ago, also played a role in characterizing the reefs' present-day appearance.

Atolls

The Maldive archipelago consists of 26 atolls. Minicoy (Maliku), once the 27th atoll in the north, was annexed by India during the regency of Sultan al-Mukarram Mohammed Imadudeen III (1750-1757). Administratively, however, there are 20 official atolls, each of which bears a simpler administrative designation in addition to its traditional name, which is often difficult for foreigners to pronounce. The Maalhosmadulu Atoll, for example, is also known as the Baa Atoll. Each atoll is also designated with a letter of the Latin alphabet; this is inscibed on the bow of every dhoni in Maldives, enabling one to tell which atoll it comes from.

The word "atoll" is the only Dhivevi term that's made it into common international usage. However, in modern Dhivevi, the language of Maldives, *atholhu* no longer designates the geological reef formation but rather the administrative entity, which can be either a single atoll or several.

In Europe, the term "atoll" was first introduced by a Frenchman, François Pyrard. On July 2, 1602, his vessel *Corbin*

was shipwrecked on the Goidhoo Atoll, and he was imprisoned for five years by the local population before he was able to escape. He wrote detailed accounts of Maldives, describing the inhabitants and their ways.

The Maldives archipelago includes the largest number of atolls anywhere in the world; the Huvadhoo Atoll in the south, extending over an area of 2,240 square kilometers, is also the largest atoll in the world. Its lagoon is 70 kilometers long, 53 kilometers across, and 86 meters deep.

By definition, an atoll is a ring-shaped coral reef surrounding a lagoon. Surrounding the whole thing is a ring reef that falls off sharply into the sea on the outer side. Dotting the seam of the reef are small individual islands consisting of coral sand and gravel. Characteristic atoll features are the channels, or *kandus*, which cut through the reef at intervals and ensure a continual flow of water between the otherwise enclosed lagoon and the open sea, thereby providing the nu-

15

trients essential for the formation and growth of new coral. While lagoons are generally between 50 and 90 meters deep, the reef falls steeply on the outer side to depths of several hundred meters. Powerful currents often spring up in the channels, their strength and direction determined by the phases of the moon, wind, tide, and the contours of the ocean floor beneath them.

Between the atolls, the largest ocean currents run at varying speeds, depending on the prevailing monsoon winds, generally in an east-west direction. In the equatorial channel of Addhoo Kandu, 74 kilometers across and 1,829 meters deep, which divides the southern Seenu Atoll from the Huvadhoo Atoll, currents can reach speeds of more than 10 kilometers an hour. Somewhat farther north, the One-and-a-Half-Degree Channel, Huvadhoo Kandu, is known for its extremely strong currents, so that this channel, 96 kilometers across, can only be navigated by larger, ocean-going vessels.

A Maldivian specialty in the world of the atolls are the small, round reef formations known as *faros*, which are small individual atolls or pseudo-atolls. Linked together, one beside another, not unlike beads on a necklace, they sometimes form the outer ring of a larger atoll. Within atolls, as well, you often spot a *faro* rising from the inner lagoon. Sand bars form on many of them, and over time these sometimes develop into islands in their own right. In addition to these *faros*, which in Dhivehi, the local language, are also called *gaa* or *baa*, there are other kinds of reef formation in Maldives. If several islands lie in the lagoon of a faro, the Maldivians describe it as a *falhu*. A *giri* is an elongated reef which, unlike a *faro*, always juts up out of the water. A *thila*, by contrast, is a perforated reef structure the top of which is always a few meters beneath the surface of the water. Channels between two reefs or atolls are also given the additional designation of *kandu* or *kandu olhi*.

Spelling of the names of atolls, islands and reefs is neither uniform nor officially consistent. Even on printed maps you encounter a number of various spellings. In general, people try to use the simplest possible form in order to make complicated or lengthy names somewhat easier to read. Thus, Ihavandhippolhoo is shortened to Ihavandiffulu, Felidhe becomes Felidu (or Felidhoo). Some names have changed completely, such as that of the Huvadhoo Atoll in the south, which is now also known as the Suvadiva Atoll.

The islands' names often indicate their geographical position or their distinctive characteristics. For example, the name of the island Thundufushi on the eastern outer rim of the Ari Atoll is a compilation of *thundhu*, "edge" or "rim," and *fushi*, "island." Some other names hearken back to important events which may have taken place on the island in question. The name of the island Dhehasanu Lonu Bui Huraa, also in the Ari Atoll, means something like "two men named Hassan drink on the salt-water island." Names such as Vihamanaafushi, Lankanfinolhu or Furanafushi, on the other hand, are of Sinhalese origin. The suffix *-fushi* indicates a large island on the outer reef of an atoll, such as Kandoomafushi or Meerufenfushi. The suffix *-finolhu* is given to an island which had, at the time it was named, only a few coconut palms, or none at all. The endings *hura* and *dhoo* are synonymous with the term "island." The two letters *-le* that conclude the names of some islands, such as Male and Hulhule, are a shortened form of the Sanskrit word *liu*, which also means "island" in that language.

In recent years, countless resort islands have abandoned their traditional names in favor of new, catchier designations or

Right: Tiny polyps have been working on building the coral reefs for about 600 million years.

hotel logos for the sake of becoming more easily marketable to foreign tourists. Thus, Medhu Finolhu has become Reethi Rah, Vihamanaafushi is now called Kurumba Village, and Velassaru today is officially known as the Laguna Beach Resort.

The names of reefs can also be significant. The name *Himmiyafaro*, for example, clues fishermen in about the geography of the reef that bears it, as *himmi* means "opening between two objects" and indicates the passage where the water divides the reef into two parts. The name of the *Koonomias faro* in the North Male Atoll signifies "reef of the rotted fish," testimony to a time long ago when a whale was beached here and came, as it were, to a bad end.

Coral Reefs

Coral reefs are formed by microscopic tiny polyps which emit calcium deposits, thereby slowly, over time, building up the reef as we see it today. Coral is ex-

tremely fragile, and only a few types of it grow as rapidly as 20 to 30 centimeters a year. Most of the stone corals that form the foundations of the truly massive reef formations grow at an annual rate of only a few millimeters.

In addition, coralline algae, which prefers modest depths, preferably in areas of surf, helps to create a solid base by "cementing together" broken and dead bits of cast-off coral.

A reef's shape is determined primarily by the depth of the ocean and the conditions on its floor, and only to a secondary degree by tides and currents, the intensity and force of the waves, and weather conditions. As the level of the ocean sank considerably during the last Ice Age, large areas of reef-building coral were left high and dry. These gradually drifted to other areas, there to build up new colonies. Extensive erosion of reefs that were now exposed to the air formed caves, crevasses and canyons in a whole range of forms and variations. As the sea level rose once again, other corals

17

formed, and various forms of marine life settled into this newly-acquired habitat. Today, divers from all over the world come to investigate and marvel at their underwater environment.

In Maldives, people distinguish between inner and outer reefs. Inner reefs lie within the ring of an atoll, and include most house reefs; while the outer reef encircles the whole atoll. In the case of islands on the edge of an atoll, the outer reef may be part of the house reef.

Shapes and Types of Islands

Depending on the characteristics of their beaches, their lagoons, and the reef structures that surround them, islands in Maldives are categorized as one of three types: the round or fried-egg type, the crescent type, and the elongated "handkerchief" type. For anyone trying to se-

Above: Coral reefs often extend to just below the water's surface. Right: Two common island shapes – crescent and kerchief.

lect the ideal vacation island, shape can play a decisive role – especially for devotees of specific water sports.

The Round or "Fried-Egg" Type

This island type is found almost exclusively on the eastern side of the Ari Atoll, and never in close proximity to the outer reef. Typical features of this kind of island are its shape, an almost perfect circle, and the vicinity of the reef, which drops off sharply into the depths of the ocean. Most of these islands have a beach that runs all the way around them (the "white" of the "fried egg"), wonderful snorkeling terrain along the edge of the reef, and breathtaking dive sites. This type of island is ideal for divers who want easy access to adventure-filled dives by a house reef.

Examples include Bandos, Banyan Tree, Bathala, Biyadhoo, Ellaidhoo, Emboodhoo, Fesdhoo, Hembadhoo, Ihuru, Kurumba, Maafushi Varu, Soneva Fushi, Villivaru.

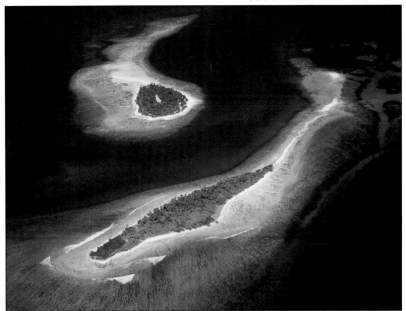

The Crescent Type

Crescent islands are found predominantly in the inner reaches of large atolls. Generally, this type of island is based on a *faru* or *falhu*. Characteristics include a broad lagoon on one side of the island, as well as a large and easily accessible house reef with steep walls. These islands tend to lie at the end of a reef complex, sheltered from strong currents. Crescent islands represent a good compromise in that they're suitable for all manner of water sports: the house reef holds underwater treasures for divers, while fans of other water sports can follow their pleasure in the lagoon. Examples include Alimatha, Angaga, Athuruga, Baros, Bolifushi, Cocoa, Dhiggiri, Eriyadhoo, Fihalohi, Full Moon, Giraavaru, Halaveli, Kudarah, Kuredhdhoo, Laguna Beach, Lhohifushi, Maayafushi, Machchafushi, Makunudhoo, Meerufenfushi, Mirihi, Nakatchafushi, Nika, Rannali, Rangali, Ranveli, Thulagiri, Vaadhoo, Vakaruvali, Velidu, Vilamendhoo.

The Handkerchief Type

Handkerchief islands generally lie atop the broad saddle of an outer reef *faru*. One characteristic of this type of island is a broad, sandy lagoon that's perfect for swimming, windsurfing, and sailing. On the inner side of the reef, the broad, flat reef roof is difficult to cross; divers have to take boats out to the house reef. But a handkerchief island's close proximity to the outer reef makes such islands particularly attractive to experienced divers; in the strong currents along the outer reefs, they can often encounter rare deep-sea fish.

Examples include Ari Beach, Dhigufinolhu, Emboodhoo Finolhu, Farukolufushi (Club Med), Fun Island, Gan Island, Holiday Island, Hudhuveli, Kandooma Fushi, Kanifinolhu, Kanu Huraa, Kuda Huraa, Kuramathi, Lankanfinolhu, Leisure Island, Lily Beach, Olhuveli, Paradise Island, Reethi Rah, Rihiveli, Summer Island, Veligandu, Veligandu Huraa.

19

THE HISTORY OF MALDIVES

The official written record of Maldivian history begins with the coming of Islam in 1153. Owing to the fact that the rulers of the period feared foreign influences, the early, pre-Islamic history of the country was deliberately suppressed, and archaeological finds and ancient writings destroyed. This explains why the country's early history is made up of such a large number of myths and legends. Maldives was first mentioned by Ptolemy (AD 85-160), the Greek astronomer, mathematician, and geographer, who spoke with astonishing accuracy of an archipelago consisting of 1378 small islands that were said to be located off the west coast of Taprobane (now Sri Lanka). In the 4th century, Scholasticus of Thebes, who was travelling down the South Indian coast of the Maldives, told of over a thousand small islands lying west of Taprobane. During the same period, Pappus of Alexandria also counted 1,370 islands in the archipelago.

The first inhabitants of Maldives are believed to have come from the Indian subcontinent and Sri Lanka. After around 500-400 BC, Maldives was inhabited by Dravidians from South India and Indo-Aryans from northwestern India, as well as Singhalese and Tamils from Sri Lanka, all of whom intermarried with each other and with a small group of natives who had been there before them. There was probably also some degree of intermarriage with two other Ceylonese groups, the Naga and the Yakka, who had evolved a pre-Buddhist culture in Sri Lanka. As a result, elements of Singhalese and Tamil entered Dhivehi, the language spoken in Maldives. Singhalese influence can also be seen in the Maldivian creation myth about "one-man monsters," who are strongly reminiscent of the lion-men in Singhalese mythology.

Left: A young girl from Male.

To this day, the Giraavaru claim to be descended from the Tamils, and are thought to be the original inhabitants of the island of Guraavaru, which was settled very early, in the North Male Atoll.

In 1985, the Maldivian government invited Thor Heyerdahl to Maldives; the Norwegian researcher hypothesized that the country's history was considerably older than had been supposed. Basing his theory on archaeological finds from the southern atoll, Heyerdahl hypothesized that Maldives was settled as early as 2000 BC by Indian, Egyptian, Phoenician, and, later on, Roman merchants.

This theory of a much earlier settlement could also help explain the origins of the legends about the Redin, a gigantic race of men described in Maldivian mythology as mysterious seafarers of unknown origin. They are said to have been highly superstitious and to have practiced pagan rituals, something that lives on in modern Maldivian society in the common belief in spirits, or *jinnis*. It is quite unlikely, however, that the Redin, who were light-skinned and red-haired, were an early Buddhist group from Sri Lanka. Far more probable is that various groups migrated to the archipelago in stages, and that these groups intermarried with the merchants and seafarers who followed them. This explains why there are so many different ethnic types, features, and skin colors to be seen in the local population.

During the early migratory period (beginning in 500 BC), various peoples were already bringing Buddhism to Maldives. The British colonial administrator H.C.P. Bell, who was stranded in the archipelago with his ship in the 1870s, spent most of his time as an amateur researcher in intense investigation of Buddhist influences on the islands' culture, backing up his conclusions with extensive archaeological findings. Between 1879 and 1920, working on various southern islands including Gaddu, Kanduhuludu

and Toddu, he discovered a number of archaeoligal sites consisting of large mounds of coral stone (*hawittas*). He took these to be the remains of stupas, domed structures housing Buddhist holy relics, because they resembled *dagoba* temples from Sri Lanka. Bell found Buddhist statues in the *hawittas*, and in graves in the southern atoll he even found Hindu sculptures. His discovery of a statue of Shiva led him to the conclusion that not only Buddhist but also Hindu influences were active throughout Maldives in the early period of its history.

The recorded history of the archipelago begins in the 9th century AD, when Maldives was "discovered" by seafarers from the Arabian peninsula. While the changeable and stormy southwest winds forced these sailors to hug the coast when

Above and right: In Male's National Museum you can see testimony to Maldives' early history on display – a stupa from the southern atolls (above) and a carved stone mask (right).

plying their trading routes to the Far East in summer, on the return trip, with the northern monsoon's favorable winds at their back, they could sail the open seas, which took them right past Maldives. The islands represented a welcome stopover where they could replenish their ships' provender. A Persian merchant named Sulaiman reported that there were 1,900 islands in the Herkend Sea, governed by a woman and boasting an immeasurable wealth of cowrie shells, the preferred unit of currency at the time. Arab sailors prized dried fish and Maldivian ropes made of coconut fibers as objects of barter, but during their sojourns they made sure to stock up, above all, on the prized cowrie shells, which may have been responsible for the archipelago's very name: *dhiva khuda* means "cowrie island." Another possible origin of the name "Maldives" are the Hindu words *mahal* ("palace" or "town") and *diva* ("island"), which are thought to be the basis of the later *Melediva* ("palace island").

In 1200, another Arab traveler reported the existence of more than 2,000 "cowrie islands" that he claimed lay between the Herkend and Lar seas.

According to legend, the Maldivians were ruled by a king in the days before the advent of Islam. When Prince Koimala Kaola, who was married to the daughter of the King of Ceylon, sailed from Sri Lanka to Maldives, the inhabitants of the island of Rasgetheemu, having learned that their guests were of noble blood, invited the prince to the North Maalhosmadulu Atoll where, shortly thereafter, they made Kaola the King of Rasgetheemu. With the consent of the powerful Giraavaru, the original inhabitants of the eponymous island in the North Male Atoll, the king later settled in Male. Another version of the same legend recounts that Koimala invited the inhabitants of Rasgetheemu and the neighboring island to a "banquet" and then had

them all massacred. He then proclaimed himself king, and went to live in Male, where he commissioned two ships to sail back to Sri Lanka in order to bring more "lion-men" to the island. His son succeeded him to the throne and reigned for 12 years before converting to Islam. After he failed to return from his pilgrimage to Mecca, his daughter became sultana. According to the legend, all the subsequent Maldivian sultans are descended from this dynasty.

A more reliable source of historical information is Ibn Battuta, a Moroccan merchant and well-known travel writer of the 14th century. He first traveled to Maldives and to "Dihabad al-Mahal" (now the capital city of Male) in 1343: "I decided to make a journey to Maldives, of which I had heard many tales... These islands are one of the wonders of the world." A planned stopover of a few days grew into a stay of many months. Sultana Khadidja took a shiine to the learned man, and as a result Ibn Battuta acceded to the position of *gazi*, the highest judge

in the land. As *gazi*, he tried to impose Islamic law with an iron fist, but later left Maldives again after quarreling with the Sultana's husband. During his stay, the Moorish guest from Tangier declared his Moroccan countryman, the Berber Jussuf al-Barbari, to be the man who converted Maldives to Islam, although the Maldivian chronicle the *Tharik* claims that it was in 1153, two centuries earlier, that a monk named Abdul Barakaath al-Barberie had converted the then-reigning king to Islam. The story goes that al-Barberie managed to drive a wicked demon out of Male forever through the power of prayer, whereupon the Maldivian king kept his promise and converted to Islam. Some 200 years after the Maldivians had adopted Islam as their religion, Ibn Battuta probably tampered with the inscription carved in the Great Mosque in Male, which stated the name of the founder of Islam on these shores, to the benefit of his countryman.

It is much more probable, however, that Islam moved into the Maldives not as the result of a spectacular or dramatic conversion but rather at a gradual pace, a natural and perhaps inevitable result of regular contact with Arab sailors and merchants over a long period of time.

Led by the Great Eunuch Cheng Ho, who initiated large-scale expeditions to the west in search of new business contacts, the Chinese passed through Maldives in 1405. A total of seven expeditions were outfitted over the next 20 years, of which the first and largest comprised nearly 28,000 men and 300 ships. In the course of these expeditions, the Chinese visited 30 countries, travelling as far from home as Persia, Mecca, Aden, and Mogadishu in Africa. The Chinese paid their first visit to the Maldivians during their fourth journey (1413-15). They were so taken with the Sultan and his court that they invited a Maldivian emissary to come to China; the emissary did not return to Maldives until the next Chinese expedition to Male brought him back.

With the coming of the Portuguese to Southeast Asia, Arabic influence diminished appreciably. As the Portuguese built up their maritime trading routes, they discovered that the Maldivian archipelago was a strategically important stopover. The Portuguese captain Vincent Sodré, a commander in Vasca da Gama's fleet, first made contact with Maldivian ships off the South Indian coast in 1503, whereupon, Portugal being at war with the Rajah of Calcutta, he promptly set fire to and destroyed the entire Maldivian fleet. Shortly thereafter, the Portuguese banned all trade between Maldives and the Indian mainland. Then, in 1517, Sultan Kalhu Muhammad allowed the Portuguese to establish a trading outpost on the island of Male, which, with the help of Mopla pirates from Malabar, was burned down one

Right: The Friday mosque of Isdhoo in the Laamu Atoll was built in the 16th century.

year later by Maldivians fearing further loss of business. A 120-man Portuguese armada under the command of João Gomes then retook Male, where a fort was built to defend the city.

In the Maldivians' ensuing struggle to free themselves of the Portuguese occupying forces, they were greatly aided by Pata Marakkar, a former merchant turned pirate from Cohin in South India. The Portuguese, not content to significantly disrupt trade by Maldivian merchants, also tried to stop pirates from raiding ships in the archipelago. In 1521, Pata Marakkar and his followers succeeded in laying siege to the Portuguese, all of whom were killed during the ensuing battle. And thus, Male was liberated again.

In 1550 a conflict erupted among the rulers of Maldives, and Sultan Hassan IX fled to Cochin, seeking refuge with his arch-enemies, the Portuguese. Two years later, he converted to Christianity, was baptized by Frances Xavier (later St. Frances Xavier), and thereby became the first Catholic sultan of Maldives. Under the pretext of helping Hassan IX (Don Manuel) to ascend to the throne, the Portuguese again tried to conquer Male by (again) sending warships. It was only on the third attempt that they succeeded in taking control of the Sultan's island, thereby making it a Portuguese colony.

As governor of this territory, the Portuguese appointed Andreas André, who was of Portuguese and Maldivian parentage. The name by which he is remembered in Maldives, Andiri Andirin, still conjures up terrible memories of the horrors associated with him. He had countless inhabitants of the archipelago murdered, and, according to the *Tharik*, the book of Islamic sultans, "colored the sea with the red of Moslem blood, and the people were heavy with despair." Andiri Andirin, who as a young man had fled Maldives and gone to India after murdering a Maldivian, soon appointed himself

Sultan and ruled the country for 15 years (1558-1573) in the name of Portuguese colonial power. Under his terrible rule, an insurrection broke out, led by Khatib Muhammad (second son of the Utheemu clan chief, who later became a folk hero) and his two brothers Ali and Hassan. Starting out from the island of Gan, where they probably built a fort, the rebels managed to drive the Portuguese occupying forces back to Male after an eight-year-long war of attrition.

Khatib Muhammad promised pirates from Malabar (who were on the rampage in Maldives at this time) a share in the spoils if they would help him to retake Male. In 1573, the rebels, who far outnumbered the occupying forces, invaded Male and massacred all 300 Portuguese soldiers, along with the hated Andiri Andirin. Khatib Muhammad, who then took the name Muhammad Bodu Thakurufaan, was named Sultan and is now regarded as the founder of the Utheemu Dynasty, which held sway for 127 years. The Maldivians still revere him as their national hero, because since his victory over the Portuguese, Maldives has never again fallen under foreign domination. The Portuguese made two last – and unsuccessful – attempts to take over Maldives in 1631 and 1649.

Sultan Ibrahmim Iskandar I, whose reign began in 1648, is also revered by modern Maldivians. Besides establishing the kingdom's first school and first minted coins, he also extensively refurbished the Hukkuru mosque, built several impressive buildings in Male, and successfully defended the island against pirates. In 1687, he was poisoned by his favorite slave, Mariyam, who took over the throne after his death and proceeded to introduce a frivolous, carefree life at court that led many devout Muslims to leave the capital altogether.

In the middle of the 17th century, the Dutch, in the name of protecting the ships of their East India Company (with which they were attempting to force the Portuguese out of the Indonesian spice trade) decided that Maldives was vital to their

25

strategic interests. The Dutch, however, never interfered in the domestic affairs of Maldives; their restraint was rewarded when, in 1645, the Maldivian government instituted voluntary payments of tribute. The amicable commercial relationship between the two countries lasted for another 150 years. The Dutch supplied Maldives with areca nuts, spices, weapons, and munitions; in return, they obtained the highly prized cowrie shells from the Maldivians.

After pirates from Malabar abducted the Sultan in 1754, the Maldivians took up contact with the French forces stationed in southern India, who drove the pirates out of Male. The French then stayed in Male for another five years to protect the island against further pirate attacks. They withdrew in 1759, once the Maldivians demonstrated that they could defend themselves effectively.

When, in 1792, the British colonized Ceylon, they automatically adopted Dutch laws in their dealings with the Maldivians. Naturally, they also recognized the potential advantages of Maldives' geographical location for their own East India Company. Even before colonization, strong business ties had developed between Colombo and Male, and the Sultan of Maldives, who wished to remain on good terms with his trading partners to the northeast, placed great importance on establishing harmonious relations with the new colonial power. Trade between Maldives and Ceylon flourished for about 50 years, primarily in dried tuna, tortoiseshell, coconuts, cotton, rice, and sugar. However, Indian merchants eventually came to dominate trade in all the most important goods coming into the country, which gave rise to popular unrest: In 1887, angry Maldivians burned

Right: Maldivian women haven't been required to wear purdah, the veil of Islam, since the 1950s – women in a health center in the Gaafu Alifu Atoll.

down the warehouses belonging to the powerful Indian Carijmjee Jafferie Company. In the same year, Sultan Muhammad Muin-uddin II signed a protectorate treaty with the British that obliged Maldives to pay tribute to the British crown. However, the treaty also granted Maldives freedom from interference in domestic affairs, and provided a guarantee of British military aid in case of attack.

In order to improve navigational safety for their own shipping, the British admiralty, at the instigation of Robert Moresby, commissioned from the Maldivians the first charts ever of the waters around certain reefs that the Maldivians, from years of experience, had long known posed a danger to ships. The Dutch United East India Company had also made a similar request years before, and as early as the 4th century, Scholasticus reported on "1,000 islands of a fickle nature, where there are magnetic stones that attract iron-hulled ships and draw them to their doom."

In 1932, a group of young Maldivian intellectuals who had studied abroad attempted, with British support, to reform the absolute sultanate and institute a constitutional monarchy. Sultan Mohammed Shamshuddeen III, who saw that this would compromise his unlimited political power and its concomitant privileges, rejected the idea; in 1934, he was exiled, again with British support, to the island of Fua Mulaku. His successor, Sultan Hassan Nuruddin II, who reigned until 1945, proved to be more open to reforms.

During World War II, the British constructed two military bases in Maldives, one on Gan in the southern Maldives, and the other on Kelai. Although the war's disruption of commercial shipping impeded the flow of goods to the island and led to many Maldivians' dying of starvation, there islands didn't actually see military conflict.

Abdul Madschid, who was elected successor to Nuruddin, declined the office of

Sultan, preferring to live abroad. His nephew Muhammad Amin, later known as Amin Didi, took over the role of Sultan in his absence. When the uncle died in 1952, Amin was elected Sultan with 98% of the vote. January 1, 1953, Maldives, saw the declaration of the first Republic of Maldives.

Amin Didi, a shining figure in Maldivian political history, abolished the office of Sultan and gained renown beyond Maldives through his reforms in the fields of education and health, as well as in the country's infrastructure. Despite these achievements, however, he was also unpopular. On the one hand, he instituted such popular reforms as granting women the right to vote and abolishing the veil; on the other, however, he increased the severity of certain criminal laws, punishing thieves, for example, by cutting off their hands. After he turned the fish export business into a government monopoly and outlawed tobacco imports, unrest broke out, and he was overthrown during a trip abroad. His at-

tempt to regain power failed when, on December 31, 1953, he delivered a speech to the people of Male. A tumult ensued, in which Amin Didi was seriously injured; he died three weeks later on Kurumba, where he is buried, and where his grave can still be visited.

Muhammad Farid Didi, the son of the previous Sultan, was extremely popular when he came to power. However, he soon abolished both the constitution and the republic, and in 1954 became Maldives' 94th and last Sultan.

In 1956, Britain was granted a new, 100-year lease on the Air Force base at Gan, since the Ceylonese, having won independence from the British, had denied them the right to use the harbor at Trincomalee and the airport at Katunayake. Ibrahim Nasir, the Sultan's new Prime Minister, withdrew from this treaty in 1957. This action led to unrest in the three southernmost atolls, which had benefited economically from the British presence on Gan. In 1959 they cut ties with the Maldivian government and

27

of ways, supporting the growth of tourism and fish exports, and substantially increasing the fees for the British to use the air and naval base on Gan. However, the fact that the country's wealth was concentrated solely on Male and that the president had already been suspected, in 1972, of embezzling state funds, high inflation proved the last straw and sparked a popular revolt in 1974. Nasir's reaction was neither slow nor particularly diplomatic: shots were fired into the crowd. Afterwards, he drastically tightened security measures to reinforce his position. Four years later he fled the country for Singapore, taking with him what one might kindly term "a generous pension for life, which he had awarded himself." Shortly thereafter, he was charged with embezzlement and corruption and was sentenced *in absentia* to 25 years of exile. Two years later, Nasim, one of Nasir's nephews, attempted to overthrow the new president, Maumoon Abdul Gayoom, with the help of English and Swiss mercenaries. The commando operation failed, however, perhpas because the Maldivians had apparently been alerted by the British.

In 1988, foreign mercenaries attempted another coup, but it was quickly put down with the help of Indian military personnel. Little is known about the background of this coup, although it is assumed that Nasir had organized it and was controlling the putsch from Singapore. Another theory is that under the leadership of Abdullaa Luthufi, an exporter of Maledivian tropical fish from Colombo, influential Maldivian businessmen had hired 90 Tamil mercenaries to overthrow the government. However, the mercenaries were only able to hold their position in Male for a few days after 1,600 Indian paratroopers landed on the island.

formed an independent state, called the United Suvadiva Islands, with Abdullaa Afif Didi as president. At first it seemed that the Sultan might negotiate an extension of the treaty with the British; in 1962, however, Ibrahim Nasir sent gunboats from Male to the south, and the president of the new nation was forced to flee into exile in the Seychelles, where he was granted political asylum.

Maldives was officially granted its independence on July 26, 1965, and became a member of the UN. 1968, after the abdication of Sultan Farid, saw the creation of the second Maldives Republic with Ibrahim Nasir as president. In that year, a new constitution went into effect that was based on the teachings of the Koran and that gave increased powers to the president. Ibrahim Nasir helped bolster his country's economy in a number

President Abdul Gayoom Maumoon, now in his fourth term, is extremely popular. In the last election, in 1993, he

Above: President Maumoon Abdul Gayoom.
Right: Modern seaplanes shorten the transfer times between the airport on Hulhule and the atolls.

received 96% of the vote. However, this figure does not have the same significance as it would in a European democracy. Powerful ruling families, religious leaders, and island chiefs make up a power elite that leaves little room for differing political views or legal opposition to the government. Moreover, Koranic law and the will of Allah watch over all.

Nevertheless, certain tendencies are beginning to manifest themselves in contemporary Maldivian society which seem to indicate a growing desire for democracy. Politics is no longer a taboo subject. People talk about abuse of power and corruption, and the newspaper *Sangu* ("Triton's Horn") openly criticizes conditions in the country.

Despite the country's intrigue-ridden and entrenched power structure, the economy is booming, with an annual growth rate of 9 percent – thanks in no small part to the increase in tourism. Improvements in social services, modern systems of education, health, and transportation, and expansion of the Maldi-

vian telecommunications infrastructure indicate that this country, which not long ago was one of the poorest in the world, is well on its way to becoming a model Asian success story.

Yet as Maldives emerges as a modern society and contact with foreigners increases, so, too, increase foreign influences on the country – a development which is not at all in line with Maldivian religious leaders' concept of what's proper for an Islamic state. In 1998, after the terrorist attack by Islamic fundamentalists in Luxor, Egypt that left many tourists dead, the Maldivian government, seeking to curb fundamentalist tendencies and to give a clear signal to the international community, appealed to Maldivian women to stop wearing the Islamic veil, which has been optional in any case since the 1950s. This measure is also a gesture ensuring that tourists on the Maldives will be safer from possible fundamentalist attacks.

In quite a different area, Maldives appears to be heading for a catastrophe.

Since 1995, this island nation has been attracting a great deal of attention at the UN's environmental conferences, because global warming and the attendant increase in the earth's sea level could prove disastrous to these low-lying coral islands. The direst predictions of some scientists have not yet come to pass. Still, if sea levels were to increase by only one meter, the outermost reefs would no longer protect the islands sufficiently from the sea, and within a few years Maldives would disappear altogether from world maps.

POLITICS, RELIGION, AND CULTURE

Government and Administrative Divisions

Maldives, which has been independent since 1965, is a republic with a president as head of state and a parliament in Male. There are 50 *majlis*, or members of Parliament: two from each administrative atoll and Male are elected directly by popular vote, and eight are appointed by the president. The president is first nominated for a renewable five-year term by the legislature, and is then elected in a national popular referendum. The president is at once commander-in-chief of the armed forces and minister of defense, national security, and finance. He also has the power to appoint to his cabinet individuals who are not members of Parliament. Since November 6, 1996, the cabinet has consisted of the Speaker of Parliament, the president of the High Council for Islamic Affairs, the Attorney General, and 18 cabinet ministers. There are no western-style opposition parties.

Maldives' political system is hierarchically structured, with a centralized government ruling from Male. The lower administrative levels are divided into 20 districts (atolls), each of which is governed by an *atoulveri* (atoll governor) and his staff. The atoll governors are appointed by the central government in Male, and most of them are natives of the capital. An *atoluveri* steers the atoll's political and economic fate, assisted by a *ghazi*, or community judge, who adjudicates minor cases according to the teachings of the Koran. More important cases are brought before the atoll courts or the Supreme Court in Male. The lowest rung of the administrative ladder is occupied by the *bodu katibu* – the mayors of the inhabited islands – and their deputies, the *kuda katibu*. Rounding out the tripartite administrative structure are the *mudimu*, who are in charge of the mosques. The mayors, also appointed in Male, take their policy cues from the central government. They are expected to lend support to the president's reelection campaign at the end of each five-year legislature session. Each *katibu* is required to radio reports of any unusual occurrences on his island to the atoll governor, who then relays this information to Male.

Islam and Society

Maldives is one of three countries in the world (Oman and Qatar are the other two) that is 100% Moslem. The branch of Islam known as Sunni, to which 92 % of Moslems adhere, is the state religion, and the president is the highest authority charged with safeguarding it. Every Maldivian is an avowed Muslim, and foreigners who want to become Maldivian citizens are required both to be Islamic and to have resided in Maldives for five years.

The precepts of Islam permeate every aspect of life in Maldivian society. Although the first Maldivian constitution of 1932 proclaimed the legal authority of secular judges, in everyday practice Mal-

Right: The circumcision of young boys, a religious duty for Moslems, is celebrated as a festival within the family.

divian law is still heavily influenced by the teachings of the Koran and the *Sharia*, the Islamic legal code. However, as the Maldivians are a peace-loving people, sentences tend to be relatively mild in comparison to those in other orthodox Islamic countries. In the 20th century, for example, the practice of cutting off hands has existed in Maldives only under President Amin Didi, and it has been many years since any convicted criminal received the death penalty. Maldivians commit few violent crimes; participants in fights tend rather to "acts of revenge," damaging property belonging to their antagonist. However, prisons do now exist for people who commit serious crimes. Punishment by flogging, though authorized by the constitution, is rarely applied, because the Maldivians, deeply rooted in their village communities as they are, find exile to a far-off island or a heavy fine a far severer punishment. Non-violent crimes such as adultery, robbery, and the consumption of alcohol earn the perpetrator a maximum of one year of exile.

The omnipresence of Islam is reflected both in the practice of praying five times daily and in an unquestioning acceptance of monotheism ("There is no God but Allah, and Mohammed is his prophet"). Most shops and offices in Male close for fifteen minutes after each call to prayer, and on Friday, the Moslem holy day, they are usually closed all day.

Maldivians are followers of the moderate Shafite Islamic school, which, named after its founder al-Shafi, sets forth the Koran's teachings by recounting the words and deeds of worthy men and of the prophet Mohammed. Accordingly, Maldivians strive to dedicate their lives "to the service of God." This means giving alms to the poor as a matter of course, as well as strictly observing the month-long fast of Ramadan (the ninth month of the Moslem calendar), and, if finances permit, fulfilling the duty of each Muslim to make the sacred pilgrimage to Mecca (the famous *hajj*) once in his lifetime during the 12th month of the Islamic calendar.

31

Family and Society

Islam also has a powerful influence on family life in this closely-knit island society. The *Sharia* clearly delineates the respective social roles of men and women. Business, religious, and legal matters fall within the purview of men, while women's responsibilities are limited to house, garden, kitchen, and raising children. For a woman, therefore, holding a religious office, or the office of a judge, is completely out of the question, as is entering a mosque together with the men; the mosque has separate rooms, of course, for women.

Women's work has historically been restricted, and continues to be today, to such occupations as fish processing,

Above and right: In Maldivian families, men and women divide the work in accordance with their traditional roles – the women and girls do the housework, while the boys who are more than 12 years old and the men go off to sea to go fishing.

weaving floor mats, spinning ropes and fishing lines from coconut fibers, and the production of sweet palm wine (*toddy*). At the age of 5 or 6, little girls begin helping with simple household tasks: they prepare coconut fibers for the braiding of rope, fetch water from the village well, sweep up outside the house, and learn to cook. Little boys of the same age are allowed to indulge in games and horseplay until the age of 12 to 14, when they begin helping their fathers on their fishing trips.

Maldivians marry young, as early as age 15 or 16, and divorce quickly; the divorce rate is 80%. In 1995, there were 2,442 marriages on Male, 1,476 of which ended in divorce; and of the 302 couples who got married between the ages of 15 and 19, 192 separated within the first year of marriage. Islamic law stipulates that a man can have up to four wives at one time, although this practice is extremely rare on Maldives, primarily due to economic considerations. Both marriage and divorce are relatively uncomplicated matters: in fact, the woman doesn't have to be present for either event. Two family members and an equal number of witnesses need only bear witness to the marriage in the presence of a judge. To divorce, it suffices for the husband to pronounce once (not three times, as is customary in other Islamic societies) the words "I cast you aside," also in the presence of a judge. Maldivians marry an average of four times, and many marry between ten and twenty times. Owing to Western influence, arranged marriages are now far less common that they once were, and marriages based on romantic love are correspondingly more common occurrences.

As Maldivian society becomes increasingly modern, the status of women is also changing: there are now several girls' schools, and women now hold 25% of all public offices. And in recognition of the International Decade of Women, a National Women's Organization and Department of Women's Affairs were set up in 1979 and 1986 respectively. In addition, the government has established a Ministry for Women and Social Affairs.

Cultural Identity and Tourism

Despite modern tendencies brought about by increased openness to the western world and the rise in tourism, the Maldivian government under President Maumoon Abdul Gayoom has been making increased efforts to protect the country's religious and cultural identity, which had begun to blur a bit under the previous president, Ibrahim Nasir. Women, who in the past never even had to wear the veil in Maldives (they even went bare-breasted until the start of this century), now mostly wear traditional Islamic dress, completely covering themselves. Marriages with foreigners find little social acceptance, even when the foreigner officially converts to Islam and becomes a Maldivian citizen.

Contact between the local population and foreign cultures is kept to a minimum. Only a limited number of Maldivians are employed on the resort islands, and the jobs (crew members on boats, bellhops, waiters, etc.) are held exclusively by men. You only see Maldivian women on the hotel islands when they're paying a family visit to an island's rich owner. Tourists visiting local villages have to register in advance, and the visit has to be over by 6 p.m.

According to the "Tourist Master Plan," 4 more atolls and 14 new resort islands will be opened to tourism by the year 2004. At the same time, in order to prevent undue foreign influence on the locals, there are plans to establish special "culture islands" for tourists. These islands are to provide foreign visitors with some insight into local life, but in a controlled atmosphere, where they can purchase traditional handcrafts and photograph and film demonstrations of local life and culture that have been set up for them in advance.

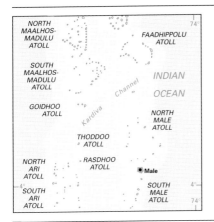

MALE

MALE

Thanks to its towering skyscrapers, Male, Maldives's up-and-coming island metropolis, is visible from afar, looming out of the water. Today, the country's capital exudes a veritably cosmopolitan flair, although it wasn't long ago that it bore more the stamp of a sleepy Asian town. Around 1900, Male boasted a mere 2,000 inhabitants, and domestic animals grazed on the little island as recently as a few decades ago.

Male is located in the North Male Atoll, offically known as the Kaafu Atoll. At the outset of Maldivian history, Male was not yet the country's political and cultural center; it wasn't until the advent of Islam in 1153 that the city gradually developed into Maldives' administrative hub.

As the earliest settlers of Maldives came from Sri Lanka, the island Rasgetheemu, in the Maalhosmadulu Atoll to the north, was the first royal island. It was here that the legendary Ceylonese prince Koimala Kaola was crowned Maldives'

Preceding pages: Male shows its modern face along Marine Drive, its traditional one at the nearby fruit and vegetable market. Left: The Islamic Center's golden domes shine over the city.

first king. The island of Gaafaru, north of the Male Atoll, settled by influential figures in the country's early years, was also important; historians believe that this island long served as the archipelago's secret capital. This changed, however, when Koimala Kalo moved his court to Male. The name Male derives from the Sanskrit word *Maaliu*, "large island" or "main island." Male later acquired the designation *Mahal*, "palace island," and it remained, after Koimala Kalo's move, the seat of Maldives' kings and sultans.

In the course of its history, Male, lying as it did on what was, in the northeast monsoon season, the perfect sailing route between East Asia and the western world, became a favorite stopover point for the leading marine powers of the day. Arabs (after 1153), Portuguese (1517-1573), Dutch (1645-1792), and British (1887-1965) all had a decisive influence on the overall development of the archipelago.

City of the Future

Male is a mere 1.85 kilometers wide and 1.2 long, and nearly rectangular in shape. The little capital is divided into four districts: Henveiru in the northeast, Maafannu in the northwest, Galohu at the center and Machchangolhi to the south.

39

The first official census of Maldives' population, in 1921, recorded 6,127 inhabitants of Male; today, that number has swollen to more than 70,000. As the island is a mere 2.2 square kilometers, this population explosion has necessitated considerable work in the area of artifical landfill.

The end of the 1980s saw a phenomenal construction boom on Male, which rapidly transformed the city into a modern urban center. The view of the golden dome and minaret of the Islamic Center, once free in virtually every direction, is gradually being obscured by the tinted glass facades of sleek new office towers. As in other Asian cities such as Singapore or Tokyo, the paucity of avaible land has forced the city to grow upward rather than outward, causing an increase in the kind of multi-story buildings that until 1990 were still regarded as rather incredible and worthy of special attention.

Another major change in the cityscape has come about through the paving of Male's streets. About 1,000 registered cars make their way through the city's narrow streets, their passage impeded by countless cyclists who prevent traffic from moving much faster than a walking pace. Everywhere there are paved roads, sidewalks and crosswalks; and the days when potholes prevented the rise of vehicular traffic along the harbor promenade are definitely gone by. As recently as 1989, Marine Drive had to be closed when, after a heavy rain shower, a car sank in a deep puddle. Today, only a few small alleyways in more remote residential areas remain unpaved. A new habor, built in 1992 with Japanese assistance, has driven many of the picturesque fishing and transport dhonis from the old harbor along Marine Drive.

Male today is a modern government center with officials, ministers and administrators; it's also the economic and cultural center of this island republic,

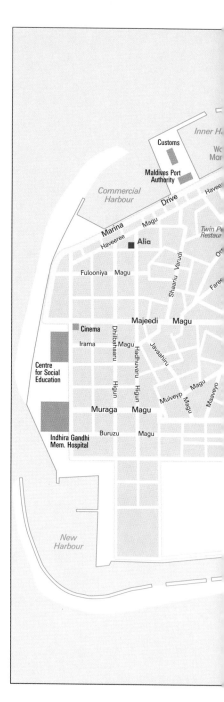

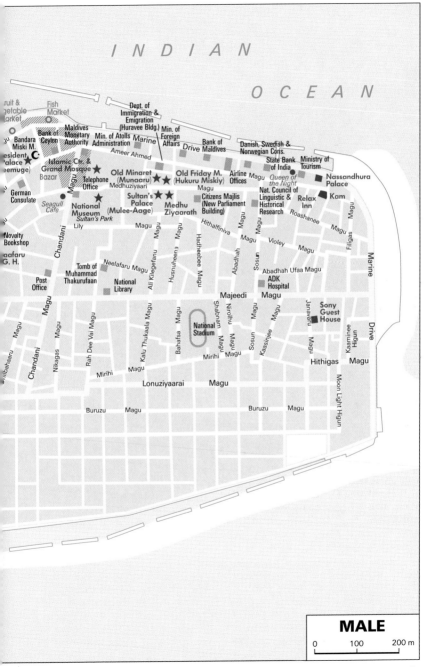

with its own radio and television stations, a large electrical power plant, and modern satellite receivers facilitating international communication. Linking Male to the rest of the world is the international airport on the nearby island of Hulhule, a mere 2 kilometers away. Many Maldivians commute from their home islands to the capital to take advantage of the broader range of medical facilities, business opportunities, banks and services, as well as better-paying jobs. Many parents send their children to Male to reap the benefits of a more comprehensive academic and vocational education than they can possibly hope for on their home islands in remote atolls.

An inevitable consequence of the city's attractiveness has been a dramatic growth in its population; the government therefore took over the nearby resort island of Villingili in 1990 and converted it

Above: Taking the day's catch to the fish market. Right: Wood is an important commodity in Male (wood market).

into a kind of suburb to create new living space for Male's residents.

The undreamt-of scale of the economic boom enjoyed by Male and, indeed, the whole country is clearly reflected in the crowds of freighters lying moored off Male between Funadhoo (Petrol Island), the prison island of Dhoonidhoo, and Villingili. As the capital doesn't have its own deep-sea harbor, any supplies or consumer goods which due to cost considerations are transported by sea have to be loaded onto smaller boats and dhonis which ferry them either to Male or directly to the other islands.

A Tour of Male

In spite of the march of progress, the countless stores, the hectic traffic and the hustle and bustle caused by this city's rapid growth, you can still, especially along Marine Drive, find visible traces of the "old Male" as the first tourists must have seen it years ago.

The **fish market**, where the vendors are still exclusively male, is best visited in the afternoon, when the dhonis arrive in the harbor with the day's catch. When the boats come in, Marine Drive springs to life, crowded with people haggling over the price of bonito, tuna, barracuda, sailfish and shark. Lying packed together are row upon row of snappers, wrasse, mackerel, and other kinds of fish often unfamiliar to the eyes of visitors from abroad. Not far from the fish market, the **wood market** is also a center for active, engaging trading in a traditional ambiance.

Another souvenir of days gone by is the **bazaar**, an amalgamation of tiny shops extending over blocks of narrow side streets, where you can buy anything you can imagine that you might need in the course of a day. Located here, too, are the signature Maldivian tea shops, which convey a sense of the typical harbor atmosphere, serving spicy dishes and

sweets, accompanied by plenty of tea and betel nuts.

Also on Marine Drive is the **fruit and vegetable market**, where the vendors offer a huge range of exotic produce and provide colorful images for would-be photographers. Other shutterbugs point their lenses at the picturesque fishermens' dhonis on the harbor as they unload the catch of the day or night and carry them across the street to the spot where prospective buyers are already collecting.

For visitors, modern Male is also a shoppers' paradise. Gung-ho consumers will have a field day here, where the selection extends to virtually everything you can imagine buying in any Asian city. Note, however, that many of the souvenirs in the smaller shops aren't from Maldives at all, but rather from Sri Lanka, India, Malaysia, Singapore, Indonesia or Taiwan. The shopping centers, by contrast, have large stocks of such items as watches, electronics and textiles, generally at bargain prices.

Thanks to the ever-increasing flow of visitors to Male and the city's improving service sector, the city's cuisine has also flourished. Modern restaurants catering to Western palates, ice-cream stores, pizza joints and other purveyors of fast food are all signs of the new times that have arrived on Maldives.

Sights

As Male continues to grow unchecked, more and more of its historic buildings and neighborhoods have had to yield pride of place to ambitious construction projects. Nonetheless, visitors to the city can still find a few interesting sights pertaining to "old Male," although such sights are steadily dwindling in number. As early as the 1960s, then-President Nasir was already having the walls of the old Portuguese fort and the harbor quay dismantled; what old cannons remained were simply thrown into the sea, and were later buried forever through the addition of subsequent layers of landfill.

Only nine of them were recovered in the course of construction of the new harbor in 1990; one stands today at the end of the wharf on Bandos. Nasir also oversaw the almost complete destruction of the venerable, historic sultan's palace. The last relics of this bygone residence are preserved in the **National Museum**, founded in 1952, actually a converted wing of the former palace, which sits in a pleasant, shady park.

Also vanished are the public bathing pools, once fifteen in number, which were generally located in the vicinity of mosques and used by the faithful for symbolic acts of cleansing and purification before prayer. These were, however, removed for a good reason, in an effort to reduce the danger of malaria on the island.

One historic sight that has survived is the **Friday mosque**, *Hukuru Miskiy*,

Above: The minaret of the Hukuru Miskiy.
Right: The Friday Mosque cemetery with its carved gravestones.

which Sultan Ibrahim Ibrahim Iskandar I built in 1656; the small, curving minaret, trimmed in green and blue, was added in 1675. It's said that this mosque was only the third such house of worship to be built in the whole country. The intricate carving of the gravestones, as well as the architectural ornaments on the building itself, attest to the high degree of virtuosity Maldivians once boasted in one of the island's traditional artisan specialties, stonecarving.

The very first mosque in the country, probably built around 1153 when Islam first arrived on these shores, originally stood in a side street not far from the Friday mosque. Foundation walls of this old building were probably incorporated into the small, new mosque that now stands on the site. Near here is the **tomb** and a **memorial** to the revered national hero **Mohammed Thakurufaanu**, who conquered the Portuguese in 1573, thereby ending the rule of Catholic occupying forces.

You can't miss Male's trademark, the **Islamic Center**, completed in 1984: its gilded dome and slender minaret tower over the city. This modern Friday mosque can accommodate more than 5,000 worshippers. Opposite the Great Mosque is the shrine of **Medhu Ziyaarath**, honring the monk Abu al-Barakat Yusuf al-Barberi, who converted the Maldivians to Islam. Unlike many other mosques, this shrine is open to visitors even outside of regular prayer hours, as long as everyone respects Islamic dress codes.

It's also worth taking a look at the **President's Palace**, *Mule Aage*, although you can only peruse the exterior, since like most government buildings it isn't open to the public. Not far from the Islamic Center, somewhat kitschy in aspect, this edifice was built in 1913 at the behest of Sultan Mohammed Shamshuddeen III for his son, the designated heir to the throne. After the Sultan and his family were forced to go into exile on a

remote island in 1936, the government began using the building as an administrative center. Since the declaration of the first Republic of Maldives on January 1, 1953, the palace has served as headquarters of the President.

Night Life and Shopping

Anyone compelled to spend the night in Male will search in vain for the kind of night life to which Europeans are accustomed: there aren't any discos or bars, not even any corner pub where you can get alcohol. In fact, you can't even find beer or wine, not even by day, not even in the duty-free shops which are only open to tourists. Up 'til the end of the 1980s, Male had two hotels licensed to serve beer and wine – the Nassandhura Palace Hotel and the Alia Hotel – but because of immoderate consumption on the part of a few locals, even these ultimately lost their licenses. Today, you can only find alcohol on the resort islands and on a few licensed safari boats.

Yet in spite of the fact that it only serves nonalcoholic beverages, the "beer garden" of the **Hotel Nassandhura**, at the northern end of Marine Drive, is a good place to head for, at least by Maldivian standards. Until relatively recently, there were hardly any restaurants or pubs for visiting foreigners, and this hotel's cuisine was an insider tip for tourists. In the last few years, however, a number of tourist restaurants have sprung up, such as the **Park View Restaurant** with tasty Chinese and Indian specialties; **Twin Peak**, serving excellent Italian food; or the small ice-cream parlour **Seagull Cafe**, where you can sit outside. In addition to the countless teaships, the **Queen of the Night** and the **Moon Café** are among the more popular hangouts with locals; as a rule, not many tourists find their way here.

Beyond the pleasures of the table and an evening stroll in the moonlight, Male offers visitors hardly any other nighttime diversion, unless one opts to venture into one of the two local cinemas in the city.

Even if you don't speak any Indian languages or Dhivehi, you can get a taste of local color and derive considerable amusement from one of the "ultra-dramatic" B-movie romances from India's film studios, some of the most popular films in the Asian world, which include a surprising amount of dancing and music.

There are plenty of places to stay the night in Male, but no accommodation on Maldives is particularly cheap. Apart from the Nassandhura Palace Hotel, the best place in town, the Kam Hotel and the Relax Inn have decent rooms.

Male, furthermore, has some 30 guesthouses and lodges which offer simpler accommodation for around US$30 and up a night. There's no centralized hotel service for visitors, but taxi drivers are happy to help you look, as they get commissions from the hotels if they're suc-

cessful in finding guests. Individual travelers should ascertain in advance whether the bed tax that's obligatory for every foreign visitor, currently (in 1998) amounting to some US$6 a night, is included in the price they're being quoted. Package tourists don't have this problem, as the bed tax is included in the price of their tour.

Shoppers for low prices and duty-free articles don't have to stick only to the very good selection in the well-stocked duty-free shop at the airport on Hulhule; electronics and watches, in particular, are generally cheap in Male, as well. But don't come to Male if your only goal is to find bargains; the time and cost of the trip far outweigh any savings on the purchase price. When buying a product, make sure that it comes with an internationally valid warranty; if not, don't buy it, especially if the object in question is a watch, camera, or video camera. When buying a video camera, also remember to check that the unit corresponds to the television system of your home country (PAL or NTSC).

Above: Men break for a lunch of traditional Maldivian dishes in a teashop near Male's harbor.

MALE

Getting There / Transportation

AIR: Fly in to the Male International Airport on Hulhule, then take a dhoni to Male (2 km), disembarking either at the harbor or in front of the Nassandhura Hotel.

NATIONAL AIRLINES: **Air Maldives**, 26 Ameer Ahmed Magu, tel. 322428, fax 325056. **Maldives Air Taxi**, International Airport Hulhule, tel. 315201, fax 315203. **Hummingbird**, MHA-Bldg., Orchid Magu, tel. 325708/9, fax 323161.

BOAT: Male is always the port of entry for the entire Maldives. Register with the port authority: Maldives Port Authority, Boduthakurufaanu Magu.

TAXIS only make sense if you have a lot to carry; otherwise, it's much faster on foot. Negotiate the price before you get in. If you're taking a taxi from a hotel, order it by phone.

Accommodation

MODERATE: **Nassandhura Palace Hotel**, Boduthakurufaanu Magu, tel. 323380, fax 320822, e-mail: nasndhra@dhivehinet.net.mv. The best place in town, renovated in 1995; 31 deluxe rooms with air conditioning, mini-bar, a good outdoor restaurant, business center, IDD telephone. **Kam Hotel**, H. Roanuge, Meheli Goalhi, tel. 322212, 320611-13, fax 320614, e-mail: kamhotel@dhivehinet. com. 31 superior rooms (small) with air conditioning, mini-bar, TV, safe, IDD telephone, rooftop restaurant, swimming pool. **Relax Inn**, Ameer Ahmed Magu, tel. 314531/2, fax 314533, 47 rooms, two of them suites, with air conditioning, mini-bar, TV, restaurant, coffee shop, sauna, jacuzzi pool, travel agency.

BUDGET: **Maagiri Tourist Lodge**, Boduthakurufaanu Magu, tel. 322576, small rooms with fans, hot showers, TV, telephone. **Transit Inn**, Maaveyo Magu, tel. 313174, 320420, nice rooms with air conditioning. **Buruneege Guest House**, Hithahfiniva Magu, tel. 322870. **Buruneege Residence**, Buruneege, Hirhahfiniva Magu, tel. 313777. **Athamaa Palace**, Majeedhi Magu, tel. 313118, 15 rooms with air conditioning, hot showers, TV. **Villingili View Inn**, Majeedhi Magu, tel. 318696, 12 rooms with air conditioning, showers, telephone.

Restaurants

Parkview Restaurant, Chandhanee Magu, tel. 328106, Indian, Chinese, and international dishes. **Queen of the Night**, Boduthakurufaanu Magu, tel. 322653, popular teashop on the harbor. **Seagull Café House**, 2 Fareedhee Magu, tel. 323792, 323332, excellent Italian ice-cream parlor with outdoor seating. **Slice Café**, Faamudheyri Magu, good burgers and other snacks. **Thai Wok**, Marine Drive, good, reasonably priced Thai cooking. **Twin Peaks**, Orchid Magu, Italian restaurant, pizza, pasta and good coffee.

Sights / Museums Mosques / Markets

Islamic Center with the Great Mosque and minaret, Medhuziyaaraiy Magu. **Shrine of Abu al-Barakat Yusuf al-Barberi (Medhu Ziyaarath)**, opposite the Great Mosque. **Friday Mosque** (Hukuru Miskiiy) and **Old Minaret**. Medhuziyaaraiy Magu, can only be visited with a permit from the National Council for Linguistic Historical Research, tel. 323206 or preferably request in writing to the fax number 326796. **National Museum** in Sultan Park, 9 am-noon and 3-6 pm, closed Fri. **Sultan Park**, Medhuziyaaraiy Magu, 4-6:30 pm. **Presidential Palace (Mulee Aage)**, Medhuziyaaraiy Magu. **Monument and Tomb of Mohammed Thakurufaanu**, between Sultan Park and **Majeedhee Magu**. **Wood Market**, **Fish Market**, **Fruit and Vegetable Market** all on Marine Drive, by the harbor.

Banks

Bank of Ceylon, Orchid Magu. **Bank of Maldives**, Boduthakurufaanu Magu. **Habib Bank**, Orchid Magu. **State Bank of India**, Boduthakurufaanu Magu.

Shopping / Bookstores

Stores are open 8 am-noon and 12:30-10 pm, Fridays 2-10 pm. **STO Shopping Complex**, Maafanu. **Umar Shopping Arcade**, Chandi Magu, Marine Drive. **A1-Bookshop**, STO Trade Center, Orchid Magu. **Books N Toys**, Majeedhee Magu. **Modern Bookshop**, Janavari Magu. **Novelty Bookshop** (largest bookstore in town), Fareedi Magu. **Multi Books**, Lonuziyaaraiy Magu.

Cinemas

Star Cinema, Majeedhee Magu, tel. 323913/322913, American action films. **Olympus**, Majeedhee Magu, shows mainly Indian films.

Hospitals / Pharmacies (Emergency Number for Male's Ambulance Service: 102)

HOSPITALS: **Indhira Gandhi Memorial Hospital** (state-owned), tel. 316647/318516, fax 316640. *PRIVATE CLINICS:* **ADK Hospital**, Sosun Magu, tel. 313553, fax 313554. **AMDC Clinic**, Dharumavantha Magu, tel. 325979, fax 325899. **Polly Clinic**, tel. 314647. *DOCTORS* who take private patients: **Dr. Imthiyaz**, eye clinic, tel. 323655. **Dr. Yaganegis**, tel. 322593. *PHARMACY:* **GKT Pharmacy 2**, tel. 318982.

Useful Addresses

Emergency Police Line: 119. **Ministry of Foreign Affairs**, Boduthakurufaanu Magu, tel. 323400-8, fax 323841. **Immigration Authorities**, Huvaree Building, tel. 323912, fax 320011.

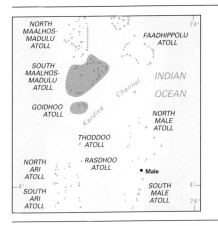

THE SOUTH MAALHOSMADULU AND GOIDHOO ATOLLS (BAA ATOLL)

THE SOUTH MAALHOSMADULU AND GOIDHOO ATOLLS

The South Malhosmadulu Atoll, which was called the Horsburgh Atoll during the period of the British protectorate, lies about 100 kilometers north of the Ari Atoll, and southwest of the Faadhippolu Atoll. Its nearest neighbor is the smaller Goidhoo Atoll, adjacent to the south. The two atolls together form an administrative unit that's officially known as the Baa Atoll.

One notable feature of the South Malhosmadulu Atoll is a channel about 1.8 kilometers wide running right through the middle of the atoll's northern section. Its sheer cliff walls, plunging to depths of as much as 200 meters, make it a favorite with scuba divers. The western side of the channel is called Kuda Kanduolhi, while its eastern section goes by the name of Kudarikilu Kandu.

Measuring some 42 kilometers by 32 kilometers, the atoll has 82 islands: 14 of these are inhabited, 67 uninhabited, and one is a resort island. The whole atoll has some 8,500 inhabitants; Eydhafushi, the main island, has a population of about 2,000.

To date, Soneva Fushi remains the only resort island in the South Maalhosmadulu Atoll. By the year 2004, however, four other islands in the eastern part of the atoll are scheduled to become resorts: Fonimagoodhoo, Kihaadhuffaru, Horubadhoo and Dhunikolhu.

In 1962, the Maldivian government began using Fulhadhoo, Fehendhoo and Goidhoo, the three southernmost islands in the oval Goidhoo Atoll, as a place of imprisonment or exile for criminals. Among the convicts was a German national who had committed a crime in Maldives. Banished to Fulhadhoo, he ultimately settled down, converted to Islam, and married a Maldivian woman. The islands effectively served as a prison or place of exile long before this; for when François Pyrard ran his ship, the *Corbin*, aground on a reef off Fulhadoo in 1602, he was held captive on the island for five years, until he finally managed to escape.

8.5 kilometers in length and 17.5 kilometers wide, the Goidhoo Atoll can only be reached from the south through a channel called Doru Kandu. During the monsoon season, therefore, fishermen are happy to seek out its sheltered anchorage.

Preceding pages: Arriving on Eydhafushi, main island of the Baa Atoll. Left: Maldivians steer their dhonis "by foot."

51

RESORT ISLAND IN THE SOUTH MAALHOSMADULU ATOLL

Soneva Fushi (Kunfunadhoo)

Off the beaten track, the South Maalhosmadulu Atoll is virtually untouched by tourism. But the atoll's sole resort, Soneva Fushi, is one of the largest and most exclusive islands of Maldives.

Seen from the air, the island's lush tropical foliage seems like a large green carpet, 1.4 kilometers long and a mere 400 meters wide, which almost conceals the 42 bungalows scattered around the island. Running around the periphery of this "carpet" is a narrow sand beach; inland, birds, lizards, and rodents dwell in the dense vegetation. Off the east side of the island is a broad reef with a beautiful lagoon: a perfect place for modern-day

Above: Comfortable and attractive, Soneva Fushi's decor is designed to pamper guests.
Right: People can live out their shipwreck fantasies on a nearby uninhabited island.

Robinson Crusoes, to say nothing of divers.

When the 50-bed Kunfunadhoo Island Resort opened in 1983, the dhoni trip to and from the airport in Hulhule, 112 kilometers away, still took almost two days. Because of it remoteness, the resort subsequently closed; it re-opened in 1995, its transportation system much improved, under the name of **Soneva Fushi Resort**. Today, a Hummingbird helicopter shuttles back and forth from the island to Hulhule in a mere 40 minutes.

In the range and luxury of its amenities, Soneva Fushi is exemplary. Bungalows are offered in three different price categories, although none of these is exactly cheap: one night, including full board, ranges from US $350 to $685. The 25 "moderate" superior bungalows, measuring 34 square meters, are all equipped with ceiling fans, showers, and private bathrooms with hot and cold running water, as well as with safes, hair dryers, mini-bars, and terraces. An additional twelve duplex bungalows of 42

square meters have bedrooms on the upper storey. Top of the line are the five Soneva villas, 54 square meters in size. These have decadently luxurious bathrooms, air conditioning, TV, video, and even a stereo.

Soneva Fushi's luxurious standards extend to its restaurant, as well; guests can find everything their palates could possibly desire. This is quite literally true, as if the restaurant doesn't have something, it can be brought in by LSG, Lufthansa's catering service.

And the exclusivity continues in the realm of sports and activities: the island boasts both a water sports center and a tennis court. Then, of course, there's the obligatory diving center. Daily diving excursions bring guests out to gorgeous and largely unspoiled diving locations. Particularly impressive are the numerous *kandus*, or channels, in the southeastern part of the atoll, right around Soneva Fushi; they offer brilliantly-colored coral formations, as well as the occasional encounter with a really big fish. Rounding out the selection of recreational options are snorkeling, sailing, windsurfing, volleyball, ping-pong, and both night fishing and deep-sea fishing.

INHABITED ISLANDS AND PICNIC ISLANDS IN THE SOUTH MAALHOSMADULU ATOLL

Bathalaa

Lying in the northern part of the atoll, Bathalaa is a small, uninhabited island with no palm trees and very little vegetation. Most attractive features include superb white sand beaches and a long sand bar that extends out into the lagoon on the western side of the island. Both beaches and the sand bar are excellent places for sun-worshippers or for a leisurely swim in the warm ocean water.

Dharavandhoo

Dharavandhoo sits right on the eastern outer reef of the atoll, and divides the entrance to the atoll's inner area into two channels, Dharavandhoo Kandu and Dharavandu Bodu Kandu. In addition to fishing, the island's inhabitants make their living primarily from the production of a range of hand-crafted articles for the tourist market, such as fans, lampshades, and woven mats. Most of their creations are sent off to the capital city of Male to be sold.

The island also sports an old mosque, as well as ruins of buildings from days long past.

Dhonfanu

Located in the eastern section of the South Maalhosmadulu Atoll, this uninhabited island is surrounded by a broad reef. Its sheltered northern end provides excellent anchorage for safari boats and fishermen's dhonis.

Eydhafushi

The main island in the South Maalhosmadulu Atoll, Eydhafushi is the atoll's commercial center and transportation hub. The island has had a relatively high population for hundreds of years. The inhabitants of Eydhafushi used to be known for their beautiful hand-woven white cotton sarongs, *fehli*; but after the introduction of synthetic fabrics, which were lighter-weight and easier to wash, these traditional *fehli* went rather quickly out of style.

Eydhafushi's Great Mosque was built two centuries ago during the reign of Sultan Mohammed Mu-eenudhee I (1799-1835). A large radio tower provides visual orientation and marks the island's position for passing ships.

Finolhas

Long and narrow, overgrown with a luxuriant tangle of tropical island, the uninhabited Finolhas lies in the inner part of

the atoll, on the eastern side. The island's wealth of coconut palms and idyllic beach attract, and delight, the occasional visitor.

Fonimagoodhoo

Fonimagoodhoo lies in the northeast corner of the South Maalhosmadulu Atoll. At present still uninhabited, the island has lush vegetation, beautiful beaches, and a house reef that's well worth a look.

At night, sea turtles often come up onto Fonimagoodhoo's deserted beaches to lay their eggs and bury them in the sand. To date, the few picnickers who now and then happen upon the island have had hardly any effect on the reproductive cycle of these rare creatures. However, this will probably change, as the government has given permission for Fonimagoodhoo to be developed as a resort island. A 200-bed hotel is to be built sometime in the near future.

Hithaadhoo

Maldivians all over the country tend to regard the inhabitants of Hithaadhoo with esteem, because of their strong Islamic faith and strict adherence to the commandments of Allah. The island has a broad enclosure reef, which forms a large lagoon in the south.

Horubadhoo

Horubadhoo is one of the islands in this atoll scheduled to be opened to tourism by 2004, at which point this tropical paradise will bear some 100 bungalows. At the moment, however, Horubadhoo's lush vegetation grows right down to the narrow beach that extends all the way around the island. This wealth of greenery draws countless migratory birds who stop off here on their annual journeys; underwater, a beautiful coral reef draws

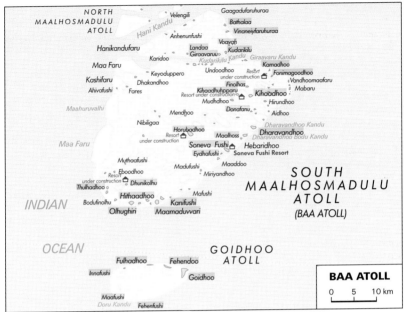

divers and snorkelers. Inland, the jungle has grown up around the ruins of an old mosque, as well as a bathing pool and an ancient graveyard where the tombstones have no inscriptions: all indications of early settlement. Horubadhoo's first residents probably moved on to Dhonfanu.

Kamadhoo

Kamadhoo lies on the northeastern side of the atoll, right on the Giraavaru Kandu. Fishermen from other islands occasionally stop off at this inhabited island to repair their boats and paint their hulls with a very smelly fish oil that protects them from barnacles and tropical woodworms. The fishermen don't appear overly sensitive to strong smells, yet it can be observed that they only do this work when there's a stiff seaward wind.

Kanifushi

Kanifushi is one of the larger islands on the southern rim of the South Maalhosmadulu Atoll. The uninhabited island's most beautiful beach is located at its northern end. At low tide, one can walk over to the neighboring islands of Medhufinolhu and Ufulingili, as well as to two sand bars a little ways offshore.

Kihaadhoo

The inhabited island of Kihaadhoo lies on the eastern side of the atoll and is surrounded by a reef about 50 meters wide. A shallow channel leads into the lagoon on the southwestern side of the island.

Kihaadhuffaru

Apart from a few young coconut palms, the island of Kihaadhuffaru has very little vegetation. What it does have is a very beautiful beach that runs all the way around it and a fabulous lagoon for swimmers. These striking features and picture-perfect island scenery are probably reasons why this is one of the islands in this atoll recently declared free for tourism; one wonders how the picture will change with the completion of a hotel with 200 beds.

Kudarikilu

The inhabited island of Kudarikilu (population 489) is located on the southeastern side of the atoll's northern section, right on the channel Kudarikilu Kandu. Sporting an abundance of palm trees right down to the edge of the beach, the island is situated in a lovely, very calm lagoon. Kudarikilu also boasts an old mosque and a cemetery. To locals, Kudarikilu bears the additional epithet *Bomuge Haasdhisaa*, or "Bomb Island," a name that refers to a tragedy that occurred here in 1915, when a land mine washed up on the beach. Drawn by curiosity, the island's inhabitants unsuspectingly brought their deadly "find" to shore and began hitting the exposed fuse with a heavy object. The resulting explosion instantly killed nine people and seriously injured fifteen others.

Landaa Giraavaru

Landaa Giraavaru, an uninhabited island, lies in the northeastern part of the atoll, just north of Kudarikilu Kandu. The uninhabited island boasts a profusion of palm trees, and a few small sand bars extend along its western side. Surrounding the island is a lovely lagoon with large formations of coral. The ruins of two buildings located on Landaa Giraavaru probably date from the time when the palm trees were planted.

Maalhoss

Located on the atoll's southeastern edge, Maalhoss is inhabited primarily by fishermen and artisans. The eastern side

Right: Children play without a care in the world on Maalhoss.

of the island is overgrown with lush vegetation. Visitors can venture into this jungle to see the island stone, the *huraagandhu*. This block of coral, some 60 centimeters in diameter, is supposed to have been as tall as a palm tree at some point in the past; the stone's origins and purpose remain unknown.

Another noteworthy "attraction" on Maalhoss is a 70-year-old palm tree that has grown so unusually it appears almost crippled.

In the western part of the island there's a small lagoon which offers boats a protected anchorage. The locals fish its waters for herring, which they either eat or use as bait.

Maamaduvvari

Medium-sized and elongated, the island of Maamaduvvari, located at the southern end of the South Maalhosmadulu Atoll, is popular with swimmers as well as with divers and snorkelers. A wonderful lagoon extends along its northwestern shore. The most beautiful reef channels are in the south.

Milaidhoo

The small, uninhabited island of Milaidhoo lies in the northeast of the atoll, southwest of Kamadhoo. Surrounding it is a reef whose roof, formed of hard and soft coral, is a paradise for snorkelers and divers.

Mudhdhoo

Mudhdhoo, located in the eastern part of the inner atoll, was once inhabited, but is no longer. Nature has erased all traces of human life here, except for two fountains, an old graveyard, and the ruins of a mosque. Today, idyllic Mudhdhoo's untouched beaches, encircling the entire island, and its dense stands of palm trees lure visitors to its shores.

Olhugiri

Olhugiri is the first island sailors use to orient themselves when they enter the atoll from the south. Quite large and uninhabited, overgrown with dense tropical foliage, the island serves as a refuge for birds and turtles. A small reef runs around Olhugiri, coming closest to shore off the eastern and northern coasts. On the east side, a deep channel allows boats to enter the lagoon.

Thulhadhoo

Thulhadhoo is a small island located in an extensive reef system in the southwest of the South Maalhosmadulu Atoll. The neighboring islands Bodufinolhu and Dhunikolhu are part of the same system. Tuhlhadhoo is one of Maldives' classic artisan centers; its residents produce a variety of objects adorned with colorful lacquer decorations, which are sold in souvenir shops and markets throughout Maldives.

Vinaneiyfaruhuraa

The tiny island of Vinaneiyfaruhuraa is located southeast of Bathalaa at Bathalaa Kanduohli, which is at the northeast tip of the Vinaneiy Faru reef. This is the perfect place to play at being Robinson Crusoe, sitting on a completely deserted tropical island and, perhaps, searching one's soul.

Voavah

Voavah lies on the northeast side of the inner South Maalhosmadulu Atoll, and is well protected from the open sea by the Vinaneiy Faru reef. Uninhabited, crescent-shaped, this island has little vegetation to speak of, aside from a few coconut palms. However, any visitor who's looking for a peaceful place in which to rest, relax and commune with unspoiled nature will be able to appreciate the gorgeous beach flanked on either side by large sand bars extending out into the lagoon.

INHABITED ISLANDS AND PICNIC ISLANDS IN THE GOIDHOO ATOLL

Fehendhoo

The long, narrow island of Fehendhoo is located on the atoll's outer reef. An inhabited island, it's been populated for many years. It's easy to reach by boat, thanks to the southern channel that runs straight through the atoll. To the south, there's a sandy lagoon studded with blocks of coral. Extending to the west of the island is a strip of sand that at low tide reaches almost all the way to the neighboring island of Fulhadhoo.

Fehenfushi

Fehenfushi is located in the south of the Goidhoo Atoll just east of the Doru Kandu, which represents the only entrance to the atoll. Rather than the typical Maldivian island of most vacationers' dreams, Fehenfushi is little more than a large accumulation of coral fragments piled up by wind, waves, and ocean currents.

Fulhadhoo

Fulhadhoo lies right on the northern edge of the reef that runs around the entire atoll. The only access to the island is by boat through the Doru Kandu. Rather thin, but quite long, this inhabited island has very lush vegetation. Extending along its southern side is a beautiful expanse of beach, as well as a shallow lagoon. Fulhadhoo is well known both to historians and experienced wreck divers because of the *Corbin*, a French ship that was stranded on the reef near Fulhadhoo on July 2, 1602, with the Frenchman François Pyrard on board. Pyrard and the 40 other surviving crew members managed to make their way to the island on a smaller boat; they were promptly cap-

Above: These typical woven chairs are popular everywhere.

58

tured and sent to various other islands, where only four of them, including Pyrard, managed to survive five years of imprisonment. According to local tradition and legend, the shipwrecked crew managed to bury the silver the *Corbin* was carrying at the foot of a large breadfruit tree before they were captured. It's also said that quite a few years ago a group of French adventurers came back to the island in search of the treasure. However, they found neither the tree nor the silver.

Goidhoo

Goidhoo lies at the southern tip of the atoll that bears its name. Measuring 1.6 kilometers across and 2 kilometers in length, it's the atoll's largest island. Numerous flattened mounds scattered around the island made of a mixture of coral and sand suggest that Goidhoo was inhabited for many centuries. In 1962, the island was officially declared to be a penal colony or place of exile, a move that was evidently in keeping with tradition: historical records indicate that criminals were banished to Goidhoo, as well as several other Maldivian islands, as early as 1602.

Innafushi

Innafushi lies in the northwest of the Goidhoo Atoll, on the inner side of the circular enclosure reef. Small and uninhabited, the island has only sparse vegetation and therefore offers little shade from the sun.

Maafushi

Located on the atoll's southern side, west of the channel Coru Kandu, Maafushi is basically a pile of coral rubble without any vegetation whatsoever. The island has a lighthouse that serves as a navigational aid to ships and boats.

SONEVA FUSHI (KUNFUNADHOO)
Soneva Fushi Resort

Opened in 1995. Male office: 4/3 Bldg. Faamudheyri Magu, 20-05 Male, tel. 326685 and 326686, fax 324660; in London: tel. 0044 181 743 0208, fax 0044 181 743 6788; island: tel. 230304/-5, fax 230374, Internet: http://www.soneva-pavilion.com. *BUNGALOWS:* 25 superior bungalows (34 sq. m) with fans; 15 bungalows also have air conditioning; all rooms have safes, bathrooms with tubs, TV, video, and private terraces. 12 duplex bungalows (42 sq. m) are equipped with extra bedrooms and CD players. 5 Soneva villas (54 sq. m) boast even more modern appointments, as well as private gardens. *AMENITIES:* bar, coffee shop, restaurant, video rental, CD rental, beauty center, water sports center, deep-sea fishing. *DIVING BASE:* Soleni Dive Centre, German, English, French, Italian; house reef; nearest decompression chamber on Bandos (110 km away); there's a doctor on the neighboring island of Eydhafushi. *CREDIT CARDS:* AE/MC/VC. *AIRPORT:* 112 km, 40 minutes by helicopter.

Soneva Fushi is one of Maldives' most exclusive and most expensive resort islands.

DHUNIKOLHU

Opened to tourism in 1998; still under construction. Male office: Sunland Hotels Pte., Ltd., # 04-01 STO Trade Centre, Orchid Magu, PO Box 20145, 20-02 Male, tel. 324658, fax 325543. *BUNGALOWS:* 100 rooms (planned). *AMENITIES:* bar, coffee shop, restaurant. *DIVING BASE:* yes. *AIRPORT:* 118 km.

FONIMAGOODHOO

Opened to tourism in 1998; currently still under construction. Male office: Mr. Ahmed Thasmeen Ali, c/o Sheeraazeege Magu, Male, tel. 327622. *BUNGALOWS:* 100 rooms (planned). *AMENITIES:* bar, coffee shop, restaurant. *DIVING BASE:* yes. *AIRPORT:* 118 km.

HORUBADHOO

Opened to tourism in 1998; still under construction. Male office: Island Travel & Trade Pte., Ltd., M. Feeroaz Lodge, Muranga Magu, Male, tel. 325721. *BUNGALOWS:* 100 rooms (planned). *AMENITIES:* bar, coffee shop, restaurant. *DIVING BASE:* yes. *FAIRPORT:* 118 km.

KIHAADHUHPPARU

Opened to tourism in 1998; currently still under construction. Male office: Mr. Shabeer Ahmed, c/o G. Prospect, Male, tel. 324658. *BUNGALOWS:* 100 rooms are currently planned. *AMENITIES:* bar, coffee shop, restaurant. *DIVING BASE:* yes. *AIRPORT:* 118 km.

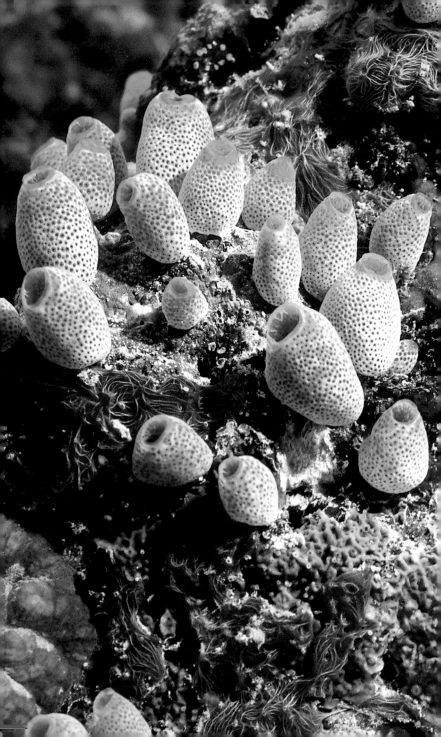

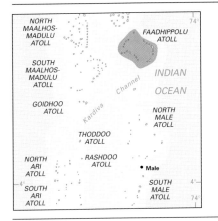

FAADHIPPOLU ATOLL (LHAVIYANI ATOLL)

THE FAADHIPPOLU ATOLL

North of the North Male Atoll and the complex reef system of Gaafaru Falhu, 120 kilometers from the capital, lies the Faadhippolu Atoll, known officially as the Lhaviyani Atoll. A dhoni takes more than eight hours to make the trip, although a helicopter takes only 45 minutes to reach the atoll, which measures some 37 kilometers across and 35 long. The islands that make up the Faadhippolu Atoll are arranged around the rim of the atoll like beads on a necklace; protecting this, as it were, on the east side is a barrier reef more than 30 kilometers long. Numerous canal-like channels (called *kandus* in Dhivevi) cut through the other sides of the reef. However, as these are rather narrow, the 7.5-kilometer-wide southern channel between Aligau and Lhossalafushi, which is far easier to navigate, serves as the main entrance to the sheltered atoll. The only obstacle in this channel, and an impossible one to miss, is the small island Maduvvari. There are no islands within the atoll itself. The westernmost

Preceding pages: Divers' paradise – the colorful underwater world of anemones, sponges and rock coral. Left: As a rule, many generations live together under a single roof.

point in the atoll, the island Kanifushi, has a lighthouse on it to warn ships. The northern entrance to the atoll is the 500-meter-wide Kuredhdhoo Kanduohli, which lies east of the resort island of the same name.

The Faadhippolu Atoll includes 54 uninhabited and 5 inhabited islands, as well as the resort island Kiredhdhoo. There are plans to open up Komandhoo (90 beds), Hudhufushi (400 beds), Madhiriguraidhoo (200 beds) and Kanuhuraa (200 beds) to tourism in the near future.

The inhabitants of the atoll make their living primarily from fishing and tuna processing; female laborers from Sri Lanka are also brought in to do this work. In days past, the islanders used to make their money from sail-making and processing coconut fiber.

RESORT ISLANDS IN THE FAADHIPPOLU ATOLL

Kuredhdhoo

Kuredhdhoo, measuring 1,500 meters by 350 meters, is one of the largest resort islands in Maldives. Currently the only holiday resort in all of the Faadhippolu Atoll, this long, narrow island is located at Kuredhdhoo Kanduohli, near the northern entrance to the atoll. Kuredh-

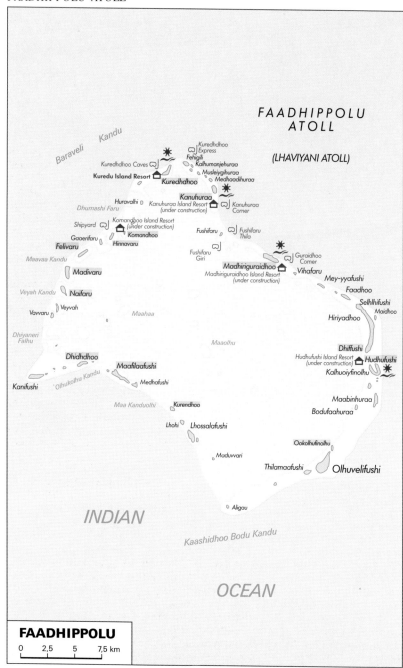

FAADHIPPOLU ATOLL

(LHAVIYANI ATOLL)

Baraveli Kandu

Kuredhdhoo
Express
Kuredhdhoo Caves
Fehigili
Kuredu Island Resort
Kalhumanjehuraa
Kuredhdhoo
Musleiygihuraa
Medhaadihuraa

Kanuhuraa
Kanuhuraa Island Resort
(under construction)
Kanuhuraa
Corner

Huravalhi
Dhumashi Faru

Shipyard
Komandhoo Island Resort
(under construction)
Gaaerifaru
Komandhoo
Fushifaru
Fushifaru
Thila

Felivaru
Hinnavaru

Fushifaru
Giri
Guraidhoo
Corner
Madhiriguraidhoo
Vihafaru
Madhinguraidhoo Island Resort
(under construction)

Maavaa Kandu

Madivaru

Mey-yyafushi
Faadhoo
Selhlhifushi
Maidhoo

Veyah Kandu
Naifaru

Vavvaru
Veyvah
Maahaa

Hiriyadhoo

Dhiyaneri
Falhu
Maaolhu

Dhiffushi
Hudhufushi Island Resort
(under construction)
Hudhufushi

Dhidhdhoo
Maafilaafushi
Olhukolhu Kandu
Kalhuoiyfinolhu

Kanifushi
Medhafushi

Maabinhuraa
Bodufaahuraa

Maa Kanduolhi
Kurendhoo

Lhohi
Lhossalafushi

Ookolhufinolhu
Maduvvari
Thilamaafushi
Olhuvelifushi

INDIAN
Aligau

Kaashidhoo Bodu Kandu

OCEAN

FAADHIPPOLU

0   2,5   5   7,5 km

dhoo is enchanting, with its lush growth of palms and tropical bushes, the untouched sand beach, which fluctuates in size as it winds around the island's perimeter, and its lovely lagoon which, since it has but little coral in it, is ideal for swimming and surfing.

The Kuredu Camping Resort was built in 1978; ten years later, after a thorough refurbishing, it was renamed **Kuredu Island Resort**; and it boasts, today, more than 250 rooms with 500 beds. It can be reached from the airport by either seaplane, speedboat, or by a helicopter that operates to and from the island's own heliport.

Of the rooms, 123 are self-contained standard class bungalows with ceiling fans and fresh- (cold-) water showers, toilets, and small terraces. An additional 126 self-contained superior class bungalows are equipped with hot and cold running water, air conditioning, and a refrigerator. The restaurant serves a range of international specialties, catering to the preferences of the hotel guests, half of whom are from German-speaking countries. However, there is also a good selection of Maldivian specialties, including fresh-caught fish. Most meals are served buffet-style, but table service is available for some evening meals.

By far the most popular sport on Kuredhdhoo is scuba diving. As there are still relatively few tourists in this area and, moreover, as Kuredhdhoo lies well off the usual safari boat routes, the island's diving spots are still virtually untouched.

Attractions for divers include, in addition to a panoply of breathtaking reefs, two large wrecks on the island's western side, which, because they lie at a shallow depth, are easy to dive to. The exact position of the sunken ships is clearly marked by the *Skipjack II*, which stands perpendicular to the ocean floor with its prow still protruding above the surface. Over the years the two ships, both of which went to the bottom in 1985, are covered with a luxuriant growth of coral, and have provided a vast array of marine life with a new home. By day, imposing moray eels float in apparant suspension between the colorful soft corals growing out of the rusted openings in the wreck. In Kuredhdhoo Kanduolhi, the 250-meter-wide channel to the west of the island, you can often glimpse sea turtles. Underwater, the channel's reefs descend like terraces for more than 25 meters, and display breathtaking growths of fan coral. Along the outer reef, which is more exposed to ocean currents and therefore requires a bit more experience to dive, large fish such as gray reef sharks often swim by. The swift currents in the channel have earned it the name "Kuredhdhoo Express."

Other sports activities on the island include snorkeling, windsurfing, sailing, soccer, ping-pong, badminton, and tennis, as well as deep-sea and night fishing. Those so inclined can also use the fitness room or browse in the souvenir and jewelry shops for mementos. Island-hopping is also a popular recreational activity. Disco and cabaret evenings, as well as beach parties, round out the picture of this appealing island, which offers a wide range of activities in an otherwise isolated region of the Maldivian archipelago.

INHABITED ISLANDS AND PICNIC ISLANDS IN THE FAADHIPPOLU ATOLL

Dhidhdhoo

Dhidhdhoo, a long, narrow island in the southwest of the atoll, is sometimes called by its traditional name of Olhukolhu Dhidhdhoo. This uninhabited island has very thick vegetation, including several coconut palms. At low tide, a number of sand bars emerge around the island, extending all the way to **Olhu-**

kolhu Kandu, on the eastern side of the island, which is one of the main channels into the atoll. Maldivians say that there was once, to the north, an island larger than Dhidhdhoo called Olhulgiri; but no trace of such an island remains today.

Dhiffushi

This elongated island lies on the eastern reefs of the atoll; together with Selhhifushi, Hiriaadhoo, and Maidhoo, it forms a complex island landscape. Dhiffushi was once inhabited; the ruins of an old mosque and a well still attest to the days when people lived here. The island is connected with a local story: in 1966, the ship *The City of Victoria*, out of Colombo, was stranded on the house reef. After the crew had managed to repair the damage and make the ship seaworthy

Above: Jewel damselfish are particularly colorful reef-dwellers. Right: Tuna processing remains an important branch of the Maldivian economy.

again, they rechristened it *Dhiffushimaadhoo*.

Felivaru

On the western rim of the atoll is Felivaru, home to a large fish processing plant. Opened in 1977 with help from Japan, it's now under Maldivian ownership. Fish processing is the main source of revenue for the Faadhippolu Atoll, the best atoll for fishing in Maldives. Many fishermen, especially those from Naifaru and Hinnavaru, bring their tuna catch to the factory in Felivaru, where the fish are processed into top-quality canned goods for worldwide export.

Hinnavaru

Somewhat northeast of the factory island of Felivaru, at the western edge of the atoll, lies Hinnavaru with its 2,706 inhabitants. The island's residents have long specialized in fishing; over the years, they've achieved a measure of

prosperity, which led to their bringing in more workers, thus increasing still further the number of residents of this densely-populated island.

Prosperity has also brought a brand-new set of environmental problems. For example, releasing untreated waste water into the lagoon has caused a steady rise in the growth of algae.

Hudhufushi

Hudhufushi, on the eastern edge of the atoll, is easy to recognize because of its V-shaped outline. In the middle there's a shallow lagoon in which mangroves grow. The island is covered with a thick growth of trees, shrubs, and coconut palms.

Hudufushi was once two islands, Hudhufushi and Kalhuoiyfinolhu, but over time sand deposits made the two islands one. The beaches on the island are truly wonderful. By 2004, if all goes according to plan, the island should sport a 400-bed resort hotel.

Kanuhuraa

Long and narrow, with dense vegetation and countless coconut palms, the strikingly beautiful uninhabited island of Kanuhuraa sits within shouting distance of the resort island Kuredhdhoo. The large, shallow lagoon is bordered by an exquisite beach. This island, too, is to get a 200-bed hotel in the near future.

Komandhoo

Komandhoo is a small, uninhabited island just opposite Hinnavaru in the inner atoll. The island has an impressive number of beautiful coconut palms and other lush tropical vegetation. By 2004, it, too, should have a resort hotel for up to 90 guests.

Kurendhoo

Kurendhoo, an inhabited island with a population of 1,019, is also called Loa-kurendhoo by the locals. It is in the

67

southwest of the atoll at the entrance to Maa Kanduohli.

Maafilaafushi

This large, elongated island lies like a barrier along the southwestern edge of the atoll by the Ohlhukolhu Kandu channel. It was inhabited as early as the late Middle Ages, during the reign of Sultan Mohammed Imaaduddeen I (1620-1648). Those inhabitants, however, abandoned the island for unknown reasons, migrating to the island of Naifaru. Today, tucked away in the lush greenery, visitors can still see silent reminders of the past, such as the ruins of a mosque or a cemetery with old gravestones.

Some years ago, in an effort to relieve overcrowding on the neighboring islands of Naifaru and Hinnavaru, the Maldivian government decided to resettle Maafilaafushi. But despite jungle-clearing pro-

Above: Naifaru's residents are known for their artisan skill.

jects and an improved infrastructure, the resettlement program proceeded slowly, in part because of the Maldivian superstitition that an abandoned island should remain uninhabited. Still, civilization has already had its effects on the once-crystalline waters of the island's lagoon, which are now overgrown with a thick stand of eel grass as a result of the release of waste water.

Madhiriguraidhoo

In addition to its traditional name, this uninhabited island has two other ones: Guraidhoo and Dream Island. There's good reason for the latter appellation. This picture-perfect island, which lies in a long and narrow lagoon on the outer reef in the northeast of the atoll, is truly gorgeous. A pristine snow-white beach runs all the way around its edge, 1,200 meters on a side. Furthermore, with its handful of small hills the island is, by Maldivian standards, veritably mountainous. Narrow at its northwest tip,

Madhiriguraidhoo broadens out toward the southwest and becomes gradually wider, thanks to sand deposits, in the south. Vegetation is not particularly dense at the northern end of the island, but the eastern side, by contrast, boasts an impressive growth of coconut palms, increasingly dense toward the end of the island.

This veritable paradise of a tropical island has not escaped the attention of the international tourist industry, however: it's to get a 200-bed hotel within the next few years.

Madivaru

Madivaru is a very narrow, crescent-shaped island that lies on the western side of the atoll near the main island, Naifaru. Hidden and unremarkable, this island is home to Maldives' National Security Agency, a kind of combination of army and police force.

Naifaru

Densely populated, with 3,132 inhabitants, Naifaru is located on the western side of the atoll, by the Veyah Kandu. Owing to its sizable population, the island's inhabitants jokingly refer to it as "Little Male." Main sources of income for Naifaru's residents are fishing and a range of artisan crafts producing souvenirs for the country's tourist markets and shops. The islanders are supposed to be particularly talented at working with black coral and mother-of-pearl. They are also known for their traditional medicine, supposed to be very effective.

Olhuvelifushi

Olhuvelifushi, which lies in the southeastern section of the atoll, is a small inhabited island with a population of only 336. It is flanked by two even smaller, uninhabited islands, Thilamaafushi and Ookolhufinolhu.

KUREDHDHOO
Kuredu Island Resort
Opened in 1978, refurbished in 1988. Male office: Champa Trade & Travels, Kum No. 5, Ahmadee Bazaru, tel. 321751, fax 326544, telex: 089666140 CHAMPA MF, E-Mail (diving school): prodiver@netlink.net.mv, Internet (diving school): http://www.prodiver.com. Island: tel. 230337, fax 230332, telex: 089666201 KUREDU MF. *BUNGALOWS:* 100 individual bungalows with fans, cold showers; 150 bungalows with air conditioning, warm showers, refrigerators. Drinking water from the island's own desalination plant. The new bungalows are furnished with modern bamboo furniture. *AMENITIES:* 2 bars, coffee shop, 2 restaurants, fitness room, tennis, accident station, jeweler, disco, large souvenir shop, surfing and sailing schools. *DIVING BASE:* Swedish, German, English, French, Italian, PADI 5 Star IDC center, E6 lab and video studio; the nearest decompression chamber is on Bandos (136 km away), house reef. *CREDIT CARDS:* AE, MC, VC. *AIRPORT:* 146 km, 45 min by helicopter, 3.5 hours by motorboat.
Kuredhdhoo is the largest hotel complex to date in Maldives, with more than 3 km of white sand beach and a playground for children. It offers a great range of activities for fans of water sports. For divers, there are more than 40 breathtaking and nearly untouched diving spots, as well as two wrecks, near the island. About half of Kuredhdhoo's clientele hails from the German-speaking world.

HUDHUFUSHI
Hudhufushi Island Resort
Opened to tourism in 1998; a 200-room hotel complex is currently still under construction. *AIRPORT:* 126 km.

KANUHURAA
Kanuhuraa Island Resort
Opened to tourism in 1998; a 100-room hotel complex is currently still under construction. *AIRPORT:* 143 km.

KOMANDHOO
Komandhoo Island Resort
Opened to tourism in 1998. Male office: Mr. Hussain Afeef, Ma. Champa Villa, Champa Brothers Maldives Pte., Ltd., tel. 313248, fax 314101. *AIRPORT:* 143 km.

MADHIRIGURAIDHOO
Madhiriguraidhoo Island Resort
Opened to tourism in 1998. Male office: Mr. Ibrahim Ali Maniku, Ma. Nooree, Jawaahiru Goalhi, tel. 314833 and 328850, fax 316922. *AIRPORT:* 140 km.

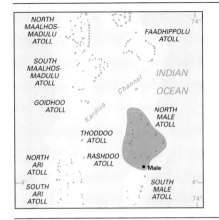

THE NORTH MALE ATOLL (KAAFU ATOLL)

THE NORTH MALE ATOLL

The North Male Atoll, which includes the capital city of Male, is the main atoll of Maldives. Thulusdhoo is its main island and the seat of the atoll's local government. Administratively a part of the Kaafu Atoll, the atoll, including the island of Gaafaru, is 69 kilometers long and 39 kilometers across at its widest point.

The North Male Atoll includes 50 "real" islands as well as various small, island-like sand bars and mounds of coral. Of its 42 islands, originally uninhabited, 27 have to date been opened up to tourism; 15 others are leased to private individuals. Eight islands, including the airport island of Hulhule, are inhabited. Many of the resort islands lie very close to the airport, so that the transfer from hotel to airport by traditional dhoni doesn't take more than a few minutes. In order to save time, tourists staying on islands that are somewhat farther away from Hulhule are generally taken to their hotels by either speedboat, plane, or helicopter.

Preceding pages: Treating stress in the shallow lagoon waters. Left: Watching and feeding the fish on the island dock – a favorite vacation pastime for children.

RESORT ISLANDS IN THE NORTH MALE ATOLL

Asdhoo

Asdhoo, a small tourist island in the North Male Atoll, lies near the island of Meerufenfushi, about 58 kilometers from the airport. Approximately 350 meters long and only 120 meters wide, Asdhoo sports a luxuriant growth of thick tropical shrubbery and a number of coconut palms. Even before the opening of the current hotel, Asdhu Sun Island, there was a modest bungalow facility here, but it soon proved unequal to the task of dealing with the geometric increase of tourism and the demands of modernity. As a result, **Asdhu Sun Island** opened for business in 1981; the hotel was completely renovated in 1988. This idyllic island also has its own desalination plant, which means that guests can drink fresh water from the taps in their rooms around the clock.

The cuisine on Asdhoo is international; the accommodations consist of row houses with relatively modest appointments. It is no surprise, then, that Asdhoo tends to attract visitors who compute their expenses carefully and travel on a limited budget. Anyone who doesn't find luxurious sleeping and living quarters

73

necessary to the enjoyment of a vacation can avail himself of the idyllic beach that encircles the entire island, the most attractive sections of which are located along the west coast. As well as diving, Asdhoo offers windsurfing, ping-pong, and volleyball. The many beautiful diving sites near the island are popular with underwater photographers.

Bandos

With a surface area of 180,000 square meters, Bandos is one of the largest islands in Maldives. Approximately 500 meters long and 400 meters in width, the island forms almost a perfect circle. Bandos has been inhabited for a very long time, and historians believe that the first people to live here were descended from a group of Indian Tamils. The

Above: Bandos – a perfectly round island paradise. Right: Doctors treat victims of diving accidents in a decompression chamber.

Frenchman François Pyrard, who on July 2, 1602 was shipwrecked on a reef in the Goidhoo atoll in his 400-ton ship *Corbin*, and therefore was compelled to remain in Maldives for a number of years, reported as early as 1602 that Bandos was inhabited and that "the island's waters are preferred to those of Male." Between 1962 and 1968, there was an orphanage on the island, but it was later moved to Villingili. The **Bandos Island Resort** opened in 1972. After Kurumba, Bandos has long been Maldives's "second" resort island; and it remains a classic among Maldivian resorts.

In 1989, the hotel was expanded to 177 deluxe rooms and 48 suites, which raised its capacity from 225 to 450 beds. The hotel management is constantly seeking ways to continue to improve its standards. A staff of some 450 people, from gardeners to managers, are responsible for seeing to it that guests enjoy a comfortable and seamless visit. The island has succeeded in modernizing without losing any of its original charm. Because

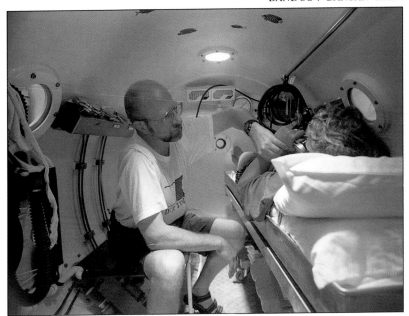

Bandos is only 20 minutes from the airport by speedboat, airlines often book it for their flight crews during layovers, which has led to the rather sarcastic nickname of "Stewardess Island."

Bandos sports the vegetation so typical of Maldives – a mix of coconut palms, agave bushes, and rubber trees – and is completely ringed with a beautiful sandy beach. Because of its shallow depth and the profusion of underwater coral growth lying just below the water's surface, Bandos's lagoon is not ideal for swimming and snorkeling – or at least, only to a limited degree. The best swimming on the island is along the edge of the house reef, where there's another attraction for divers in the form of a small wreck.

Bandos gained some notoriety in the 1980s when the popular German scuba diving teacher Herwarth Voigtmann ran the diving base here and attracted international attention with his spectacular but not altogether uncontroversial shark feedings, which some critics dubbed "Voigtmann's shark circus."

Scuba diving is still the number-one sport on Bandos, and with good reason: a beautiful house reef and the proximity of another 40 first-rate diving sites virtually guarantee an unforgettable underwater vacation. The hotel also offers windsurfing, sailing, waterskiing, volleyball, and tennis.

Right next to Bandos is a small, uninhabited island called **Little Bandos**, perennially popular with day-tripping hotel guests; the island was allegedly used a few years ago for the filming of a TV commercial for a well-known brand of Caribbean rum. The nearby island of **Kuda Bandos**, which is inhabited, is popular with inhabitants of Male as a desination for holiday excursions.

Banyan Tree (Vabbinfaru)

Banyan Tree is located in the southern part of the North Male Atoll, forming a geographical triangle with the islands of Ihuru and Baros. It is one of the smallest of Maldives to be developed for tourism:

75

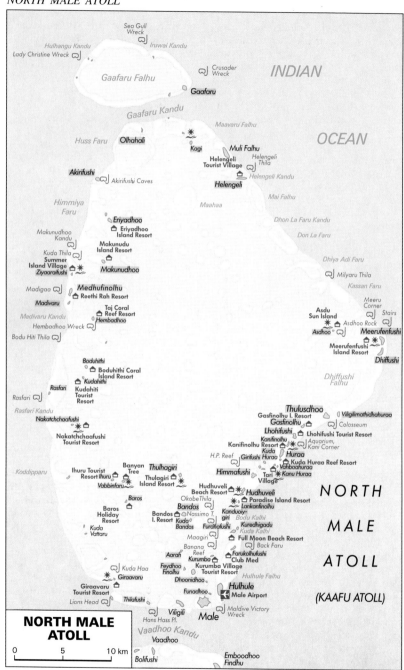

NORTH MALE ATOLL

0   5   10 km

almost circular in form, it measures a mere 150 meters in diameter. Because its position in the atoll is relatively well protected from wind and waves, Banyan Tree boasts a broad sand beach, which extends all the way around the island, helping to create a picture-perfect Maldivian idyll. Rounding out the picture of tropical island perfection is the lush vegetation, studded with countless palm trees, in the island's "interior."

Unfortunately, the island's house reef is not among Maldives's diving highlights; at most, it's suitable for simple, relaxing dives. More attractive and challenging diving reviers are located somewhat farther away. A large lagoon guarantees good swimming; at low tide, visitors can take in the absolute quiet that prevails at the island's two sand bars.

There has been a hotel on **Banyan Tree** since 1977. After an extensive course of remodeling in 1994, the island now boasts 48 round thatched bungalows, built in Asian style, and luxuriously furnished. Each bungalow has a terrace and its own small garden. The island offers a full complement of sports activities; the large lagoon, sheltered from the wind, is especially suitable for beginning surfers. Most of Banyan Tree's visitors come either from France or Italy.

Baros

Baros was once inhabited, long ago, but the crescent-shaped island was abandoned for unknown reasons around 1700. Measuring some 60,000 square meters in area, the island is approximately 300 meters long and 200 in width. Situated in the middle of the North Male Atoll, it is only 15 kilometers from the airport, a trip that takes 60 minutes by dhoni or 20 by speedboat.

The island may have taken its name from the kingdom of Baros in northwestern Sumatara, a realm with which the Maldivians once maintained trade con-

nections. However, it could also come from the island's earliest inhabitants. Baros was once used as a quarantine island for people with infectious diseases, and housed many people with *baros-bali,* a disease similar to leprosy.

Baros is also among the first generation of resort islands: it went into the tourist business in 1973. Today, the grounds and amenities of the **Baros Holiday Resort** are attractive and well-tended: palms and shrubbery, flower beds and bungalows harmonize in a successful blend of tropical idyll and modern tourism. Of the 59 bungalows facing the large, shallow lagoon, 16 have been set up as so-called "water bungalows." After a thorough renovation and remodeling, many of the rooms now have air conditioning, telephones and minbars; and the high standards continue in the well-appointed bathrooms, all of which have hot and cold running water. A staff of some 120 people, mostly Maldivians, see to the needs of the guests. The restaurant offers a range of excellent international dishes, including a large buffet several times a week. For divers, meanwhile, there's an attractive house reef with three different dive sites a mere 20 meters away from the diving base.

Boduhithi

Boduhithi was long uninhabited; not until 1979 was it opened up and developed for tourism as the **Boduhithi Coral Island Resort**. Slightly sickle-shaped, the island, measuring approximately 52,000 square meters in area, is situated on the western side of the North Male Atoll. It takes a motor dhoni about two hours to make the trip from the airport, 29 kilometers away. This modern resort with its pleasant atmosphere, with 86 individual bungalows and 4 pile bungalows, is one of the classic "Italian islands"; it's marketed almost exclusively by travel agents south of the Alps. Of

course, one can also reserve rooms directly, either by telephone or in person in Male.

Boduhithi is called "Coral Island," with good reason: the long house reef that extends along the island's southern side drops down steeply, a virtual guarantee for superb diving. Among the other excellent diving spots around the island is the underwater conservation area of **Rasfari**. However, visitors are often obliged to share this popular area with divers from neighboring islands. The lagoon on the western side of the island is particularly well suited for surfing, sailing, fishing, and waterskiing. The best places to swim are the two sand bars at the island's tips, as well as the shallow lagoon.

Night life here centers around a disco that caters to the Italian temperament. The attractive restaurant provides susten-

Above: Emperor angelfish lead solitary lives on the reef. Right: Faru (Club Med), one of Maldives's renowned club facilities.

ance with a certain Italian flair: it's an open secret that Boduhithi serves the best pizzas in Maldives.

Eriyadhoo

Eriyadhoo, the northernmost island on the western side of the North Male Atoll, lies in very close proximity to the outer reef. The oval-shaped island is 300 meters long and 180 meters wide, and it can comfortably be circumnavigated on foot in about 10 minutes. About half of the island is still in its natural state; the other half is occupied by the hotel, which has about 70 employees.

Eriyadhoo's principal focus is scuba diving. No diver can fail to be enthusiastic about the island's spectacular, intact house reef, which runs all the way around the island, beginning about 50 meters out from the beach and extending down to depths of up to 30 meters. Easily accessible from several different diving locations, the reef features a wide range of coral structures, an abundant fish popula-

tion, and spectacular dropoffs. Farther out, other diving spots, to which boats run out twice a day, also offer an intoxicating wealth of colorful coral. Because Eriyadhoo is relatively far away from other resort islands, in Maldivian terms, divers don't generally have to share these outlying sites with divers from other centers. Divers are invariably enchanted by these little-frequented reefs with their seemingly infinite variety of underwater flora and fauna. And the proximity of Eriyadhoo to **Gaafaru Falhu**, the largest reef system in Maldives, in the northern end of the North Male Atoll means that you can take day excursions out to superb diving areas featuring breathtaking dropoffs as well as four historic wrecks for divers to explore.

The hotel, which is called the **Eriyadhoo Island Resort**, is clean and practically furnished. It also has a charming restaurant that invites guests to linger; while at night you can sometimes hear music issuing from the island's small disco. However, the principal activities

on this natural, unspoiled island remain quiet relaxation and, of course, scuba diving.

Faru (Farukolhufushi / Club Med)

Farukolhufushi is located north of the airport island of Hulhule, near the capital city of Male. The crescent-shaped "Faru," approximately 800 meters long and 150 meters wide, has gained worldwide renown as a **Club Med** island. In Dhivehi, the island's name means something like "island on the edge of a reef," a reference to the island's proximity to the outer reef. Uninhabited for many years, the island was later rented out as a vacation home to a Maldivian family. Faru was opened up to the tourist trade in 1973, making it one of the oldest resort islands in Maldives. Subsequently, Club Mediterranée took over the island; the organization remains one of the few club-type facilities that's been able to establish a foothold in Maldives. After Farukolhufushi's main building burned down to the

ground in 1994, management decided to renovate the entire resort. The new facility opened in 1995.

Because of the wide range of activities and entertainment it offers, as well as a state-of-the-art disco, this resort, which is often booked up for months in advance, can't be described as the most tranquil in Maldives. Traditionally, the *lingua franca* at the Club is French, but English is spoken as well.

Water sports, of course, figure prominently on Faru. These include surfing, snorkeling, and the inevitable diving, as well as other active sports such as windsurfing, catamaran sailing, and kayaking. Extending south and west of the Club is a large lagoon, ideal for snorkeling.

Running between Farukolhufushi and the neighboring island of Furanafushi is **Kuda Kalhi**, a narrow channel which gets quite a lot of boat traffic. At times,

Above: Furana (Full Moon Beach Resort).
Right: The women of Giraavaru wear intricate embroidered collars.

especially during the northeast monsoon, Kuda Kalhi's tricky currents can create difficulties for smaller dhonis. However, these same currents make the channel extremely popular with scuba divers, who come here to dive to such world-famous locations as Banana Reef and Back Faru. On a lucky day, you can sometimes spot large schools of dolphins around Kuda Kalhi as they make their way through the atoll.

Full Moon (Furanafushi)

Along with Kurumba and Farukolhufushi, Furanafushi (more commonly known as Furana) was one of the first resort islands in Maldives – possibly because of its proximity to the airport in Hulhule, a mere 7 kilometers away. The first guests arrived here in 1973.

In the early days of Maldivian history, the island was home to a Buddhist monastery named Puranna Pura.

Located in the southern part of the North Male Atoll, the island, measuring some 600 meters long and 350 wide, was completely modernized and refurbished in 1994. New, improved standards called for a new name; the luxurious new facility is now known by the more euphonious designation of **Full Moon Beach Resort**, and marketed as such by tour operators around the world.

Since the renovations, Full Moon offers 156 rooms with deluxe furnishings in double bungalows and "water bungalows." There's also a large fresh-water pool, a shopping center, and a sports and fitness center, as well as three restaurants serving Mediterranean and Thai cuisine, several bars, and a disco. The island has one of the most extensive entertainment and sports programs in Maldives, as well as a lovely lagoon perfect for swimming. South of Full Moon is a striking underwater landscape of coral that makes for terrific snorkeling. Several privately-owned buildings, pile houses on the beach near the entrance to the lagoon, are used as warehouses for the export of tropical fish.

Gasfinolhu

Gasfinolhu, a small island only 200 meters long, is located in the southeastern North Male Atoll, on the outer reef. Only 23 kilometers from the airport, it's easy to reach from both Hulhule and Male by speedboat; the trip takes about 30 minutes.

Gasfinolhu Island Resort opened for business in 1980. Today, it offers 40 simple but efficient bungalows, their terraces all with views of the ocean. At low tide, you can walk over to the neighboring island of **Lhohifushi**; be advised, however, that sharp pieces of coral lie along the route, making some kind of appropriate footwear essential as protection against cuts.

No more than 80 guests at a time can enjoy Gasfinolhu's exclusive club-like atmosphere (Club Valtur). The island's

comfortable restaurant serves primarily Italian cuisine, although some Maldivian dishes, notably delicious seafood, are on the menu as well. The price of a meal even includes the house wine.

Most popular sports on the island are catamaran sailing, windsurfing, and, of course, scuba diving. Some of the best diving in the entire atoll is practically next door to the island's outer reef, including the so-called Colosseum, Aquarium, Kani Corner and the famous HP reef, which is often visited by diving boats from neighboring islands. Just offshore, the island's house reef drops steeply into the water, providing a perfect background for simple shallow-water dives and snorkeling. Gashfinolhu also offers other water sports, including sailing, waterskiing, canoeing, and fishing.

Giraavaru

The name Giraavaru stems from far back in Maldivian history. In the very early days of the island kingdom, the

81

name was used as a designation for the first inhabitants of the entire archipelago. *Gira* means "island" or "piece of land that has been washed away," and *varu* means "a group of people." The inhabitants of the island, which is located in the southwestern North Male Atoll, on the outer reef, were at one time the most powerful and influential population group in Maldives. They themselves trace their ancestry back to a branch of the Tamils in southern India.

Fate has not smiled upon Giraavaru's people: driven from their island, they were subsequently compelled to move from one island to another. In 1968, they were forced to leave Giraavaru, and migrated to Hulhule, where they settled down. When the airport was built, they were again forcibly relocated, this time to Male, where there's still a small com-

Above: Fun on a Hobie Cat. Right: Bunga-lows on stilts – lack of space can lead to some imaginative solutions (Hembadhoo, Taj Coral Reef Resort).

munity of these islanders. They're easy to recognize from the older women's long dresses, adorned with striking embroidery around the collars.

Only 200 meters long by 150 wide, Giraavaru is one of the smaller resort islands in Maldives. The **Giraavaru Tourist Resort** was opened up for tourism in 1980. Giraavaru is only 11 kilometers from Hulhule, or 30 minutes by speedboat. Accommodations are in two-storey row bungalows equipped with air conditioning, showers, telephones, mini-bars, and refrigerators. For evening entertainment, there's also a restaurant, a small disco, and an even smaller bar. By day, visitors can get a first-hand glimpse of Maldivian city life on excursions to the nearby capital city of Male.

Giraavaru is one of the few resort islands in Maldives with a fresh-water pool. Next to this, the large beach offers a place to sunbathe and relax, and a lagoon provides further swimming opportunities. The island offers an extensive selection of water sports, including sailing, surfing, canoeing, fishing, and waterskiing. Other sports, such as volleyball and tennis, are also available. As on most other islands in Maldives, however, diving is the activity of preference. Both the spectacular house reef and a number of dive locations along the outer reef entice and mesmerize divers. Just off Giraavaru, to the south, begins the famous Vaadhoo Kandu, which divides the North Male Atoll from the South one. This geographical location explains the popularity of the diving fields in this Vaadhoo channel: large fish often swim through on their way from the ocean, much to the delight of divers.

Helengeli

Located 51 kilometers from the airport in Hulhule, Helengeli is the most isolated and remote of the resort islands in North Male Atoll. A dhoni makes the trip from

the airport in about 3 1/2 hours, and by speedboat it's about 1 1/2 hours. By seaplane, however, it's only a 15-minute trip. Helengeli, some 800 meters long by 200 wide, loosely translates as "the island that trembles" or "trembling island reef." In all likelihood, this evocative name came about because of the island's exposed position; especially during the northern monsoon, Helengeli is pounded by the rough seas along the outer reef. However, its location on the northeastern part of the outer reef means that this island has wonders in store for those visitors who arrive with a taste for underwater vistas.

Helengeli is tailor-made for individualists and passionate divers. Around the island are nearly untouched diving areas where one rarely encounters visitors from other islands. At most, an occasional safari boat make its way across Helengeli's particularly fascinating submarine landscape. It isn't just the renowned **Helengeli Thila**, with its superb coral landscapes and high frequency of passing manta rays; the two channels on the outer reef sport six marked diving locations for memorable descents. In fact, boats from Helengeli run out to some 40 diving sites. The area's strong currents are both a blessing and a curse. On the one hand, they bring an abundance of plankton that helps the coral to "bloom" especially well. On the other, however, the currents can be unpredictable, which means that some diving experience is required.

Helengeli is also a fascinating place for wreck diving. In February, 1991, a wooden ship from the Laccadives sank at Dhon La Faru Reef off the island's southern coast; and the *Dharuma*, a schooner belonging to the Maldivian government, was wrecked on the Helengeli reef on January 24, 1962. Another victim of this latter reef was the 1,397-ton vessel *Swiss*, which split apart on May 20, 1890 on its way from Pondicherry to Marseille; but this wreck has never been found. Other wrecks from the 19th and 20th centuries lie on the ocean floor around the Gaafaru Falhu reef.

83

Helengeli began its life as a resort island in 1979. Eight years later, its hotel, **Helengeli Tourist Village**, was completely renovated, and the resort was again remodeled in the mid-1990s. Every room has hot and cold running water as well as air conditioning. Above the water, the island manages to be both natural and well-tended; the attractive bungalows harmonize well with the natural environment. Lynchpin of the island's sports center is its state-of-the-art diving school; but Helengeli is not for divers only; it offers a wide range of other water sports and activities. A good blend of activities, a peaceful, relaxed atmosphere, and the merciful absence of the nightly pounding of a disco combine to make Helengeli an ideal refuge for anyone seeking genuine rest and relaxation.

Hembadhoo

The unforested island of Hembadhoo was opened to tourists in 1982 under the name Hembadhoo Island Resort. This hotel was closed at the beginning of 1997, and reopened a year later, after extensive renovations, under the new name of **Taj Coral Reef Resort**.

Diminutive Hembadhoo is almost perfectly circular, and measures a mere 200 meters across. Located on the northwest edge of the North Male Atoll, 32 kilometers from the airport (2 1/2 hours by dhoni), it's an ideal venue for divers. Its house reef offers a panoply of exquisite segments of coral, between which countless fish cavort above the sandy ocean floor. Although the broad reef was somewhat over-dived in the past, it remains very attractive and still offers a range of exciting and varied experiences.

One of the island's diving highlights – which experienced snorkelers can also

Right: Hulhule Airport. To accommodate modern jumbo jets filled with tourists, the runway was extended out into the sea.

enjoy – is the "wreck" of a small tugboat, 16 meters long, sitting at a depth of between 15 and 22 meters, upright on the ocean floor. In 1988, the operators of the island's diving school deliberately sank the boat near the landing stage to create an artificial reef. Today, more than a decade later, it's home to populations of every conceivable type of marine life. One particularly popular tenant is the moray eel who's taken up residence in the engine room. The ship's bridge is monopolized by huge swarms of glassfish.

Hudhuveli

Hudhuveli is 13 kilometers (one hour by dhoni) from the airport, on the eastern side of the outer edge of the North Male Atoll. The island's name means "white beach," and Hudhuveli, 350 meters wide by 80 meters long, does in fact have a spectacular white beach, as well as a large lagoon ideal for swimming. A few breakwaters of coral fragments extending perpendicularly into the lagoon have served to extend the usable beach area.

Opened to tourism in 1980, the **Hudhuveli Beach Resort** is patronized primarily by Italians; and Italians also run the dive center. Both the house reef and the spectacular diving areas along the outer reef draw visitors to Hudhuveli. The hotel has 44 rooms of average comfort, in double bungalows built in the shade of the palm trees.

South of Hudhuveli is the island of **Lankanfinolhu**, which can be reached on foot at low tide, if you wear the appropriate shoes. In all probability, these two small islands were originally one island that was cut in half over the years by erosion. "Island-hoppers" can pay visits to the neighboring resort islands on the east side of the atoll, such as Tari, Kuda Huraa, Leisure Island, Paradise Island, or Furanafushi.

Himmafushi, an inhabited island also located near Hudhuveli, is known as a

good place to buy hand-crafted souvenirs.

Hulhule

Hulhule provides virtually every visitor to Maldives with his or her first sight of a Maldivian island. Its international **airport**, modernized several years ago with the help of Japanese investors, is, symbolically speaking, the gateway both to the Maldivian archipelago and to the fulfillment of many vacationers' dreams. All flights within the archipelago also originate from Hulhule, which is approximately two kilometers from the capital city of Male.

Originally, the island was divided into two parts, called Hulhule and Gaadhoo. Before Maldives became a republic in 1965, the Sultan used both of these islands as his personal holiday resort. Before him, so legend has it, the island was inhabited by dragons.

As early as 1960, a British firm surveyed Hulhule with a view to constructing a small airport, Male having proven too small for this purpose. In the same year, work was begun on a provisional runway. In 1968, Hulhule and Gaadhoo were joined once again in order to lengthen Hulhule's runway. This was the first crucial step that opened up the airport to international air traffic and allowed Maldives to be marketed around the world as a tourist resort.

The boom in mass tourism in the 1970s necessitated further expansion of the airport. Construction on the first phase began in 1981, and the work was continued in a second phase of building in the mid-1990s.

Following an unsuccessful putsch by foreign mercenaries in 1988, the Indian paratroopers who had been sent to the island at the request of the Maldivian government remained stationed on Hulhule for some time.

The airport island has no hotels: only the facilities needed to handle more than 370,000 travelers a year, as well as an infrastructure capable of dealing with

30,000 commercial flights and 24,000,000 tons of freight.

Opening up new atolls to tourism has meant a concomitant increase in domestic helicopter and seaplane flights, a development that's brought the airport at Hulhule to the limits of its capacity. In order to remedy this situation, a plan has been developed to have the former British air force base on Gan in the southern Maldives handle more international flights. Furthermore, a third international airport, in the northern Maldives, is also in the works.

Divers associate Hulhule with the most famous of all Maldivian wrecks, the *Maldive Victory*. On the night of February 13, 1981, this British container ship, 82 meters long and weighing in at 1,420 GRT, rammed into the southern coast of the island and sank rapidly to the bottom, where it lies today, between 8 and 47 meters below the ocean's surface. Off the southwest side of the island lie the remains of another old wreck, often referred to as the "Portuguese Wreck." However, it's more likely that the vessel is an Indian *baggala* that ran aground during a storm in 1820 and went to the bottom along with 30 other ships.

Ihuru

The **Ihuru Tourist Resort** welcomed its first guests in 1978. Located in the west of the North Male Atoll, on the atoll's inner side, the island is nearly oval in shape and measures 200 meters in diameter. Ihuru is very popular with divers. For one thing, it lies in close proximity to a considerable number of superb diving areas; for another, the absence of mass tourism on the island appeals to individualists. Due to Ihuru's limited supply of fresh water, the number of guests is limited to 88 at any one time, which makes for a more personal, even familial atmosphere. Its pretty round thatched bungalows give the island a distinctive, unique stamp. Overgrown with a veritable jungle of lush growth, Ihuru has a beautiful turquoise lagoon surrounded by a barrier reef. While the furnishings are more practical than luxurious, the rooms provide adequate comfort. Visitors can spend their time pursuing the familiar roster of Maldivian activities, including volleyball, aerobics, waterskiing, catamaran sailing, and fishing.

The island's name is derived from the Divehi word *ihuru*, which is synonymous with "fanditha man," a figure who is on the one hand a magician and sorcerer, and at the same time a man of great spiritual wisdom. He's also a healer with a profound knowledge of plants and herbs, and it's he who must be the first to bring out the seeds for the year's planting. Later, after the grain has grown, it is his task to divine, from signs from nature, the right moment to harvest it; and he has to cut the first sheaf. From this grain he makes a kind of cake, which he then eats as a symbolic offering to the gods.

Kanifinolhu

Kanifinolhu, a crescent-shaped island, is 800 meters long and 250 wide. It sits on the outer reef in the southeastern North Male Atoll, in an area heavily frequented by tourists. Called Kani by locals, the island is 19 kilometers from the airport; the trip takes 30 minutes by speedboat, 90 by dhoni. Kanifinolhu boasts a lush growth of palm trees and tropical shrubs, nestled in the midst of which are beautiful row bungalows built of white coral stone, some of them thatched with palm fronds. All told, the **Kanifinolhu Resort** has 154 rooms in a range of price categories.

The shallow lagoon is ideal for swimming; while the house reef, 400

Right: The Safari Lodge – just one example of the exclusive interior decoration at the Kudahithi Tourist Resort.

meters offshore (with regular boat service), offers a wealth of fascinating sights for snorkelers and scuba divers. Divers are well served thanks to a number of other exquisite diving spots in the area. Kanifinolhu is one of the largest resort islands in Maldives, and offers a varied program of sports and recreational activities, as well as a range of evening entertainment.

Kudahithi

Only 600 meters south of Boduhiti is Kudahithi, a very small but exquisite island with long white sand beaches and an exceptionally broad reef. The **Kudahithi Tourist Resort** is one of the most exclusive in Maldives. It is located on the west side of the inner North Male Atoll, 27 kilometers (1 hour by speedboat) from Hulhule. Once nothing more than a long sand bar, this patch of land developed into a full-blown island after palm trees and shrubs were planted and a resort opened in 1984 that guarantees exclusivity and

aspires to the very highest standards of hostelry. There is room for no more than 14 guests at a time in Kudahithi's seven bungalows. Each bungalow is individually, and luxuriously, decorated, something revealed in the descriptive names: Balinese Cottage, Safari Lodge, Maldives Apartment, Sultan's Lodgings, Village Queen Bungalow, Captain's Cabin, and Maharani Suite.

Luxury, understatement and exclusivity are the order of the day on this island, a perfect place for those who love to be spoiled and who expect nothing less than the very best. *Dolce far niente* – the sweetness of idleness – is not only a perfect description of this island's relaxing and relaxed atmosphere, but also gives a good indication of its clientele: Kudahithi is overwhelmingly Italian. Active sports such as diving, snorkeling, and sailing assume something of a secondary role here. The island's diving school is located on neighboring **Boduhithi**, as is the disco, which also caters to a predominantly Italian public, and provides guests with

some variety in the evening, and a change of pace. Other water sports on Kudahihti include sailing, surfing, parasailing, waterskiing, and fishing.

Kuda Huraa

This island, which lies in the southeastern part of the North Male Atoll, was originally linked to the inhabited island of Huraa; however, the two islands were later separated by erosion. A mere 20 kilometers, or 30 minutes by speedboat, from the international airport in Hulhule, the 500-meter-long by 100-meter-wide island opened its beaches to sun-starved foreign tourists in 1977 under the name Little Huraa. The resort was renovated in 1994, and expanded anew in 1997, at which time it changed its name to **Kuda Huraa Reef Resort**. As the island is owned by the Concorde Hotel chain, it's

Above: Parasailing affords a bird's-eye view of the archipelago. Right: The joy of swimming on Kurumba's beach.

also sometimes called the Concorde Reef Resort.

Today, the facility is a thoroughly modernized hotel that offers pampered guests every comfort they could possibly wish for. These include water bungalows on pilings, luxury beach cabanas, bungalows decorated in a number of different ways, a conference center, and, last but not least, the largest swimming pool in Maldives. A large diving center offers training courses and dives with oxygen tanks. And it goes without saying that this most up-to-date of all Maldivian islands also offers its guests the chance to indulge in a full array of water sports.

Kurumba

The seas of history have brought a variety of names to Kurumba's shores. In ancient times, its was called Viharanapura. As this name comes from Sanskrit, it is believed that there was once a Buddhist monastery on the island. Later, the island was known as Vihamanaafushi.

Viha means "poison" in Dhivehi, and *maana* means "forbidden."

The first president of Maldives, Mohammed Amin Didi, was buried here after his assassination in 1954. His simple grave is located near the reception building.

In 1972, this island, 500 meters long and 250 wide, became the first in Maldives to open a hotel for tourists. At that time, the island changed its name to Kurumba Village, which means "coconut village" – in Dhivehi, *kurumba* means "young coconut."

In the 1980s, the hotel was completely renovated and remodeled from the ground up. Today, the **Kurumba Village Tourist Resort**, which is advertised in tourist brochures all over the world, is one of the most sought-after hotels in Maldives. This isn't just because of the top-class accommodations in five-star bungalows, but also thanks to such amenities as two fresh-water swimming pools, five restaurants, a fitness center with a sauna, two illuminated tennis courts, and a conference center that's especially popular among businesspeople. In addition, each of the 168 rooms has a terrace with a view of the sea; there are also six junior suites and four Presidential suites. The bungalows are harmoniously integrated into the surrounding landscape, which abounds in coconut palms and dense tropical shrubbery.

The best beaches are located near the landing stage. On the southern coast, the lagoon is particularly good for snorkeling, as the coral here, housing a wealth of tropical fish, grows to just below the water's surface. Divers can pursue their hobby either at the house reef, which lies between 50 and 100 meters away, or at any of the many well-known dive locations near the island, easily accessible by boat. Of course, Kurumba also offers the usual panoply of water sports.

Lhohifushi

Lhohifushi was opened up to tourism in 1979. After a thorough renovation in

89

1993, the **Lhohifushi Tourist Resort** now offers 130 bungalows, both row houses and self-contained, with a total of 260 beds. Some 800 meters long and 350 wide, the island boasts a dense growth of lush tropical foliage. Officially, there are two different categories of bungalows, standard and superior class, but they seem to differ little in their appointments, apart from the fact that the former have ceiling fans and the latter are equipped with air conditioning. All of the bungalows have small terraces with a view of the water.

Sports enthusiasts will find plenty to keep them busy in Lhohifushi's excellent range of activities. The island has both tennis and squash courts, as well as a fitness center; guests can also play soccer or ping-pong. Water sports, of course, top the list of popular pastimes on Lhohifushi. Surfing, sailing, and diving are available as a matter of course. The superb diving spots on the east side of the North Male Atoll have already enchanted thousands of divers. At low tide, you can walk over to the neighboring island of Gasfinolhu, some 500 meters away. There are also boat excursions to Male and to the surrounding inhabited islands.

Makunudhoo

Makunudhoo is located near the outer reef in the northern reaches of the North Male Atoll. The island, whose shape is reminiscent of a teardrop, is only 210 meters long and 100 meters wide, and lies 39 kilometers distant from the airport in Hulhule. In Dhivehi, *maku* means a kind of leech. The word *makunudhoo* also means "monkey's tongue," a more likely derivation of the island's name in that it could be a reference to Makunudhoo's form.

Right: Oriental sweetlips, observed and photographed on a dive at Lhohifushi's outer reef.

In the years before tourism came to Makunudhoo, dhonis traveling between the northern atoll and Male often used it as a stopover thanks to its convenient, and sheltered, location. The Frenchman François Pyrard spent a night on the island on his way to Male in 1602 after his ship, *Corbin*, ran aground on the Fulhadhoo Reef.

It was in 1983 that the **Makunudu Island Resort** first opened its doors to tourists. After a complete renovation in the meantime, the resort now has a typical Maldivian atmosphere, with such comforts as air conditioning and hot showers. The 36 self-contained palm-thatched bungalows, besides offering all the comforts of home, harmonize well with the island's natural environment, which, characterized by lush vegetation, creates a veritable tropical paradise.

Makunudhoo is a perfect place for passionate divers. The outer reef offers a tantalizing abundance of marine life; underwater nature reserves hold the promise of encounters with rare denizens of the deep; and in its channels, divers can experiment with drift dives in the strong currents. Nearby **Gaafaru Falhu** is the largest single reef in Maldives. It also bears the dubious distinction of being the most crowded ship's graveyard in the entire archipelago.

Meerufenfushi

Meerufenfushi, which means "fresh water island" in Dhivevi, is the largest island in the North Male Atoll. It is located on the atoll's eastern side, and measures 1,400 meters long and 450 meters wide. Dhonis take about 2 1/2 hours to reach it from Hulhule airport, 37 kilometers away; a speedboat can cover the distance in just under 60 minutes. Covered with a dense growth of palms and evergreen shrubbery, almost completely encircled by a lovely sand beach, the island is especially popular with families. A stroll

around the perimeter of Meru, as the island is affectionately known, takes between 45 and 60 minutes. The large lagoon on the western side of the island is perfect for waterskiing, surfing and, of course, swimming, all the more so because there aren't any sharp pieces of coral lying on the lagoon's fine sandy floor.

Although Meerufenfushi was opened up to tourists in 1978 and is therefore among the oldest generation of Maldivian resorts, the **Meerufenfushi Island Resort** looks and feels much newer. It has 190 superior-class rooms in row housing, and an additional 24 deluxe rooms with air conditioning and hot showers. The hotel's restaurant, which opens onto the sea, pampers its guests with superb continental cuisine.

The hotel offers the usual gamut of sports activities that can be found on most of Maldives' resorts. Anyone so inclined can take an excursion to the neighboring inhabited island of **Dhiffushi** to stock up on a range of typical Maldivian

souvenirs. The house reef is only 250 meters away from the island; the outer reef, some 500 meters. As this is too far for most snorkelers, boats run out from the dive base to the house reef as well as to the many diving areas around the island. Many experienced divers on Maldives cherish Meerufenfushi for the abundance of good dive locations in the island's immediate vicinity, especially along the outer reef.

Nakatchchaafushi

The name of this island, 350 meters long and 100 wide, stems from the Dhivehi word *nakatchcha*, which refers to the court astrologer in the Sultan's palace who had a strong influence on island politics. The Maldivians themselves also translate the island's name as "island of the wandering sands." Nakatchchaafushi is located about 26 kilometers from Hululhe on the western side of the North Male Atoll; it takes two hours to reach "Nakatcha" from the airport by dhoni.

Tourism first came to the island in 1979. The 51 bungalows, some of them with two storeys, are furnished in a variety of styles, from simple to luxurious. German visitors, in particular, are regular clients of the **Nakatchchaafushi Tourist Resort**. Attractive features here include a superb beach located on the island's northern coast, as well as the extensive beaches on the island's longer side; the width of these latter varies with the season, according to the strength of the monsoon winds. The relatively small lagoon, a mere 9 meters deep, is ideal for water sports. There's very good snorkeling around the house reef, with two entrances, which is located only 150 meters off the island's southeast shore. Anyone drawn to greater depths can join one of the daily diving excursions to the outer reef or to the many spectacular diving lo-

Above: In 1994, Paradise Island Resort got 40 new pile bungalows. Right: Playing pool is one way for guests to while away the time after they've soaked up enough sun.

cations in the atoll. Another exciting option is taking a drift dive in the channels between the atoll and the outer reef.

Paradise Island (Lankanfinolhu)

Lankanfinolhu, located in the east of the North Male Atoll, is only 12 kilometers, or 15 minutes by speedboat, from Hulhule International Airport. Some 900 meters long and 200 wide, the island's resort was expanded and completely refurbished in 1994; today, under the name of **Paradise Island Resort**, it offers guests a thoroughly modern facility that leaves nothing to be desired. In the course of renovation, the number of bungalows here rose to 260, and 40 bungalows were built on pilings out in the lagoon. Lankanfinolhu's many visitors can choose from a large variety of sports and recreational activities, including billiards, karaoke, crab races, and dance competitions. At low tide, visitors can walk over to the neighboring island of **Hudhuveli** or embark on a shopping trip and sightse-

eing tour to **Himmafushi**, the nearest inhabited island.

A lovely beach on the island's northern coast is perfect for swimming, while the wonderful lagoon is ideal for surfing and sailing. But Lankanfinolhu is best of all for diving. It lies amid countless well-known and oft-visited dive areas; and the house reef on the western side of the island is still completely intact. The outer reef is only 500 meters off the island's eastern shore, and boasts some breathtaking underwater scenery. From June through October, you can often spot huge manta rays on the southeastern side of the large lagoon, hanging out by the reef. They can reach spans of up to 7 meters; and the sight of them is something that no diver can ever forget.

Reethi Rah (Medhufinolhu)

This elongated island, some 800 meters long by 100 meters wide, is perched right on the northwestern edge of the North Male Atoll, about 41 kilometers from Hulhule Airport, or about an hour by speedboat. The island's name is comprised of two Dhivevi words meaning "medium-sized" (*medhu*) and "sand island" (*finolhu*).

Opened to tourists in 1979 under the name Medhufinolhu Tourist Resort, the facility here was later renamed **Reethi Rah Resort**, which translates as "pretty island." The name suits the island perfectly, as Medhufinolhu does indeed have a wonderful island atmosphere, complete with lush vegetation of coconut palms, blossoming papayas, and a range of tropical shrubs with colorful blooms. Thanks to its wonderful lagoon, Reethi Rah has become extremely popular with windsurfers. The best swimming is to be found at the eastern end of the lagoon, as the western side, where the water bungalows are located, is somewhat too shallow for good swimming.

The resort includes 50 self-contained bungalows, each with its own beachfront, and 10 water bungalows built on stilts out over the lagoon. The self-contained bun-

galows are furnished practically, but with an eye to detail; and the water bungalows are equipped with air conditioning. Under Swiss management, Reethi Rah is set up club-style. Clean and well-tended, the resort fits harmoniously into the surrounding tropical environment.

There's a wide range of sports to choose from on this island; the most popular, not surprisingly, are surfing and diving. The island's position on the outer edge of the atoll is a guarantee for memorable diving. There are numerous well-known diving spots within easy reach of the island, which are also frequented by diving boats from neighboring islands.

Summer Island (Ziyaaraiyfushi)

There are two traditional versions of the island's history. One version has it

Above: Beloved of sailors – Summer Island.
Right: Radiant blossoms of the sea hibiscus adorn many Maldivian resorts.

that this island, which measures 250 meters long and 60 meters wide, wasn't even on the map as recently as a century ago; the other maintains that the island has been around for centuries. According to this version, *ziyaaraiy* means "resting place" or "burial site of a holy man," and legend has it that a man named Mathukkalaa' is buried here. It is believed that he was the grandson of the Christian Maldive King Hassan IX (who was christened in Cochin in 1552). The story goes that during the reign of Ibrahim Iskandar I (1648-87), Mathukkalaa' and his brother sailed from India to Male to take over the Sultan's throne. Once they got to the capital, the brother was murdered, and Mathukkalaa' drowned; his body later washed up on the beach at Ziyaaraiyfushi.

Modern times came to this island on the western edge of the North Male Atoll when **Summer Island Village** opened here in 1983. Ziyaaraiyfushi has one of the most beautiful beaches in all Maldives, with a large, shallow lagoon. Practically but not unattractively furnished, the bungalows sit in the shade of the palm trees, and their terraces take in gorgeous views of the sea. Because of its location on the outer reef, the island also offers plenty of memorable diving spots. Other water sports available on Summer Island include sailing, waterskiing, fishing, and canoeing. Dhonis take about 3 hours to travel from the airport to Summer Island, 42 kilometers away; a speedboat takes a third of the time.

Tari (Kanu Huraa)

Kanu Huraa, which was uninhabited until 1981, is located on the southeastern and outer side of the North Male Atoll. *Kanu* means "corner" or "edge" in Dhivevi, and *huraa* denotes an island that is comprised of more coral than sand. In 1981, a hotel was built on the narrow 600-meter-long island and christened

Leisure Island Resort; later, it was re-named **Tari Village**. Located on the east side of the North Male Atoll, where there's a lot of tourist development, the island can be reached from the airport by speedboat in 30 minutes. An immaculate beach and the exquisite lagoon in front of it make Tari an inviting place for relaxing, swimming, and snorkeling. Both the lovely restaurant, which serves superb Italian and Maldivian cuisine, and the 24 comfortable two-storey bungalows blend in harmoniously with the island's lush tropical greenery.

Between April and November, prevailing winds from the southwest transform Tari into a mecca for surfers. These enthusiasts lie on their stomachs and paddle their boards out to where the breakers meet the reef ("Pasta Point"). In summer, the waves have real power and speed, and world-renowned surfers congregate here to experience them. As well as superb surfing, the island, of course, has its own dive center, as well as a complete range of other sports and recreational activities,

including its own tennis court. Visitors can also shop for souvenirs on the nearby inhabited island of **Huraa** or, at low tide, stroll across the sands to neighboring **Kuda Huraa**.

Thulagiri

Opened in 1980 and completely done over in 1990, Thulagiri was originally managed by Club Med. Today, however, the hotel on this island, which measures 300 meters by 200 meters, is under Maldivian management. Lying in the southern third of the North Male Atoll, this is an island with class. The 58 residential units of the **Thulagiri Island Resort** are round, and stand in the shade of huge coconut palms. All rooms have hot showers, air conditioning, and telephones.

Thulagiri further excels through its gorgeous beaches, which extend all the way around the island and seem veritably to pose for the cameras of snap-happy visitors. Anyone who doesn't feel like

95

swimming in the lagoon can take a dip in the hotel's salt-water pool.

In addition to diving and surfing, activities on offer here include waterskiing, sailing, ping-pong, volleyball, and badminton. The diving school also offers regular excursions to the many beautiful reef landscapes in the immediate vicinity.

INHABITED ISLANDS AND PICNIC ISLANDS IN THE NORTH MALE ATOLL

Aarah

Aarah is located northwest of Male, only a few kilometers away from the resort island of Kurumba. Because it is used as a private holiday resort for the president of the Republic of Maldives, this small island is not open to the public.

Above: A paradise for sun-worshippers.
Right: Both boys and girls take part in the scout meeting on Feydhoo Finolhu.

Akirifushi

The name Akirifushi means "coral island." This uninhabited island is located in the northwestern part of the North Male Atoll, and is a popular stopover for fishing boats. Just off the island's shore extends a reef called Himmiya Faru. In Dhivevi, *himmiya* means the area between two reefs: a kind of lagoon, that is, with two channels, where boats can anchor there in safety. Such areas are particularly well protected during the southwest and northern monsoons. The reef around Akirifushi offers excellent opportunities for both diving and snorkeling. The **Akirifushi Caves**, a well-known dive site, are located off the southern tip of the island.

Dhiffushi

The inhabited island of Dhiffushi is located near the resort island Meerufenfushi on the eastern edge of the North Male Atoll. South of the island extends the **Dhiffushi Falhu** reef, a very popular diving terrain. Fishing is the largest source of income for the island's inhabitants, and dhonis with freshly caught tuna fish make their way almost daily from Dhiffushi to the fish market in Male.

Three baggalas were shipwrecked on the reef just off the island: the *Dheen Ganja* went down in 1898, the *Deylaa* in 1902, and the *Jandar* in 1911.

Dhoonidhoo

This tiny island is located north of Male on an imaginary line between Male and Kurumba. In Dhivehi, the island's name means "bird island," although today the island is home not to birds with wings but to jailbirds, specifically political prisoners. Until 1964, the colonial-style mansion that stands on Dhoonidhoo was the residence of the British governor of Maldives.

Feydhoo Finolhu

Northwest of Male, not far from the capital, lies Feydhoo Finolhu. The island is also known as "education island," because children come here for summer vacations, taking part in courses, seminars, and scout meetings. In 1960, the island was completely washed away, partly because so much sand had been removed from it for construction projects on the surrounding islands. However, the island was later resurrected, as it were, thanks to natural ocean currents depositing sand on the one hand, and additional dredging from the lagoon by the hand of man on the other.

Funadhoo

Funadhoo, which lies north of the capital city of Male, has always been a strategic point that's historically played a key role in the various struggles for political power in the Maldivian archipelago. In Dhivehi, *funa* is the word for a

hardwood tree with white blossoms (*Calophylluminophyllum*), and *dhoo* means "island." In earlier times, ships used to drop anchor both in the outer harbor on the island's western side, and farther north, up to Dhoonidhoo and Galu Falhu. As a result of bad weather, strong currents, wind, and waves, but also due to inattention, many of these ships went down. Today, with a little luck, divers can stumble upon the remains of these sunken vessels.

History buffs who come to Funadhoo can visit several graves, such as that of Captain J. C. Overend, who died in Male in 1797 after his ship, the *Tranquebar*, had run aground on one of the islands. The wreck itself has yet to be found.

Another well-known figure in Maldivian history is also buried on Funadhoo – but not quite all of him. The "him" in question is Utheemu Ali Thakurufaan, a 16th-century Maldivian freedom fighter. Together with his brothers Muhammed, still famous today as the national hero of Maldives, and Hassan, he fought for

97

eight years in the underground against the Portuguese occupation. In 1573, they finally succeeded in driving the Portuguese out of Male, but at a high cost to Utheemu Ali: shortly before the liberation of Male, the occupying forces murdered him and gave his head to the Portuguese governor as a gift. However, the Maldivians managed to steal his head back, and secretly buried it in Funadhoo. Utheemu's torso, however, is buried elsewhere, on Thakandhoo in the Haa Alifu Atoll.

The government has found a range of uses for Funadhoo in the years since. The island has variously housed a shark-oil refinery, a mill for coconut fibers used in making ropes, and a poultry farm. Today, Funadhoo is a state storage facility for domestic oil reserves.

Gaafaru

Gaafaru is a remote inhabited island in the North Male Atoll, with a total population of 698. This secluded island is located on **Gaafaru Falhu**, which is the largest free-standing reef in Maldives. This oval-shaped reef measures 8 kilometers in length and 15 in diameter, with two deep natural channels at its northern end as well as a shallower one near the island of Gaafaru. The inhabitants of the island, most of them fishermen, are extremely hospitable, and for a modest sum are prepared to entertain visitors with a performance of the traditional Maldivian dance known as *boduberu*.

For many years, the channel **Kaashidho Kuda Kandu**, which runs past Gaafaru to the north, has been one of the most important water routes through Maldives.

In stormy weather, high waves and falling spray all but obscure the reef, and

Right: Bodu-beru drummers strike up the beat for a dance.

many a captain has run aground on Gaafaru Fahlu in these tricky waters. On August 12, 1873, the *Arcan* out of Glasgow, a 1,174-ton ship on its way from Rangoon to London, ran aground here with a full load, including 9 passengers and a 34-man crew. The *Clanalpine*, a 363-ton ship with a wooden hull, which was carrying sugar from Mauritius to Bombay, also ran aground on this dangerous reef in 1879. The same fate befell the German ship *Erlangen* on August 20, 1895, when it ran aground about a kilometer west of Iruwai Kandu, which is the second entrance into the lagoon. In 1879, the *SS Sea Gull* sank a little bit farther to the east; this 1,012-ton ship with a crew of 32 and 3 passengers aboard was on its way from Calcutta to London. In 1905, a steamship, the *SS Crusader* (4,210 GRT), which was carrying sugar, sank near the shallow entrance to Gaafaru. And the 863-GRT *Lady Christine* ran aground on April 16, 1974, about 200 meters west of Hulhangu Kandu, which is the first entrance to Gaafaru's inner lagoon.

Girifushi

Girufushi lies in the eastern part of the atoll, near one of the most specatular diving locations in the entire region, the **HP reef** or **Girifushi Thila**, which is frequented by visiting divers from the resort islands of Gasfinolhu, Kanifinolhu, Kuda Huraa, Hudhuveli, and Paradise Island. However, as the Maldivian government uses Girifushi as a military training base, the area around the island is often closed off, at which times diving at one of the most fascinating reefs in Maldives is prohibited.

Himmafushi

The inhabited island of Himmafushi, located in the east of the North Male Atoll, currently has a population of 521.

Himmafushi was once an important fishing island, but the island's inhabitants have since shifted their attention to tourism; their main source of revenue today is the production and sale of handcrafted items and souvenirs. The island is visited regularly by tourists from the neighboring resort islands of Hudhuveli, Tari and Kanifinolhu.

At one time, Himmafushi was joined to the island of Gaamaadhoo. However, over the years the ocean currents shifted and deposited sand, and ultimately created two separate islands.

In the early stages of tourism in Maldives, there was a reasonably-priced guest house on Himmafushi catering to tourists of more modest means. However, the government closed this facility in 1984 out of concern for the possible adverse influence the foreign visitors could have on the local Maldivian population. Today, the island is only open until 6 p.m., and only to day-trippers who have registered in advance. And in lieu of the hotel, Gaamaadhoo now has a prison on

it, instead. Himmafushi's outer reef would be perfect for surfers; unfortunately, due to considerations of safety, it's off limits to enthusiasts of water sports.

Kagi

Kagi, a small, uninhabited and picturesque island, lies to the north in the inner atoll, northwest of Helengeli, and is privately owned by Maldivians. The little island has a shallow lagoon and a gorgeous snow-white sand beach. An intact house reef teeming with fish attracts large numbers of divers and snorkelers. A narrow channel in the reef allows ingress to the protected lagoon for the diving and safari boats that regularly bring picnickers and sportsmen to the island. Anyone who wants to picnic or spend the night on Kagi is expected to pay a token fee to the island's owner.

According to recent information, a petroleum storage facility and a landing pier are scheduled to be built on the island, which should change its face considerably.

Kanduoiygiri

Thanks to the large poultry farm that operates here, Kanduoiygiri is also known as Chicken Island. Kanduoiygiri is located in the southern section of the atoll, near Bandos and northwest of Full Moon Island (once known as Furanafushi).

Time and again, there are reports of nocturnal sightings of the very rare mammal known as the sea cow, or dugong, called *kandu-geri* in Dhivehi. In the Maldivian mysticism, these animals are regarded as *dhevi*, spirits which are sometimes visible and at other times not. Their variable function means that they may be bearers of evil, or of good – you never can tell which. For this reason, people make sacrificial offerings to them, such as flowers or the blood of birds or other animals. When they're spotted on moonlit nights, dugongs are generally regarded as being bearers of ill fortune, and Maledivians unlucky enough to see these animals at such times fear for their lives and the well-being of their families. Dugongs used to be sighted occasionally near Vihamanafushi in the North Male Atoll, as well as by Fihalohi and Gulhi in the South Male Atoll; and one was also spotted in 1986 on Vattaru in the Felidhoo Atoll. Today, dugongs are not only rare in the Indian Ocean; they're threatened with extinction throughout the world.

Kuda Bandos

The inhabited island of Kuda Bandos, which means "little Bandos," lies in close proximity to the resort island of Bandos, just to the southeast of it. Kura Bandos,

Right: By Kuredhigadu, divers can sometimes encounter a whale shark.

which, true to its name, is indeed quite small, is a favorite day-trip destination for residents of nearby Male, especially on Fridays (the day of rest in the Moslem week) and holidays, when people flock here from the capital.

In the past, the narrow waterway between Bandos and Kuda Bandos was reserved for the Sultan's ship, so that he could send messages to Male quickly, if need be. Thus, too, the Sultan could be kept abreast of events if something came up in the northern atolls or pirates were on the move.

Kuredhigadu

The very small island of Kuredhigadu is located on the northern side of the Furanafushi reef, near the resort island Full Moon. During the southwest monsoon season, divers might, with a bit of luck, spot huge whale sharks gliding by the outer rim of the reef past Kuda Kahli and Bodu Kahli.

On December 25, 1923, a baggala laden with a range of wares sank in stormy seas on Kuredhigadu's reef. The only sign of the wreck today is the ship's anchor, lying at some distance, north of Furanafushi, on the reef, 32 meters below the ocean's surface.

Madivaru

The island of Madivaru is on the western side of the North Male Atoll, very near to Madivaru Kandu, which is often visited by diving ships from the nearby resort islands of Reethi Rah and Hembadhoo. This beautiful island is privately owned by Maldivians.

Olhahali

This small, uninhabited island lies in the north of the North Male Atoll, just opposite the Gaafaru Falhu reef complex. Although the island has little vegetation,

it is quite popular with day-trippers, snor-kelers, and scuba divers. Along the island's northern side extends a shallow channel, called Olhahali Kandu. The Huss Faru reef complex provides boats with a sheltered place to anchor at night.

Rasfari

Rasfari, located in the west of the North Male Atoll, is noteworthy for the beautiful reefs lying around it. Uninhabited island, with little vegetation, the island is surrounded by a broad, flat reef. Owing to the unspoiled character and great beauty of the underwater landscape here, the Maldivian government has officially classified Rasfari and the surrounding reefs as a nature reserve.

Thamburudhoo

Thamburudhoo is located on the outer reef in the east of the North Male Atoll, near the resort island of Tari, which used to be known as Kanu Huraa. The island is named after a flowering plant (*Biloba pescaprae*) that has heart-shaped leaves and purple blossoms. Typical of tropical flora, this plant generally spreads like a weed in sandy soil, and the fruit it produces – also heart-shaped – is used in traditional medicine. During the southwestern monsoon, the wind and waves on the outer reef generally form the ideal conditions for surfers.

Thilafushi

Thilafushi is not a natural island. Lying between Giraavaru and Villingili in the southernmost North Male Atoll, it was created in 1992 by dredging and dumping sand. And today, it's the fastest-growing island in Maldives, geographically speaking, as it receives all the garbage from the capital city. Since the island was officially cleared as a garbage dump, there has been regular boat and barge traffic shuttling back and forth between Male's new harbor and the "garbage island."

101

Thulusdhoo

At the moment, 676 people live on Thulusdhoo. This inhabited island is encircled by long sandy beaches. Northeast of Hulhule, the island is both the administrative center for the North Male Atoll and an important commercial center for trade in the region. Many traders travel here from other islands to sell *lonu mas* (pickled fish) to the state-owned warehouses. Countless freighters, dhonis, and safari boats ride at anchor in the island's deep lagoon. And at Thulusdhoo's renowned shipyards, modern dhonis are built with new fiberglass hulls.

The inhabitants of Thulusdhoo are famous for their traditional *bodu-beru* dances, which is performed exclusively by men to the beat (*baburu*) of a large drum. The dance, which probably originated in Africa, begins with a slow, steady beat that gets faster and faster until it cul-

Above: My daddy catches really big fish!

minates with the dancers reaching a state of ecstasy and exhaustion. The drums are fashioned out of the hollowed-out trunk of a coconut palm covered with the skin of a ray.

Vahboahuraa

Vahboahuraa is in the southeastern part of the atoll, right next to the resort island of Kuda Huraa. The island is rented out to a private individual. Noteworthy here is the unusually long pier that links the island with the neighboring sand bar island of Rahgandu.

Villingili

Villingili is located in the southern part of the North Male Atoll, and has been inhabited since the earliest history of the region. Time and again, this unprotected island was plundered and pillaged by the infamous Malabar pirates, enraged at their inability to storm the fortifications of Male.

In 1961, the inhabitants were forced to leave their island and move to Hulhule; a year later, a prison was built on the island. One of the first resort hotels in Maldives was built on Villingili in 1973, but it closed its doors for good in 1990. Today, Villingili is again being settled with local Maldivians, with a view to easing the pressure of overpopulated Male nearby.

Viligilimathidhahuraa

Viligilimathidhahuraa, located in the southeast of the North Male Atoll, is uninhabited. It was once comprised of two islands, but shifting sands over the years transformed it into one. The epitome of tropical isolation, the island has a shallow lagoon that's suitable for boats with shallow drafts. Because of its remoteness, it's a popular destination for day-trippers looking for a wilderness experience.

ASDHOO
Asdhu Sun Island
Opened in 1981, refurbished in 1988. Male office: H. Kaamineepoolge Irumatheebai, Kurangi Goalhi, tel. 322149, fax 324300. Island: tel. 445051, fax 445051, E-Mail: info@asdu.com.mv. *BUNGALOWS:* 30 rooms with fans, cold-water showers. *AMENITIES:* bar, coffee shop, restaurant. *DIVING BASE:* Italian team, PADI, house reef. *CREDIT CARDS:* AE/MC/VC. *AIRPORT:* 58 km, 2.5 hours by motorboat.

BANDOS
Bandos Island Resort
Opened in 1972, refurbished in 1989. Male office: Bandos Male Office, tel. 325529, fax 321026. Island: tel. 440088, fax 443877, E-Mail: bandos@dhivehi.net. mv and bandos@netlink.net.mv. *BUNGALOWS:* 177 rooms in double bungalows and row houses; 48 suites w. living rooms, bedrooms, baths. *AMENITIES:* 2 bars, coffee shop, 3 restaurants, 3 souvenir shops, tennis courts, pool, sauna, steam room, fitness center. *DIVING BASE:* German-run, 9 languages, CMAS, PADI, NAUI, SSI, decompression chamber, doctor, house reef. *CREDIT CARDS:* AE/MC/VC. *AIRPORT:* 8 km: 35 min by dhoni, 15 min by speedboat.

BANYAN TREE (VABBINFARU)
Banyan Tree
Opened in 1977, refurbished in 1994. Male office: Dhirham Travels &Chandling, Faamudheyri Magu, tel. 323369, fax 324752. Island: tel. 443147, fax 443843. Internet: http://banyantree.com, E-Mail: maldives@banyantree. com. *BUNGALOWS:* 47 single bungalows, 1 President's suite. *AMENITIES:* bar, 3 restaurants, E6-lab. *DIVING BASE:* German, Engl., French, Ital., PADI, SSI, house reef. *CREDIT CARDS:* AE/MC/VC/ DC/EC/ JCB. *AIRPORT:* 13 km, 20 min by speedboat.

BAROS
Baros Holiday Resort
Opened in 1973, renovated in 1987. Male office: Universal Enterprises Pvt. Ltd., 38 Orchid Magu, tel. 323080, 322971, fax 322678, 320274. Island: tel. 442672, fax 443497, E-Mail: sales@unisurf.com, Internet: http:// www.unisurf.com. *BUNGALOWS:* 32 rooms in double bungalows with fans; 31 deluxe single bungalows with A/C, 12 pile bungalows with A/C, telephones. *AMENITIES:* bar, coffee shop, 3 restaurants. *DIVING BASE:* German-Dutch, PADI, VIT, house reef. *CREDIT CARDS:* AE/MC/VC/DC. *AIRPORT:* 15 km: 1 hr by dhoni, 20 min by speedboat.

BODUHITHI
Boduhithi Coral Island Resort
Opened in 1979, renovated in 1989. Male office: 4th floor, Alia Bldg., Orchid Magu, tel. 313938, fax 313939. Island: tel. 442637, fax 442634, E-Mail: hcmmale@dhivehinet.net.mv. *BUNGALOWS:* 86 standard single bungalows, 4 superior pile bungalows. *AMENITIES:* 2 bars, coffee shop, restaurant. *DIVING BASE:* Germ., French, Ital., CMAS, FIPS, PADI, house reef. *CREDIT CARDS:* AE/MC. *AIRPORT:* 29 km, 1 hr by speedboat. Excl. to Club Vacanze.

ERIYADHOO
Eriyadhoo Island Resort
Opened in 1975, renovated in 1983 and 1998. Male office: A.A.A. & Trading Company, STO Trade Center, 3rd Floor, Orchid Magu, tel. 324933, fax 324943. Insel: tel. 444487, fax 445926. *BUNGALOWS:* 46 rooms in double bungalows with fans and cold showers, 2 rooms with air conditioning. *AMENITIES:* bar, coffee shop, restaurant. *DIVING BASE:* German, English, French, very good house reef, CMAS, PADI, SSI, VDST. *CREDIT CARDS:* AE/MC/VC. *AIRPORT:* 44 km, 3 hrs by dhoni, 1 hr by speedboat.

FARU (FARUKOLHUFUSHI / CLUB MED)
Opened in 1973, renovated in 1995. Male office: 1 Ibrahim Hassan Didi Magu, Majeedhee Bazaru, tel. 322976, fax 322850. Island: tel. 444552, fax 441997, E-Mail: edmaldop@dhivehinet.net.mv, Internet: http://www. euro-divers.com. *BUNGALOWS:* 123 double rooms, 27 triples, all with fans and cold showers. *AMENITIES:* 2 bars, coffee shop, restaurant, pool, fitness center, *DIVING BASE:* PADI 5 Star IDC, English, French, Italian, Japanese; house reef, decompression chamber, and in-house doctor. *CREDIT CARDS:* AE/MC/VC/ JCB. *AIRPORT:* 4 km, 25 min by dhoni. Exclusive to Club Med.

FULL MOON (FURANAFUSHI)
Full Moon Beach Resort
Opened in 1973, renovated in 1994. Male office: Universal Enterprises Pvt. Ltd., 39 Orchid Magu, tel. 323080, fax 320274. Island: tel. 442011, fax 441979, E-Mail: sales@unisurf, Internet: http://www. unisurf.com. *BUNGALOWS:* 104 rooms in double bungalows, 52 rooms in double bungalows on pilings, all with bathtub and whirlpool. *AMENITIES:* bar, coffee shop, 3 restaurants, fitness center, sauna, tennis court, pool. *DIVING BASE:* House reef. *CREDIT CARDS:* AE/MC/VC/DC/JCB. *AIRPORT:* 7 km, 25 min by dhoni, 10 min by speedboat.

GASFINOLHU
Gasfinolhu Island Resort
Opened in 1980. Male office: Imads Agency, Chandhee Magu, tel. 323441, fax 322964. Island: tel. 442078, fax 445941. *BUNGALOWS:* 40 single bungalows with fans. *AMENITIES:* coffee shop, restaurant. *DIVING BASE:* Italian-run, CMAS, house reef.

CREDIT CARDS: AE/MC/VC. *AIRPORT:* 23 km, 30 min by speedboat, 1.5 hrs by dhoni. Exclusive to Club Valtur.

GIRAAVARU
Giraavaru Tourist Resort

Opened in 1980, renovated in 1987. Male office: Giraavaru Male Office, Hotel Alia, tel. 318422, fax 318505. Island: tel. 440440, fax 444818, E-Mail: giraavaru@ dhivehinet.net.mv, Internet: http://giravaru.com. *BUNGALOWS:* accommodations in double bungalows and row bungalows with a total of 65 rooms. *AMENITIES:* bar, coffee shop, restaurant, tennis court, fresh-water pool. *DIVING BASE:* E-Mail: max@dhivehinet.net.mv, PADI, house reef. *CREDIT CARDS:* AE/MC/VC. *AIRPORT:* 11 km, 60 min by dhoni.

HELENGELI
Helengeli Tourist Village

Opened in 1979. Male office: H. Karanakaa Villa, Boduthakurufaanu Magu, tel. 328544, fax 325150. Island: tel. 444615, fax 442881, E-Mail: engeli88@ dhivehinet.net.mv. *BUNGALOWS:* 30 rooms with fan in double bungalows. *AMENITIES:* bar, restaurant, coffee shop. *DIVING BASE:* Swiss-managed, PADI, house reef. *CREDIT CARDS:* AE/MC/ VC. *AIRPORT:* 51 km, 1.5 hours by speedboat, 3.5 hours by dhoni.

HEMBADHOO
Taj Coral Reef Resort

Opened in 1982, renovated in 1997. Male office: Taj Maldives Pte. Ltd., 10 Medhuziyaaraiy Magu, tel. 317530, fax 314059. Island: tel. 443884, fax 441948. *BUNGALOWS:* 70 deluxe rooms with modern furnishings. *AMENITIES:* bar, coffee shop, restaurant. *DIVING BASE*: PADI, house reef. *CREDIT CARDS:* AE/MC/VC. *AIRPORT:* 32 km, 70 min by speedboat, 2.5 hrs by dhoni.

HUDHUVELI
Hudhuveli Beach Resort

Opened in 1980, renovated in 1994. Male office: Hudhuveli Male Office, H. Jazeera, Boduthakurufaanu Magu, tel. 322844, fax 321026. Island: tel. 443982, fax 443849. *BUNGALOWS:* 44 rooms in double bungalows. *AMENITIES:* bar, coffee shop, restaurant. *DIVING BASE:* Ital., PADI, house reef. *CREDIT CARDS:* AE/MC/VC. *AIRPORT:* 13 km, 20 min by speedboat, 1 hr by dhoni.

IHURU
Ihuru Tourist Resort

Opened in 1978, renovated in 1989. Male office: H. Bodukosheege, Ameer Ahmed Magu, Male 20-05, tel. 326720, fax 326700. Island: tel. 443502, fax 445933,

E-Mail: ihuru@dhivehinet.net.mv. *BUNGALOWS:* 41 single bungalows with fans, 3 with air conditioning. *AMENITIES:* bar, coffee shop, restaurant. *DIVING BASE:* German, English, Italian, Spanish, Nitrox, PADI, SSI, CMAS, house reef. *CREDIT CARDS:* AE/MC/VC/JCB. *AIRPORT:* 19 km, 25 min by speedboat, 75 min by dhoni.

KANIFINOLHU
Kanifinolhu Resort

Opened in 1978, renovated in 1989. Male office: Cyprea Pte., 25 Boduthakurufaaanu Magu, tel. 322451, fax 323523. Island: tel. 443152, tax 444859, telex 66026, E-Mail: cyprea@dhivehinet.net.mv. *BUNGALOWS:* 154 standard and superior rooms with fans and cold showers; deluxe rooms with air conditioning. *AMENITIES:* 4 bars, coffee shop, restaurant, tennis court. *DIVING BASE:* multi-lingual, PADI 5 Star IDC, house reef 400 m away. *CREDIT CARDS:* AE/MC/VC/JCB. *AIRPORT:* 19 km, 30 min by speedboat, 1.5 hrs by dhoni.

KUDAHITHI
Kudahithi Tourist Resort

Opened in 1984. Male office: 4th floor Alia Bldg., Orchid Magu, tel. 313937, fax 313939. Island: tel. 444613, fax 441992. *BUNGALOWS:* 7 luxury suites, individually furnished. *AMENITIES:* bar, coffee shop, restaurant. *DIVING BASE:* located on the neighboring island of Boduhithi. *CREDIT CARDS:* AE/VC. *AIRPORT:* 27 km; 1 hr by speedboat. Exclusive to Club Vacanze.

KUDA HURAA
Kuda Huraa Reef Resort

Opened in 1977. Male office: Bandos Office, Boduthakurufaanu Magu, tel. 325529, fax 318992. Island: tel. 444888, fax 441188, telex 77032, E-Mail: info@ kudahuraa.com, Internet: http://www.kudahura.com. *BUNGALOWS:* 72 beach villas, 34 water villas, 4 water suites. *AMENITIES:* bar, coffee shop, restaurant. *DIVING BASE:* German, English, Nitrox, NAUI, PADI, IANDTD, house reef. *CREDIT CARDS:* AE/MC/VC. *AIRPORT:* 20 km, 30 min by speedboat, 1.5 hrs by dhoni.

KURUMBA
Kurumba Village Tourist Resort

Opened in 1972, renovated in 1988. Male office: Universal Enterprises Pte., Ltd., 39 Orchid Magu, tel. 323080, fax 320274. Island: tel. 442324, fax 443885, E-Mail: sales@unisurf.com, Internet: http://www. unisurf.com. *BUNGALOWS:* 168 standard rooms, 6 junior suites, 4 President's suites. *AMENITIES:* 2 bars, coffee shop, 6 restaurants, 2 pools, fitness center, sauna, tennis court. *DIVING BASE:* numerous lan-

guages, PADI, house reef. *CREDIT CARDS:* AE/
MC/VC/DC/EC/JCB, *AIRPORT:* 4 km.

LHOHIFUSHI
Lhohifushi Tourist Resort

Opened in 1979, renovated in 1993. Male office: Altaf
Enterprises Ltd., 3 Majeedhee Baazaaru, Goalhi No.
1, tel. 323378, fax 318025. Island: tel. 443451, fax
441908, E-Mail: lohifushi@dhivehinet.net.com. *BUN-
GALOWS:* 43 standard rooms with fans, 87 superior
and deluxe rooms. *AMENITIES:* restaurant, coffee
shop, bar, tennis, squash, pool. *DIVING BASE:* German, Engl., French, Ital. Japanese, CMAS, PADI, SSI,
house reef. *CREDIT CARDS:* AE/MC/VC. *AIRPORT:*
23 km, 30 min by speedboat, 90 min by dhoni.

MAKUNUDHOO
Makunudu Island Resort

Opened in 1983. Male office: Sunland Travel Pvt., Ltd,
#04-01 STO Trade Center, Orchid Magu, tel. 324658,
fax 325543. Island: tel. 446464, fax 446565, E-Mail:
makunudu@dhivehinet.net.mv. *BUNGALOWS:* 36
single bungalows w. fans, hot showers. *AMENITIES:*
bar, coffee shop, restaurant. *DIVING BASE:* Swiss-
run, PADI, house reef. *CREDIT CARDS:* AE/MC/VC.
AIRPORT: 39 km, 1 hr by speedboat.

MEERUFENFUSHI
Meerufenfushi Island Resort

Opened in 1978. Male office: 3rd Floor, Champa
Bldg., Ahmadhee Bazar, tel. 314149, fax 314150. Island: tel. 443157, fax 445946, E-Mail: meeru@dhive-
hinet. net.mv. *BUNGALOWS:* row bungalows, 190
rooms with fans, 24 deluxe rooms with air conditioning. *AMENITIES:* 4 bars, 2 coffee shops, restaurant.
DIVING BASE: Eurodivers, PADI 5 Star IDC, no
house reef. *CREDIT CARDS:* AE/MC/VC, *AIRPORT:*
37 km, 1 hr by speedboat, 2.5 hrs by dhoni.

NAKATCHCHAAFUSHI
Nakatchchaafushi Tourist Resort

Opened in 1979, renovated in 1995. Male office:
Universal Enterprises Pvt. Ltd., 38 Orchid Magu, tel.
323080, fax 320274. Island: tel. 443847, fax 442665,
E-Mail: sales@unisurf.com, Internet: http://www.
unisurf.com. *BUNGALOWS:* 51rooms. *AMENITIES:*
bar, coffee shop, 2 restaurants, pool. *DIVING BASE:*
German, English, CMAS, PADI, house reef. *CREDI
CARDS:* AE/MC/VC/DC. *AIRPORT:* 26 km, 45 min by
speedboat, 2 hrs by dhoni.

PARADISE ISLAND (LANKANFINOLHU)
Paradise Island Resort

Opened in 1979, renovated in 1994. Male office: Villa
Hotels, 3-04 STO Trade Center, Orchid Magu, PO Box
2073, tel. 316161, fax 3144565. Island: tel. 440011,

fax 440022, E-Mail: paradise@dhivehinet.net.mv.
BUNGALOWS: 220 deluxe rooms in single and
double bungalows, 40 deluxe pile bungalows.
AMENITIES: 4 bars, coffee shop, 5 restaurants,
tennis, badminton courts, fitness room, sauna, steam
room. *DIVING BASE:* Dutch, German, English,
French, PADI, BSAC, Baracuda, house reef. *CREDIT
CARDS:* AE/MC/VC/DC. *AIRPORT:* 12 km, 15 min by
speedboat, 40 min by dhoni .

REETHI RAH (MEDHUFINOLHU)
Reethi Rah Resort

Opened in 1979, renovated in 1991. Maleoffice: Ma.
Sheerazeege, tel. 323758, fax 328842. Island: tel.
441905, fax 441906, E-Mail: rrresort@dhivehinet.
net.mv. *BUNGALOWS:* 50 single bungalows with
fans, 10 pile bungalows with air conditioning.
AMENITIES: 2 bars, coffee shop, restaurant. *DIVING
BASE:* German, English, French, Italian, PADI, house
reef. *CREDIT CARDS:* AE/MC/VC, *AIRPORT:* 41 km,
45 min by speedboat, 2 hrs by dhoni.

SUMMER ISLAND (ZIYAARAIFUSHI)
Summer Island Village

Opened in 1983, renovated and expanded in 1991.
Male office: Kaimoo Travels & Hotels Pvt., Ltd., tel.
318005, fax 318057. Island: tel. 443088, fax 441910.
BUNGALOWS: 120 rooms in double bungalows and
row houses; superior rooms with telephones and fans.
AMENITIES: bar, coffee shop, restaurant. *DIVING
BASE:* German, English, CMAS, PADI, house reef.
CREDIT CARDS: AE/MC/VC/DC. *AIRPORT:* 42 km, i
hr by speedboat, 3 hrs by dhoni .

TARI (KANU HURAA)
Tari Village

Opened in 1981, renovated in 1988. Male office:
Phoenix Hotels and Resorts Ltd., tel. 323181, fax
325499. Island: tel. 440012, fax 440013, E-Mail:
phoenix@ dhivehi.net.mv. *BUNGALOWS:* 24 single
bungalows with fans. *AMENITIES:* bar, coffee shop,
restaurant, tennis court. *DIVING BASE:* Italian, English, French, PADI, house reef. *CREDIT CARDS:*
AE/MC/VC. *AIRPORT:* 17 km, 25 min by speedboat,
75 min by dhoni.

THULAGIRI
Thulagiri Island Resort

Opened in 1980, renovated in 1990. Male office: H.
Jazeera, Boduthakurufaanu Magu, tel. 322844, fax
318992. Island: tel. 445960, fax 445960. *BUNGA-
LOWS:* 58 rooms in single and double bungalows.
AMENITIES: bar, coffee shop, restaurant, pool. *DI-
VING BASE:* English, French, Italian, house reef.
CREDIT CARDS: AE/MC/VC/DC, *AIRPORT:* 11 km,
25 min by speedboat, 75 min by dhoni .

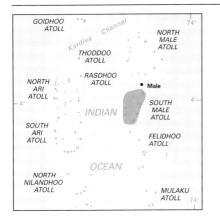

SOUTH MALE ATOLL (KAAFU ATOLL)

SOUTH MALE ATOLL

Measuring 36 kilometers long and 19 wide, the South Male Atoll is part of the Male Atoll, which is officially administered under the name of Kaafu Atoll. Of its 30 islands, 3 are inhabited, 11 uninhabited, and 16 are used as tourist resorts. The atoll's main island is called Maafushi. Separating the South Male Atoll from the North Male Atoll is the Vaadhoo Channel (Vaadhoo Kandu), 4.5 kilometers wide and 1,000 meters deep, whose waves can sometimes be extremely rough. Most trips between the airport and the islands in the South Male Atoll are made by speedboat; although those islands closer to the airport are serviced by motor dhoni.

RESORT ISLANDS IN THE SOUTH MALE ATOLL

Biyaadhoo

Biyaadhoo is a tiny dream of an island located in the inner reaches of the eastern South Male Atoll. Tropical gardens

Preceding pages: Sri Lankan artists provide spectacular evening entertainment. Left: A hammock under the palms – quintessential relaxation for body and soul.

bursting with colorful flowers and generously shady palm trees help convey the feeling of in a classic tropical paradise. The island teems with mangroves, papaya trees and banana plants, and the island's own gardens even produce fresh vegetables.

Long ago, local people lived on Biyaadhoo; but the island was subsequently uninhabited for quite some time, after which it was used temporarily as a leper colony. Tourism came to the island in 1981 with the construction of the **Biyaadhoo Island Resort**, which was completely renovated and remodeled in 1993. Oval in shape, Biyaadhoo has a total surface area of about 10 hectares, and measures about 400 meters in diameter. As the island is enclosed by a narrow reef, there are beautiful dive sites off the east and west coasts. Biyaadhoo also has a simply wonderful small lagoon with an idyllic white sand beach that's perfect for sunbathing, swimming, and just lazing around. Right next to the island, a mere 300 meters away, is another resort island, Viligilivaru, also known as Villivaru Island. A ferry runs between the two islands four times a day, free of charge.

Well-tended and immaculate, Biyaadhoo's resort is among the best that Maldives has to offer. Characteristic features

109

include comfortably furnished two-storey bungalows, which can accommodate up to 192 overnight guests in rooms equipped with air conditioning and hot and cold showers. The six bungalow complexes are all close to the beach and command breathtaking ocean views, both from the ground-level terraces and the upper-storey balconies. The well-appointed rooms are all equipped with minibars, refrigerators, and direct-dial telephones. With its large outdoor terrace and superb continental cuisine, the air-conditioned restaurant is a popular gathering place for guests, as is the open-air bar on the beach. Two attractive boutiques invite browsers and serious shoppers alike; and there's also a television room, a clubhouse, and a disco that's held once a week.

Sports and leisure pursuits on Biyaadhoo center around diving, which on this

island is a year-round activity, even during the monsoon season. In addition to the two house reefs, the numerous diving sites around Biyaadhoo offer breathtaking coral landscapes. More than 60 different sites await the diver, among them inlets in the outer reef, wrecks, drop-offs and channels with strong currents. Because nearby Villivaru's diving school is run by the same management as Biyaadhoo's, there are regular and well-coordinated boat connections from both islands to these sites.

Other sports and recreational activities include parasailing, waterskiing, surfing, sailing, and helicopter sightseeing trips from nearby Guraidhoo.

Bodu Hura

Once uninhabited, Bodu Huraa has been linked by a pier to the resort island Veligandhoo since 1998, and is now part of the Palm Tree Island Resort. A total of 36 water bungalows and a diving school are currently under construction.

Above: Biyaadhoo – seen above and below the water.

Bolifushi

Bolifushi is located near the outer reef, in the northwest of the South Male Atoll. This miniscule island, measuring a mere 100 meters long and 50 meters wide, first opened to tourists in 1982, is only 15 kilometers away from Male. The word "boli" means shells, and it's been inferred that this island once boasted large quantities of the cowrie shells which in the past were used as currency on the islands.

In 1982, the **Bolifushi Island Resort**, consisting of eight detached bungalows and a hotel, was built on this tiny island; twelve years later, in 1994, the facility was completely remodeled. In addition to the eight bungalows, there is now a two-storey building on the island with 32 beautiful rooms.

A white sand beach runs all the way around the diminutive islet, and the large lagoon here is a favorite meeting-place for water sports enthusiasts.

The hotel's restaurant serves both international and local dishes. Built out over the water on pilings, the hotel bar invites guests to linger in the evenings and socialize.

Diving is, it goes almost without saying, the island's most popular sport. The island has a superb house reef teeming with aquatic life, and there are a number of other inviting diving locations nearby. Among the many highlights here is an excursion to **Vaadhoo Kandu**, where divers can often spot large fish such as sharks and rays. Bolifushi is also very popular with surfers; aficionados consider it one of the best surfing venues in the northern South Male Atoll. Waterskiing, fishing, sailing, volleyball and ping-pong are also on offer.

Cocoa Island (Makunufushi)

Cocoa Island, a long, narrow island located in the southeastern South Male Atoll, is 400 meters long and approximately 60 meters wide. Abutting on it to the east is a large, picturesque sand bar. The shallow southern end of the lovely lagoon is excellent for swimming, while the deeper northern end is perfect for snorkeling.

Cocoa Island's original name, Makunufushi, means "Island of the Apes"; but as no apes live here at all, the name is somewhat enigmatic. In addition to trees and dense tropical shrubs, there is also a beautiful palm grove at the center of the island, which is effectively Cocoa's trademark.

Cocoa is one of the most expensive islands in Maldives, and is fast becoming a popular high-society vacation spot favored by the affluent and the jet-set. This exclusive island, which has just 16 beds in eight bungalows, opened in 1981 as the **Cocoa Island Resort**. Built in a Polynesian style, the two-storey bungalows are thatched with palm fronds, and harmonize perfectly with the surrounding landscape. The rooms have been kept deliberately simple, without air conditioning, but they're airy and comfortable, nonetheless. The sand that covers the ground outside continues within on the ground floors of each bungalow; the bedrooms are upstairs, in a kind of gallery that forms the top floor.

A French chef from Strasbourg sees to the guests' culinary needs; the food here is widely held to be the best in Maldives. The open-air restaurant is right on the beach, and there's a small bar built on pilings extending out into the lagoon, over the water.

Diving on Cocoa is no less exclusive than the food and board. Each guest has his or her own assigned boat and guide who will bring her out to the destination of her choice. At the nearby outer reef, spectacular underwater landscapes await scuba divers, while the house reef offers opportunities for superb snorkeling. Among other sports activities available

are surfing, waterskiing, parasailing and catamaran sailing.

Dhigufinolhu

Dhigufinolhu is situated on the eastern edge of the South Male Atoll. Together with Veligandhoo Huraa and the tiny supply island of Guhliggaathuhuraa (Bushy Island), it forms a triangle, connected by means of wooden piers. Bushy Island serves as a supply depot for the two resort islands, and is also home to the islands' scuba diving school.

In the local language, Dhigufinolhu means something along the lines of "sand bar island." Long and narrow – 400 meters long by 60 meters wide – this island is the largest of the three. Tourism arrived here in 1980. Dhigufinolhu is almost completely surrounded by a sand beach; inland, there's plenty of shade thanks to a wealth of awnings, tall

Above: Feather anemones entrance divers with glowing color.

bushes, and trees. In addition, there's great swimming in the shallow, calm areas of the island's large lagoon, which makes Dhigufinolhu an ideal holiday venue for families traveling with children.

Since the summer of 1997, **Dhigufinolhu Island Resort** has had 97 rooms equipped with air conditioning, showers, and bathtubs. Of these 97 rooms, 57 are classified as standard and 40 as deluxe. The island also has two restaurants, both offering superb international and local specialties, as well as barbecues and buffets, to their well-fed guests. In the evening, the entertainment can include anything from magic shows and fire-eaters to performances involving live snakes. Anyone who's interested in seeking out more than simply peace and quiet can dance to the music of live disco bands. In terms of sports, the island, together with neighboring Veligandhoo Huraa, offers everything any athlete could possibly desire: scuba diving, surfing, sailing, waterskiing, fishing, ping-pong, and volleyball. The area around Dhigufinolhu is also excellent windsurfing territory. The best sites for divers lie somewhat farther out, by the house reef and the sunken wreck off Kuda Giri, or in the many channels along the eastern side of the outer reef.

Emboodhoo

Emboodhoo (or Embudhu) has been one of the most popular resorts on Maldives for quite some time. **Embudhu Village** opened in 1979 on this small and lovely tropical island, which is 285 meters long and 145 meters wide. This idyllic little spot is situated in the northeastern part of the South Male Atoll, at the end of the famous Emboodhoo channel, the Emboodhoo Kandu. This island has it all: beautiful palms, lush vegetation, and a superb white sand beach that runs into two tongues of sand thrusting out into the large, flat lagoon. Close to

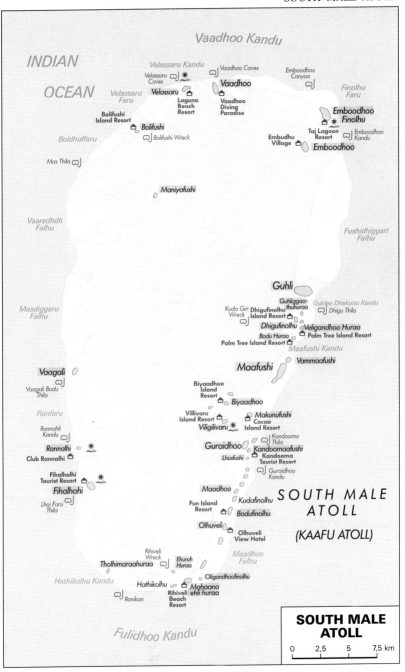

Vaadhoo Kandu

INDIAN

OCEAN

Velassaru Kandu

Velassaru
Caves

Vaadhoo Caves

Emboodhoo
Canyon

Finolhu
Faru

Velassaru
Faru

Velassaru

Vaadhoo

Laguna
Beach
Resort

Vaadhoo
Diving
Paradise

Emboodhoo
Finolhu

Bolifushi
Island Resort

Bolifushi

Taj Lagoon
Resort

Emboodhoo
Kandu

Boldhuffaru

Bolifushi Wreck

Embudhu
Village

Emboodhoo

Mas Thila

Maniyafushi

Vaaredhdh
Falhu

Fushidhiggari
Falhu

Guhli

Maadiggaru
Falhu

Guhliggaa-
thuhuraa

Guhlee Dhekunu Kandu

Kuda Giri
Wreck

Dhigufinolhu
Island Resort

Dhigu Thila

Dhigufinolhu

Veligandhoo Huraa

Bodu Huraa

Palm Tree Island Resort

Palm Tree Island Resort

Maafushi Kandu

Maafushi

Vammaafushi

Vaagali

Vaagali Bodu
Thila

Biyaadhoo
Island
Resort

Biyaadhoo

Ranfaru

Villivaru
Island Resort

Makunufushi
Cocoa
Island Resort

Rannahli
Kandu

Viligilivaru

Rannalhi

Guraidhoo

Kandooma
Thila

Kandoomaafushi

Club Rannalhi

Lhosfushi

Kandooma
Tourist Resort

Fihalholhi
Tourist Resort

Guraidhoo
Kandu

Fihalhohi

Maadhoo

Lhoi Faru
Thila

Kudafinolhu

SOUTH MALE
ATOLL

Fun Island
Resort

Bodufinolhu

(KAAFU ATOLL)

Olhuveli

Olhuveli
View Hotel

Maadhoo
Falhu

Rihiveli
Wreck

Ehuruh
Huraa

Tholhimaraahuraa

Oligandhoofinolhu

Hathikolhu Kandu

Hathikolhu

Mahaana
ehli huraa

Ranikan

Rihiveli
Beach
Resort

Fulidhoo Kandu

SOUTH MALE
ATOLL

0   2,5   5   7,5 km

the shore, the house reef, which drops steeply down for about 20 meters and then slopes off more gradually to the floor of the inner atoll, is particularly suitable for snorkeling: it has lovely growths of coral and a wealth of different kinds of fish.

The resort is extremely well-managed. Of the 124 rooms rated standard and superior, 84 are air-conditioned and 40 are equipped with fans. There are also 16 "open water bungalows" built out on pilings in the lagoon. Located further inland, as it were, the restaurant serves both the usual à la carte dishes and lavish Maldivian-Indian buffets. An inviting bar lures would-be drinkers to extend their cocktail hour, and there's also disco music every once in a while. Emboodhoo offers the full panoply of sports common to most Maldivian resorts: waterskiing,

Above: Diving into the lagoon from one's private terrace. Right: Exotic drinks in the cozy, friendly ambience of the Taj Lagoon Resort.

fishing, volleyball, surfing, sailing, and diving. There are a number of good diving spots in close proximity to the island, and they're all extremely popular. One highlight for divers is the wreck of the *Maldive Victory*, a mere 45 minutes away by boat, near the airport on Hulhule. Male, the capital city and a popular place for holiday shopping, is also close at hand. One special attraction Emboodhoo offers are sightseeing flights on a seaplane, allowing visitors to take in a bird's-eye view of the beautiful atoll.

Emboodhoo Finolhu

Narrow and sickle-shaped, the island of Emboodhoo Finolhu, which is often erroneously confused with Embudhu Village, its neighbor to the south, is 700 meters long and 50 meters wide. The island lies a mere 13 kilometers or so from Hulhule on the northeastern edge of the South Male Atoll; the trip from the airport takes 45 minutes by dhoni, 20 minutes by speedboat.

The island's name is a corruption of an earlier designation, Ebboodhoo, which stems from the Maldivian word *eboo*, denoting a delicious berry that grows wild on many Maldivian islands. This berry is the fruit of a thorny bush that reaches heights of up to two meters. Bushes and palm trees comprise most of the vegetation on Emboodhoo Finolhu, where about 70% of the surface area has been left undeveloped, in its natural state. Because the island is so narrow, many bungalows have been built on pilings out into the lagoon; by the front door of each of these, there's a ladder going down to the agreeably warm water. Emboodhoo Finolhu has a wonderful sand beach that goes around the whole island, and a beautiful large lagoon that is ideal for all manner of water sports. There is also a small wreck at the bottom of the lagoon, which is an interesting and rewarding challenge for beginning divers.

The island was opened up to tourists in 1983; the resort was remodeled in 1987, and further expanded in 1995, when it acquired its current name of **Taj Lagoon Resort**. All of the apartments are extremely comfortable, equipped with air-conditioners, showers, and bathtubs as a matter of course. International standards dominate the restaurant's menu; light meals and snacks are also available in the coffee shop. You can have a perfectly wonderful time on Emboodhoo Finolhu by simply relaxing and putting your mind in neutral. But if that's not your style, another option is to take advantage of the wide range of sports available on the island, including daily diving outings to the breathtaking outer reef, waterskiing, windsurfing, sailing, fishing, boating, and various types of ball games. There is, however, no house reef here for would-be snorkelers.

Fihalhohi

Tourism first came to the Arcadian island of Fihalhohi in 1981. *Fihal* means "to fry"; and since this island is the last one at the southwestern edge of the South

Male Atoll, it's thought that it may have gotten its name from the fishermen who used to cook their last meal here before sailing westwards to the Ari Atoll. Situated hard by the outer reef, Fihalhohi boasts lush vegetation with a wealth of tall coconut palms and dense foliage in the interior: Fihalhohi, in fact, is often referred to as "Green Island." Oval in form, lying about 75 minutes from Male by motorboat, the island is about 450 meters long and 280 wide. Its northern section features a beautiful beach for bathing; the southwestern end is dominated by a shallow lagoon.

Fihalhohi Tourist Resort has 92 rooms in palm-thatched bungalows, each of which has two or four units for a total of 190 beds. Accommodations are available in smaller A-class or larger B-class bungalows. Every room has its own ter-

race, shower and toilet, as well as drinking water on tap and a ceiling fan; eighteen rooms are also air conditioned. The restaurant, built in the round, offers local dishes as well as the standard international tourist fare, with a particular emphasis on seafood.

Visitors to Fihalhohi can participate in almost any sport that Maldives has to offer. Especially noteworthy are the island's beautiful diving sites, as well as the house reef, only 15 meters distant, making this a paradise for underwater enthusiasts. Sometimes, there's organized entertainment in the evenings: live music, films, a disco, karaoke, crab races, and magic shows are among the possible options. But for anyone who just wants to be alone, Fihalhohi also has a number of more isolated spots perfect for daydreaming and relaxing.

Fun Island (Bodufinolhu)

Bodufinolhu – "the big sand bar" – is a modern resort island that opened its

Above: Afternoon sun gilds Fihalhohi. Right: Tanking up on sun before the next round of snorkeling.

doors for business in 1995 under the name **Fun Island Resort**. However, tourists have been coming to the island since as early as 1980. Long and narrow, measuring approximately 700 meters long and 100 wide, the island is situated in the southeast of the atoll. The speedboat from Hulhule airport takes about an hour, though a dhoni needs around three hours to cover the 40 kilometers. Anyone who's really in a hurry can opt for a seaplane or helicopter, at, of course, a price. At low tide, beachcombers on Fun Island can wander over to two adjacent small, uninhabited islands that become sand bars when the waters recede.

Bodufinolhu has beautiful vegetation, predominantly pandanus trees (or screw palms) and coconut palms, as well as fan flower bushes. All of the beaches that line the island's coasts are perfect for sunbathing, swimming, or simply whiling away the day.

The hotel has 100 rooms in row bungalows and double bungalows; each room is furnished both tastefully and practi-

cally. They're all equipped with either an air conditioner or fan, a mini-bar, hot and cold showers, and a terrace overlooking the water. The hotel's cuisine caters to the tastes of an international clientele, most of them hailing from Switzerland, Italy, Great Britain, and Germany. In addition to the regular menu, a buffet three times a week features a range of delicious local specialties such as fish and other seafood, as well tasty and spicy (mild to hot) Indian and Maldivian curries.

Scuba diving is the number-one sport on Fun Island. Exploring the fascinating underwater world of the house reef is a relatively simply matter, as it's linked to the island by a long jetty. The real highlights for enthusiastic divers here, however, are the spectacular scuba diving sites along the outer reef, as well as the Kuda Giri wreck. Other sport-related options include windsurfing, sailing, waterskiing, badminton, ping-pong, and volleyball. One special attraction are the helicopter trips the hotel offers from Guraidoo, letting guests survey the surrounding islands. Night fishing, trips to inhabited and uninhabited islands, and shopping excursions to Male are other popular activities.

Kandoomaafushi

Kandoomaafushi lies to the southeast, by the outer reef of the South Male Atoll, near the inhabited island of Guraidhoo. The **Kandooma Tourist Resort** here opened its doors to foreign visitors in 1985. Some 500 meters long and 400 meters wide, the island lies 28 kilometers from Male, a distance which a dhoni travels in about 2.5 hours. The island's name translates as "mangrove island": *kandoo* denotes a mangrove plant, and *maa* is a general term for flowers. Indeed, the island boasts a marvelous profusion of tropical vegetation. A small lagoon lures swimmers, and the two man-made beaches are superb for basking in the sun.

Accommodations at this resort are thatched with palm fronds, and include several self-contained, air-conditioned bungalows. Self-contained or not, all the rooms are equipped with a full range of modern comforts. Visitors can indulge in any of the usual panoply of sports, although the island's diving is famous far beyond the borders of Maldives, and that activity therefore tends to dominate. Right around the island, divers have a wealth of beautiful dive locations to choose from, particularly on the outer reef; the latter is a popular destination with diving ships from neighboring islands, as well. Unfortunately, however, Kandoomaafushi's house reef is some distance away from the island itself.

Laguna Beach (Velassaru)

Velassaru, about 400 by 130 meters in size, was once uninhabited. But the first

Right: A range of sports and a disco make Olhuveli popular with a younger crowd.

tourists arrived here as early as 1974, and the island quickly became a familiar spot among early travelers to Maldives. Situated in the northern South Male Atoll, the island is only 11 kilometers from the capital. Ringing it is a superb, broad sandy beach, and it's also surrounded by a broad lagoon. Reaching maximum depths of up to 16 meters, the lagoon is shallower toward the northeast end of the island, near the landing stage.

After the entire resort was rebuilt and expanded in 1990, it was renamed **Laguna Beach Resort**. Until recently, it was rated as one of the 300 best hotels in the world; however, it was deliberately converted into a tourist village of the better sort. One striking feature is an attractive curved swimming pool skilfully integrated into the natural surroundings. Each of the complex's 115 rooms and its two suites, all located in attached, double, or self-contained bungalows, has a small terrace with ocean view, air conditioning, a fan, a shower, IDD telephone, and a mini-bar. The hotel also has a snack bar and three restaurants serving international, Chinese, and Italian dishes. After dinner, you can repair to the island's disco to work off the extra calories to the strains of recorded music, or even, three times a week, live music.

Due to the proximity of the channel **Vaadhoo Kandu**, where strong currents bring in a wide range of aquatic species and a number of large fish, diving is the number-one sport on Laguna Beach. Other sports include snorkeling along the house reef, windsurfing, catamaran sailing, volleyball, tennis, ping-pong, and fishing.

Olhuveli

Olhuveli lies to the southeast, at the outer perimeter of the South Male Atoll. Not only was the island once inhabited; it was even the atoll's second most densely-populated island. But the inhabi-

tants were ultimately relocated, and Olhuveli opened as a resort in 1979.

The island's name is a composite of two local words. *Olhu* denotes a channel in a reef deep enough to allow boats to pass through. *Veli* means "new sand," and is here probably a reference to the sandy entrance to the inner lagoon. The island is about 700 meters long and 90 wide, and is encircled by a narrow beach some 2 kilometers long. To the west, a large lagoon extends from the house reef on one side and the outer reef on the other; strong currents often sweep around the latter. At low tide, visitors can walk across the exposed lagoon bed to a tiny nearby island lying offshore.

Olhuveli is popular with younger tourists, especially visitors from Japan and Italy. Most of the accommodations of the **Olhuveli View Hotel**, which is managed by Japanese owners, are concentrated on one half of the island; they consist of two-storey buildings with terraces or balconies taking in views of the ocean. Olhuveli also offers so-called offshore or water bungalows, built on pilings. All of the rooms are fitted out with "mod cons" such as air conditioning, mini-bars, and telephones. The reception desk and large restaurant are located in the middle of the island. Most of the cooking here is geared to international tastes; guests can choose to dine in a Japanese restaurant or a "gourmet" one.

In addition to diving, recreational activities offered here include windsurfing, waterskiing, catamaran sailing, fishing, volleyball, badminton, and tennis. Anyone who doesn't want to swim in the lagoon can do his laps in one of the island's two swimming pools. In the evening, Olhuveli's residents convene in the island's two bars, then go on dance the night away in the island's disco.

Rannalhi

Rannalhi is situated near the outer reef, on the western side of the South Male

Atoll. It is about 37 kilometers from the airport, a distance that can be covered by speedboat in just under an hour. The island is approximately 320 meters long and 90 meters wide. On the southern end of the island there is a beautiful beach with a shallow lagoon that extends all the way to the house reef. Tourism arrived on these shores in 1977; **Club Rannalhi** was renovated in 1992-93 and again in 1996. Today, the spacious quadruple bungalow units are all fitted out with air conditioning, showers and bathtubs, and either a balcony or a terrace. A large open-air restaurant facing the sea serves international dishes and occasionally delicious and copious buffets, as well.

The island's name, Rannalhi, is probably derived from two different words. *Ran* means "gold" and *nalhi* is an old Maldivian unit of measurement. In the

Above: Tasty fish dishes served at a beach barbecue. Right: Because of its protected lagoon, Rihiveli is known as a good place to vacation with children.

past, wares such as rice were weighed with a *nalhi*, a round object weighing about a kilo, made, in some cases, of solid gold. The island may have gotten its name because it is shaped not unlike a *nalhi*.

In the past, before the reign of Sultan Mohammed Shamshuddeen III (1903-1934), there were many islands in the South Male Atoll where no coconut trees grew at all. Through the efforts of Minister Sayyidh Kilegefanu, who had leased the North and South Male Atolls, there began a systematic program of tree planting and cultivation, on Rannalhi and a number of other islands. Coconut palms were brought in from the Addhoo Atoll, which was known for the quality and size of its trees. Today, Rannalhi is supposed to have the largest palm trees in any of the northern atolls.

On Rannalhi, as on so many other islands, scuba diving is the sport of preference. One popular spot is the house reef, which runs almost completely around the island; another is the western

outer reef, which is perennially popular, even more so than some of the more distant sites within the atoll. Waterskiing and windsurfing are also both very popular pastimes on Rannalhi.

Rihiveli (Mahaana ehli huraa)

Rihiveli means "silver sand," although the local name of the island, Mahaana ehli huraa, has a rather different signification: Island of the Graves. Here, it was once believed, stood the sacred burial site of a deceased fisherman. Located at the southern end of the South Male Atoll, the island is 450 meters long and 150 wide. Rihiveli began its life as a tourist island in 1980 under the name **Rihiveli Beach Resort**. The island is distinctive not only by virtue of its lush vegetation; it also stands out thanks to its unique French atmosphere. It's no coincidence that many honeymooners find their way to its shores. It is one of the most attractive resorts in Maldives, although its self-contained bungalows are somewhat deficient

in modern comforts. Rihiveli's real attractions are its flair and French charm, which its owner deliberately cultivates, and its outstanding cuisine.

Because the island has an unusually large lagoon – as much as 700 meters wide in places – as well as gorgeous beaches, it is very popular with families, who respond to the staff's openness to children, and with watersports enthusiasts who like the lagoon's sheltered waters. The main recreational activities available include fishing, windsurfing, waterskiing, catamaran sailing, volleyball, aerobics, tennis, and ping-pong. The close proximity of the outer reef, easily accessible thanks to a wooden pier, makes Rihiveli a paradise for scuba divers. The reef is also excellent for snorkeling, although visitors must exercise caution due to unpredictable ocean currents. Boats run out to other more distant dive sites. One highlight is Rihiveli's wreck, a small coastal freighter, sunken deliberately, lying on the ocean floor on the atoll side of the island.

Vaadhoo

Vaadhoo is the northernmost island in the South Male Atoll, and lies very close to the tourist island of Laguna Beach, once called Velassaru. Though extremely small (250 meters long by 100 meters wide), Vaaadhoo is popular with divers owing to its proximity to the famous channel of **Vaadhoo Kandu**, with its wealth of underwater attractions.

Vaadhoo, which used to have a larger surface area, was once inhabited by aboriginal Maldivians. Thanks to the remains of a temple and some statues that were unearthed in the course of construction work about a decade ago, archaeologists have established that Buddhists lived on the island some 1,500 years ago.

Tourism came to Vaadhoo in 1978. The channel between Velassaru and

Above: The Vaadhoo Diving Paradise is popular with Japanese visitors. Right: A memorable sight – red-tailed butterfly fish in front of a red sponge.

Vaadhoo, which leads into the South Male Atoll, is still the route most frequently used by sailboats and dhonis on their way to Male from the south.

Over the years, the **Vaadhoo Diving Paradise** has been modernized to keep up with the rapid increase in the number of tourists visiting the island. Today, the resort offers guests considerable comfort, even luxury. The bungalows, some split-level, are equipped with air conditioning, refrigerators, showers, and bathtubs. In addition, there are seven luxury water bungalows which are built on pilings out into the lagoon – as, indeed, is the bar.

The large restaurant, built Maldivian-style, serves a range delicious international and local dishes, as well as a wide variety of specialties from the grill. Diving is the main sport on the island. Part of Vaadhoo's house reef lies right along the outer reef of the channel, which makes for exciting dives and raises a diver's chances of encountering large fish. Since most of the tourists here are from Japan, the diving school is under Japanese management. In addition to diving, fishing, surfing, sailing, and water-skiing are also available.

Veligandhoo Huraa

Directly adjacent to Dhigufinolhu, Veligandhoo Huraa is an extremely small but lovely island, measuring only about 150 meters in diameter. Small, too, is the number of guests; this intimately scaled island has only 16 bungalows with a total of 32 beds. The island's name means "sand castles."

In 1984, Veligandhoo Huraa was converted into a picturesque hotel called **Palm Tree Island**. All of the rooms are fitted out with a full range of modern comforts, including hot and cold showers, air conditioning, and direct dial phones. Spreading in front of the hotel is a broad sand beach running down to the waters of a broad, shallow lagoon.

Wooden piers connect the island to the neighboring island of Dhigufinolhu (see p. 112) and the supply depot of Bushy Island, so guests can take advantage of the facilities on Dhigufinolhu, as well.

Despite the fact that Veligandhoo is a small island with relatively few beds, it nonetheless boasts two restaurants for the dining pleasures of its guests, one serving excellent Asian cuisine, the other offering a variety of international dishes. Evening activities are coordinated on the larger island of Dhigufinolhu, including disco nights. The two islands also share the diving center on the pier and the dive sites accessible by their boats.

Villivaru (Viligilivaru)

Once called Viligilivaru, the island's name was changed in 1981, when it became a tourist island and took on the simpler designation of **Villivaru Island Resort**. In 1994, this resort received a thorough remodeling. Small and nearly circular in form, the island is almost a twin of Biyaadhoo, which is only 300 meters away and also located in the inner atoll. Like its "twin," Villivaru boasts a dense covering of lush vegetation, including a number of lovely palm trees; it also has a long reef that extends out to the south of the island. Running around the coast is a pristine sand beach, and there is a large lagoon for swimming on the island's northwest side.

Viligilivaru was once inhabited, but the inhabitants evidently abandoned it in 1830. Later it, like the neighboring island of Biyaadhoo, was used as a leper colony. At first, lepers of both sexes came to Villivaru, but later the men and women were separated: the women stayed on Villivaru, and the men were moved to Biyaadhoo.

This is all long past, however, and today the island's untouched beaches and the large lagoon on its northwest side attract tourists from all over the world. Skilfully integrated into the natural landscape around it, the hotel complex consists of 60 apartments within ten row

bungalow units. Each has a full complement of modern sanitary facilities, a telephone, and either air conditioning or a ceiling fan. In addition, all the apartments have terraces and their own small strips of private beachfront.

Air-conditioned and comfortable, the restaurant offers a full range of international dishes with some really delicious specialties; guests can also repair to the coffee shop for a selection of light meals and snacks. Other diversion is provided by a television room and a so-called "clubhouse."

Diving is the sport of preference on Villivaru. In addition to the island's own house reef, divers can explore the house reef of its nearby "twin" island, Biyadhoo; there's also a range of other spectacular dive sites both close to the island and a bit farther away, within the atoll

Above: A great day for tuna – a successful fisherman. Right: Karem, a board game popular with both children and adults, is played all over the country.

and along the outer reef. Other recreational activities available include fishing, sailing, windsurfing, waterskiing, ping-pong, and volleyball.

Anyone who wants a bird's-eye view of the atoll can depart from the neighboring island of Guraidhoo on a helicopter flight over the Maldivian archipelago.

A shuttle ferry service operates between Villivaru and Biyaadhoo, free of charge.

INHABITED ISLANDS AND PICNIC ISLANDS IN THE SOUTH MALE ATOLL

Ehuruh Huraa

This uninhabited island lies in the southern part of the atoll, on the outer side of the reef. It's also close to the Rihiveli wreck, a ship deliberately sunk for the amusement of divers. Because of the many herons and terns that nest here, the island is also known as Bird Island.

124

Guhli

Guhli, with a population of 504, is located on the east side of the South Male Atoll, north of the resort island of Dhigufinolhu. It has been inhabited for a very long time, and is famous for its fishing. The island's name is derived from the word *guhlu*, which denotes a traditional earthenware vessel with a capacity of between three and four liters that holds the drinking water on many dhonis.

During the reign of Sultan Mohammed Shamshuddeen III (1904-34), Guhli received a new mosque. Thanks to a deep access channel, large ships can dock at the island without any problem. 1984 saw the opening of a boatyard with slips for docking vessels. However, Guhli is also surrounded by dangerous reefs, and the waves breaking over them get especially high during the southwest monsoon. These waves are not to be trifled with: a number of boats have come to grief either on their way to Guhli or on the trip through the Guhlee Dhekunu

Kandu, which is the channel leading through the outer reef to the atoll and the island. Several years ago, a dhoni carrying a family of six was shipwrecked on this reef and sank.

Between the inhabited island of Gulhi and the resort island of Emboodhoo lies a very popular and much-frequented dive site called **Fushidhiggari Falhu**. Extending over several kilometers, this area also represents the easternmost part of the atoll. During the northern monsoon, as well as when the seas are rough, travelling by boat around Fushidhiggari Falhu is extremely hazardous, as the high waves render the reef practically invisible. Numerous ships and dhonis are said to have gone to the bottom here, as they have along the reef of Gaafaru Falhu.

Guhliggaathuhuraa

This small island on the eastern side of the South Male Atoll houses equipment, boats, and the diving school for the resort islands of Dhigufinolhu and Veligandu Huraa. Also called a "supply island," Guhliggaathuhuraa is linked to its fellow resort islands by means of a long pier.

Guraidhoo

Also located on the eastern side of the South Male Atoll, Guraidhoo is a venerable island that's one of the most historically interesting in the area. In the past, it was a favorite vacation spot of the sultans; in times of rebellion or invasion by foreign enemies or pirates, furthermore, the sultans fled here to take refuge, as the island was and is protected by an enclosing reef that was and is virtually impenetrable. The 65th sultan, Hussein Faamuladeyri Kilagefannu (1609-1620), is even buried here.

In 1971, a guest house for tourists opened on the island; but it was closed again in 1984, as was the one on Himmafushi in the North Male Atoll, due to the undesirable impact western tourists had or could have on the local population. Nonetheless, the island still boasts more than 25 souvenir shops today, as it's remained popular with souvenir-hunting visitors who come over from the nearby resort islands on shopping trips.

Scattered around Guraidhoo are countless very small individual reefs, their tops concealed just below the water's surface. As a result, only people who have a thorough first-hand local knowledge of this complex labyrinth of reefs are really able to navigate these waters safely.

The lagoon at Guraidhoo offers excellent shelter during the northern monsoon. Safari dhonis also stop off here quite frequently, since they can anchor very close to the beach, allowing their passengers to disembark without undue hassle.

Right: If you want to be a good fisherman, you have to start young.

Lhosfushi

Located in the southeastern section of the South Male Atoll, Lhosfushi is a small, uninhabited island frequented only by a handful of free-range chickens run wild. At low tide, people can walk over the island on a narrow tongue of land that extends out from the inhabited island of Guraidhoo.

Maadhoo

Maadhoo lies at the northern end of a large reef formation in the eastern part of the South Male Atoll. The island is also known as Maadhoo Falhu. Over time, much of Maadhoo has fallen victim to the sea, the tides, and the vagaries of its currents. Once one of the most densely populated islands in the South Male Atoll, Madhoo has lost much of its surface area to erosion by the sea, and its former population has prudently picked up and left.

Maafushi

Inhabited for quite some time, this island is known for its fishing industry. A government trade organization called the State Trade Organization, or STO, has its headquarters here. The STO purchases dried tuna, a prized culinary delicacy in Maldives, from the fishermen of the surrounding islands.

Dried tuna comes in two varieties, prepared in different ways. For the kind known as *lonumas*, tuna fish, as well as some other reef species, are pickled and then rinsed in salt water. The fish are then put out in the sun until they are dry and adequately preserved.

The second variety, *hikimas*, is a quartered tuna fish that is cooked, first in salt water and then in fresh water, for two to three hours. After this, it is smoked for an entire day, and then left out to dry in the sun.

Maniyafushi

Located in the middle of the northern third of the South Male Atoll, Maniyafushi is officially classified as uninhabited. However, the island is used nowadays as a base for the export of the fish known as grouper.

Oligandhoofinolhu

This uninhabited island located in the southern section of the South Male Atoll is also called the "island of the rising sun."

At one time, there was another island with a few coconut palms very near to Oligandhoofinolhu, but it was washed away in 1983.

Tholhimaraahuraa

Today, Tholhimaraahuraa lies under water and is only a small reef.

Once, however, long ago, the island was renowned for its excellent fishing,

which may explain the name Tholhimaraahuraa. A *tholi* is a long fish of the pike family, such as a trumpet fish or a barracuda, and *maraa* means either "death" or "to be captured" – presumably one and the same to the hapless fish to which the word is applied.

Vaagali

Located on the western side of the South Male Atoll, this island is uninhabited. Its name comes from its unusually dense growths of coral: *vaa* means "jungle" and *gali* means "branched coral." Its sheltered lagoon offers excellent, sheltered anchorage for fishing boats and safari boats alike.

Vammaafushi

Vammaafushi is a small, uninhabited island on the eastern side of the South Male Atoll. The island boasts impressive coral gardens along its northern flank, by the channel of Maafushi Kandu.

127

BIYAADHOO
Biyaadhoo Island Resort
Opened in 1981, renovated in 1993. Male office: H. Maarandhooge, tel. 324699, fax 327014. Island: tel. 447171, fax 447272. *BUNGALOWS:* 96 rooms in 6 two-storey row bungalows of 16 units each, with air conditioning, minibar, phone, hot and cold showers. *AMENITIES:* open-air bar, coffee shop, restaurant, 2 boutiques, clubhouse. *DIVING BASE:* German, English, French, Italian, Japanese, PADI 5 Star IDC, house reef. *CREDIT CARDS:* AE/MC/ VC/DC. *AIRPORT:* 29 km, 1 hour by speedboot, 2.5 hours by dhoni.

BOLIFUSHI
Bolifushi Island Resort
Opened 1982, renovated in 1994. Male office: Gateway Maledives Pte., Ltd., tel. 317526, fax 317529. Island: tel. 443517, fax 445924. *BUNGALOWS:* 32 rooms in row bungalows with air conditioning, minibar, fresh-water showers; 8 large single bungalows are also equipped with safe and telephone. *AMENITIES:* bar, coffee shop, restaurant, windsurfing school; arrangements can be made for babysitters and childrens' beds. *DIVING BASE:* Maldivian owners, German, English, French, Italian, Spanish, Japanese, PADI, house reef some 20 m from the diving school. *CREDIT CARDS:* AE/MC/VC. *AIRPORT:* 15 km, 20 min by motorboat, 90 min by dhoni.

BODU HURAA
Palm Tree Island Resort
Opened in 1998. Male office: PO Box 2014, tel. 327058, fax 327058. Island: tel. 443882, fax 440009. *BUNGALOWS:* 36 pile bungalows built out into the lagoon, air conditioning, telephone, safe. *AMENITIES:* Facilities shared with Dhigufinolhu and Velingandhoo Huraa. *DIVING BASE:* German, English, Italian, PADI, no house reef. *CREDIT CARDS:* MC/VC. *AIRPORT:* 24 km, 40 min by motorboat, 1.5 hours by dhoni. The clientele is almost exclusively Italian.

COCOA ISLAND (MAKUNUFUSHI)
Cocoa Island Resort
Opened in 1981; no Male office. Island: tel. 443713, fax 441919. Exclusive favorite of the jet-set. *BUNGALOWS:* 8 large, airy bungalows (two-story), air conditioning, fans. *AMENITIES:* bar, restaurant. *DIVING BASE:* German, Engl., French, PADI; a boat for each guest; house reef. *CREDIT CARDS:* AE/MC/VC/EC. *AIRPORT:* 33 km, 40 min by motorboat.

DHIGUFINOLHU
Dhigufinolhu Island Resort
Opnend in 1980, renovated in 1987 and 1997. Male office: H. Athereege Aage, tel. 327058, fax 327058.

Island: tel. 443599, fax 443886. *BUNGALOWS:* 97 rooms in two- and three-unit bungalows, air conditioning, telephone, minibar, fresh-water showers. *AMENITIES:* 2 bars, coffee shop, 2 restaurants, grill. *DIVING BASE:* German, English, French, Italian, Japanese, PADI, house reef. *CREDIT CARDS:* AE/MC/VC. *AIRPORT:* 22 km, 40 min by speedboat, 2 hours by dhoni.

EMBOODHOO
Embudhu Village
Opened in 1979, renovated in 1989. Male office: Kaimoo Travels & Hotel Services (Pte) Ltd., H. Roanuge, tel. 322212, fax 318057. Island: tel. 444776, fax 442673, E-Mail: embvil@dhivehinet.net.mv. *BUNGALOWS:* 60 standard rooms in row bungalows with fans and folding doors; 48 superior rooms in row bungalows with air conditioning, minibar, shower; 16 pile bungalows in four-unit buidings, with bathtubs. *AMENITIES:* bar, coffee shop, restaurant, windsurfing school. *DIVING BASE:* German, English, French, CMAS, VIT, PADI, house reef (some 2.5 km long) some 20 m from the diving school. *CREDIT CARDS:* AE/MC/VC. *AIRPORT:* 10 km, 20 min by motorboat, 1 hour by dhoni.

EMBOODHOO FINOLHU
Taj Lagoon Resort
Opened in 1987, renovated in 1995. Male office: Taj Maldives Pte., Ltd., tel. 317530, fax 314059. Island: tel. 444451, fax 445925. *BUNGALOWS:* 48 pile bungalows with air conditioning, minibar, telephone, fresh-water shower, 8 double bungalows on the beach. *AMENITIES:* 4 bars, 2 coffee shops, restaurant. *DIVING BASE:* Dutch, German, English, French, PADI, no house reef. *CREDIT CARDS:* AE/MC/VC. *AIRPORT:* 13 km, 20 min by motorboat, 45 by dhoni.

FIHALHOHI
Fihalhohi Tourist Resort
Opened in 1981, renovated in 1998. Male office: Dhirham Travels & Chandling Co. Pvt., Ltd., Faamudheyri Magu, tel. 323369, fax 324752. Island: tel. 442903, fax 443803, E-Mail: fiha@dhivehinet.net.mv. *BUNGALOWS:* 92 rooms in double and row bungalows, 18 of them with air conditioning, hot water, minibar, 74 of them with fans only. *AMENITIES:* 3 bars, coffee shop, restaurant, 2 souvenir shops. *DIVING BASE:* German, Engl., CMAS, house reef (c. 40 m from diving school) with 2 wrecks. *CREDIT CARDS:* AE/MC/VC/DC. *AIRPORT:* 39 km, 75 min by motorboat, 3 hrs by dhoni.

FUN ISLAND (BODUFINOLHU)
Fun Island Resort
Opened in 1980, renovated in 1995. Male office: Villa Hotels, 3rd Floor, STO Trade Center, tel. 316161, fax

314565. Island: tel. 444558, fax 443958, E-Mail: vilahls@dhivehinet.net.mv. *BUNGALOWS:* 100 rooms in double and row bungalows, air conditioning, hot & cold showers (fresh water), minibar, telephone. *AMENITIES:* 3 bars, coffee shop, 2 restaurants. *DIVING BASE:* Dutch, German, English, French, BSAC, PADI, house reef. *CREDIT CARDS:* AE/MC/VC/DC. *AIRPORT:* 40 km, 1 hr by motorboat, 3 hrs by dhoni.

KANDOOMAAFUSHI
Kandooma Tourist Resort

Opened in 1985. Male office: M. Zebey Magu, tel. 323360, fax 326880. Island: tel. 444452, fax 445948. *BUNGALOWS:* 41 standard rooms with fans in row bungalows, 20 single bungalows with air conditioning. *AMENITIES:* beach bar, coffee shop, restaurant, tennis court, souvenir shop. *DIVING BASE:* German, English, French, CMAS, PADI 5 Star IDC, outlying house reef. *CREDIT CARDS:* AE/MC/VC. *AIRPORT:* 28 km, 15 min by helicopter, 40 min by motorboat, 2.5 hours by dhoni.

LAGUNA BEACH (VELASSARU)
Laguna Beach Resort

Opened in 1974, renovated in 1990. Male office: Universal Enterprises Pte., Ltd., Orchid Magu, tel. 323080, fax 320274. Island: tel. 443042, fax 443041, E-Mail: sales@unisurf.com, Internet: http://www.uni-surf.com. *BUNGALOWS:* 115 rooms in single, double, and row bungalows with air conditioning, freshwater showers, minibar, telephone, 2 suites. *AMENITIES:* bar, coffee shop, 4 restaurants, pool, tennis court. *DIVING BASE:* German, English, Italian, CMAS, PADI, SSI, VIT, house reef. *CREDIT CARDS:* AE/MC/VC/DC/JCB. *AIRPORT:* 11 km, 1 hour by dhoni.

OLHUVELI
Olhuveli View Hotel

Opened in 1979, renovated in 1992. Singapore office: #02-07/07A IBM Towers, 80 Anson Road, Singapore 079907, tel. 2232157, fax 2231673. Island: tel. 441957, fax 445942, E-Mail: olhuveli@dhivehinet.mv. *BUNGALOWS:* 80 standard rooms, 32 larger rooms and 13 even larger pile bungalows (50 m^2). *AMENITIES:* 2 bars, coffee shop, 3 restaurants, pool, mini-golf, sauna, steam bath, tennis court. *DIVING BASE:* Japanese, English, Italian; no house reef. *CREDIT CARDS:* AE/MC/VC/EC. *AIRPORT:* 41 km, 70 min by motorboat. Some 20% of the tourists here are German.

RANNALHI
Club Rannalhi

Opened in 1977, renovated in 1996. Male office: Jetan Travel Services Co. (Pvt) Ltd., tel. 323323, fax 317993, Island: tel. 450629, fax 450619, E-Mail:

rnl4628@dhivehinet.net.mv. *BUNGALOWS:* 100 rooms in two-story four-unit bungalows with air conditioning and showers, 16 pile bungalows. *AMENITIES:* 2 bars, coffee shop, restaurant. *DIVING BASE:* Ital., Engl., PADI, house reef. *CREDIT CARDS:* AE/MC/VC, *AIRPORT:* 37 km, 45 min by motorboat.

RIHIVELI (MAHAANA EHLI HURAA)
Rihiveli Beach Resort

Opened in 1980, renovated in 1995. Male office: Ahmadhee Bazar shop No. 4, tel. 322421, fax 322964. Island: tel. 443731, fax 440052. *BUNGALOWS:* 47 single bungalows with fans, fresh-water showers, hammocks outside. *AMENITIES:* bar, 2 restaurants, one built out over the lagoon, bookstore, boutique. *DIVING BASE:* E-Mail: edmaldop@dhivehi.net.mv, Internet: http://www.eurodivers.com, English, French, house reef. *CREDIT CARDS:* AE/VC. *AIRPORT:* 41 km, 1 hour by motorboat.

VAADHOO
Vaadhoo Diving Paradise

Opened in 1978, renovated in 1988. Male office: H. Maarandhooge Irumatheebal, Filigas Magu, PO Box 20159, tel. 325844, fax 325846. Island: tel. 443976, fax 443397. *BUNGALOWS:* 24 rooms in 8 triple units with air conditioning and minibar, 7 deluxe pile bungalows with exclusive furnishings and phone. *AMENITIES:* 2 bars, restaurant. *DIVING BASE:* Japanese, English, NAUI, house reef. *CREDIT CARDS:* AE/MC/VC. *AIRPORT:* 8 km, 20 min by motorboat, about 1 hour by dhoni. Predominantly Japanese clientele, with an admixture of about 10% Germans.

VELIGANDHOO HURAA
Palm Tree Island Resort

Opened in 1984. Male office: Lotus Goalhi, PO Box 2014, tel. 314008, fax 307058. Island: tel. 440011, fax 440022. *BUNGALOWS:* 16 single bungalows with air conditioning, minibar, telephone. *AMENITIES:* bar, 2 restaurants. *DIVING BASE:* German, English, French, Italian, Japanese; house reef some 400 m away, small wreck. *CREDIT CARDS:* AE/MC/VC. *AIRPORT:* 23 km, 40 min by motorboat, 1.5 hours by dhoni.

VILLIVARU (VILIGILIVARU)
Villivaru Island Resort

Opened in 1981, renovated in 1994. Male office: H. Maarandhooge, tel. 324699, fax 327014. Island: tel. 447070, fax 447272. *BUNGALOWS:* 60 rooms in row bungalows with air conditioning, minibar, telephone. *AMENITIES:* bar, restaurant. *DIVING BASE:* German, English, French, Italian, PADI, house reef. *CREDIT CARDS:* AE/MC/VC/ JCB. *AIRPORT:* 33 km, 1 hr by motorboat, 2.5 hours by dhoni.

NORTH ARI ATOLL
RASDHOO ATOLL
(ALIFU ATOLL)

THE ARI ATOLL

The Ari Atoll, 96 kilometers long and 33 wide, is located to the southwest of the North Male Atoll, between the Goidhoo Atoll in the north and the Nilandhoo Atoll in the south. Administratively, since 1998, the Ari Atoll (official name: Alifu Atoll) has been split into the North Ari Atoll, including Rasdhoo and Thoddoo Atoll, and the South Ari Atoll. The main island of the North Ari Atoll is Rasdhoo; that of the South Ari Atoll is Mahibadhoo.

The number of islands in the atoll is defined afresh every year; one can assume that there are about 70 islands. The differences in the numbers are due to the sand bars in the atoll, which may or may not be counted. In the Ari Atoll, there are 18 inhabited native islands, which are home to about 8,500 Maldivians. In addition, there are 52 uninhabited islands in the atoll, of which 27 are resort islands; two of these are in the atoll's neighbor to the north, the Rasdhoo Atoll.

The Maldivians in the Ari Atoll have a reputation as good fishermen. Earlier,

Preceding pages: A child reads the Koran aloud to her grandmother (Rasdhoo Atoll). Left: Soldierfish and glassfish glitter in the spotlight.

they put out to sea mainly to fish for turtle and sharks, whose oil they used as a protective coating for the hulls of their dhonis. Part of the population devoted themselves to weaving high-quality sails and collecting corals. Some of the corals were used for constructing houses; smaller shells were also used as a unit of currency or barter in the markets of Male.

The cultivation of coconuts and other agricultural products is considered very important in the Ari Atoll. Today, many natives pursue more lucrative jobs on the resort islands, whether as boat captains, diving guides, or as employees in the hotels. The development of tourism in the Ari Atoll reached a peak in 1990, at which point the government decided to put a temporary stop to the opening of any more hotels in the atoll.

All the hotel islands in the Ari Atoll lie relatively far away from the international airport at Hulhule, and in the past, guests had to travel for several hours on the traditional dhonis in order to reach their dream islands. This transfer time has been cut down considerably since the introduction of speedboats. Furthermore, helicopters of the Hummingbird fleet can reach the Ari Atoll from the airport in about 30 minutes. Today, most guests avail themselves of modern "air taxis," or twin-engine seaplanes, which will prob-

133

ably replace helicopters completely in the foreseeable future. In addition, the government is planning to implement rapid hovercraft, which can carry up to 120 persons each. In the Ari Atoll, then, there are already clear indications of the route that will lead into a future of ever-increasing tourism in the region.

RESORT ISLANDS IN THE NORTH ARI ATOLL

Athurugau

Shaped like a crescent, the island of Athurugau lies about 95 kilometers from Hulhule airport, in the middle of the Ari Atoll, and about 9 kilometers from Moofushi, the nearest resort island. About 250 meters long and 100 wide, Athurugau boasts a number of beautiful palm trees, and mangroves and tropical bushes complete the impressive, picture-book vegetation. The island also has a beautiful sand beach that runs almost completely around its circumference, with an offshore lagoon that is wonderful for bathing.

The name of the island, Athurugau, means something like "unordered stones." It may be a nod to the enormous variety of corals in the impressive house reef, which runs along the island to the southeast, and is equally suitable for diving and snorkeling.

Opened in 1990, the resort started tourist operations under the name of **Athurugau Island Resort**. However, Italian tour operators, whose customers form the main bulk of the island's visitors, market it as the **Maldiviana Sea Club Hotel**. With its accommodation and the typical Maldivian flair, it's one of the better class of hotels, distinguished by its comfort and its correspondingly appealing atmosphere. All of the 42 rooms have air conditioning and fans. A minibar, IDD telephone and music system are as much a matter of course as the bungalows' lux-

urious appointments, which include a large, furnished terrace looking out over the ocean.

Athurugau is mainly frequented by Italians, a fact that's reflected not only in the hotel's uninhibited atmosphere, but also in the selections on the menu. Breakfast consists of a large buffet, at noon, there is a hot and cold buffet, and dinner alternates between buffets and sit-down meals. A snack bar on the beach fills up the chinks between meals, and there is a cozy bar for whiling away time in the evening. The island also boasts a boutique and a small drugstore.

Since 1996, the hotel has offered an all-inclusive package with full board, so that the rate includes all drinks, even outside of mealtimes, and all sports activities. Exceptions are made for beverages such as champagne and sports activities such as scuba diving, waterskiing and deep-sea fishing; for these, participants are charged extra.

Apart from diving and snorkeling, there are other active sports available, including windsurfing, waterskiing, sailing, canoeing, aerobics, soccer, ping-pong, badminton and volleyball. Other recreational activities include night-fishing, deep-sea fishing and excursions to other islands.

Avi Island (Velidhoo)

Avi Island is centrally located in the northern quarter of the North Ari Atoll, near Nika, Gangehi and Madoogali. The airport of Hulhule is 76 kilometers away; it takes a helicopter about 20 minutes to travel from the airport to the helipad, from which a dhoni bears guests to the island, a trip that takes another 30 minutes or so.

The original name of the island, Velidhoo, means something like "sand island." It's easy to see why – a glance from the helicopter shows that the entire island is surrounded by fantastic sand beaches and

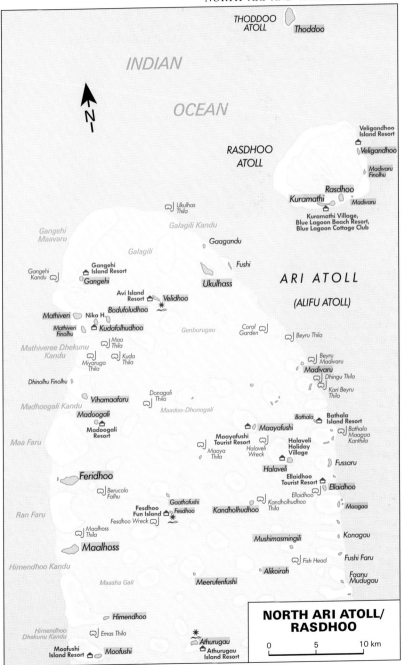

THODDOO
ATOLL
Thoddoo

INDIAN

OCEAN

N

Veligandhoo
Island Resort
Veligandhoo

RASDHOO
ATOLL

*Madivaru
Finolhu*

Rasdhoo
Kuramathi
Madivaru

Kuramathi Village,
Blue Lagoon Beach Resort,
Blue Lagoon Cottage Club

*Ukulhas
Thila*

*Gangehi
Maavaru*

Galagili Kandu

Galagili

Gaagandu

Fushi

Gangehi
Kandu

Gangehi
Island Resort
Gangehi

Ukulhass

ARI ATOLL

(ALIFU ATOLL)

Avi Island
Resort   *Velidhoo*

Mathiveri   Nika H.   *Bodufoludhoo*

*Mathiveri
Finolhu*   *Kudafolhudhoo*

Genburugau

Coral
Garden

Beyru Thila

*Mathiveree Dhekunu
Kandu*

*Maa
Thila*

*Miyaruga
Thila*   *Kuda
Thila*

*Beyru
Madivaru*

Madivaru

Dhingu Thila

*Kari Beyru
Thila*

Dhinolhu Finolhu

Vihamaafaru

*Donagali
Thila*

Madhoogali Kandu

Madoogali

Madoogali
Resort

Maadoo-Dhonogali

Bathala   Bathala
Island Resort

*Bathala
Maagaa
Kanthila*

Maa Faru

Maayafushi
Tourist Resort

Maayafushi

*Maaya
Thila*

Halaveli
Wreck

Halaveli
Holiday
Village

Fussaru

Feridhoo

*Berucolo
Falhu*

Halaveli

Ellaidhoo
Tourist Resort   *Ellaidhoo*

Ran Faru

Fesdhoo
Fun Island   *Fesdhoo*

Gaathafushi

Fesdhoo Wreck

Kandholhudhoo

Ellaidhoo

Kandholhudhoo
Thila

Maagaa

*Maalhoss
Thila*

Maalhoss

Mushimasmingili

Konagau

Fush Faru

Himendhoo Kandu

Fish Head

Maasha Gali

Meerufenfushi

Alikoirah

*Faanu
Mudugau*

Himendhoo

*Himendhoo
Dhekunu Kandu*   Emas Thila

Athurugau

Moofushi
Island Resort   *Moofushi*

Athurugau
Island Resort

**NORTH ARI ATOLL/
RASDHOO**

0   5   10 km

a large, protected lagoon. Triangular in form, Velidhoo is about 350 meters long and 250 meters wide. The island is covered by lush vegetation, including numerous coconut palms. Tourism arrived here in 1989, and Velidhoo was soon renamed Avi Island. In 1995, the hotel resort was completely renovated and partially rebuilt.

Today, the **Avi Island Resort** has more than 80 round bungalows, thatched with palm fronds, laid out with considerable imagination, and corresponding to the standards of high-class comfort. Air conditioners or fans keep room temperatures constant and pleasant; and hot and cold showers are part of the package, as are a minibar and a remarkably spacious terrace. In every element of the resort's decor, even in the coffee shop and the reception area, there is a predominance of rattan elements, which serve to underline

Above: Bathala is surrounded by a gorgeous white beach. Right: Scorpion fish are a not uncommon sight in the Ari Atoll.

the island's markedly tropical atmosphere.

The restaurant is open on all sides. Its cuisine, as is the case on so many of the Maldivian islands, is a skillful blend of international and local dishes. Since most of the visitors are from Europe, the varied menu is mainly oriented toward European tastes. There is a large and varied breakfast buffet every morning, while lunch and dinner alternate between a buffet and a sit-down meal.

The principal recreational activities available on Avi Island are scuba diving, waterskiing, windsurfing, canoeing and snorkeling. Apart from the classical water sports, there are facilities for volleyball, night fishing, ping-pong, and badminton, as well.

There is also a small disco for those visitors who feel like a change of pace in the evenings. And anyone who wants to take a look at the lifestyle of the Maldivian people and examine their artisan skills can join one of the regular excursions to a nearby inhabited island.

Bathala

Bathala is situated in the northeast of the Ari Atoll, right on the outer side of the hem reef. Because of its location and outstanding diving spots, this island holds a special place in the hearts of scuba divers. The word *bathala* stands for a kind of sweet potato that is cultivated on Maldives.

Bathala is a picture-perfect illustration of the classic "fried-egg" type of Maldivian island – no travel prospectus could illustrate it better. Oval in form, it measures about 200 by 150 meters and is completely surrounded by a broad and blindingly white sand beach. Typical of the "fried-egg" type island, there is no lagoon, only a shallow bathing area that extends around the entire island. For divers, this means that there are terrific rock walls and reef slopes, dropping off to depths of up to 30 meters, all around.

The **Bathala Island Resort** here opened in 1983, and was extensively renovated in 1991. Despite the island's small size, almost half of its area has remained undeveloped and virgin because of the small number and compact arrangement of its bungalows; the lush evergreen bushes and palms make it a tropical idyll of the finest order.

All of the 38 bungalows look towards the sea and are thatched with palm fronds. Self-contained and round in form, each house offers a full complement of modern comforts, such as an air conditioner, a fan and a minibar. Every hut also has its own little garden, with the somewhat unusual but undeniably pleasant feature of an open-air shower. Also typically Maldivian in decor is the large restaurant, which is open on the sea side. Right next to the restaurant stands the island's small bar, which in the evening becomes a gathering place where guests can enjoy a round of drinks, conversation, or simply the island atmosphere. In addition to international cuisine, the res-

taurant also offers a number of local dishes. Fresh fish, poultry or grilled meats are regularly on the menu.

Diving has pride of place among the sports offereed on Bathala. Following it in popularity are such sports as waterskiing, fishing, sailing, volleyball, darts, tennis and ping-pong. In addition, the hotel also organizes visits to inhabited islands and excursions to nearby hotel resorts, including Maayafushi, Halaveli or Ellaidhoo, which are also among the atoll's most renowned diving islands. You can take a round-trip flight around the atoll or fly to Male to go shopping. The state capital is about 62 kilomters away, and can be reached by air taxi in 15 to 20 minutes.

Ellaidhoo

Ellaidhoo, with its dense vegetation, is the "sister island" of neighboring Bathala. Since it opened as a resort in 1985, Ellaidhoo has become one of the best-known diving islands on Maldives. On hardly any other resort island is the ratio of divers and non-divers among the guests so clearly in the divers' favor. Oval in form, the island extends over an area of about 500 by 350 meters, and is covered in luxuriant vegetation that grows almost right up to the beach. Prominent features of Ellaidhoo are breakwaters made of coral stones that project out of the water all around the island. They have been put there to prevent further erosion of the beach by the monsoon winds and ocean currents; this is a problem that many Maldivian islands have to contend with. The coral breakwaters have thus far proven their usefulness on Ellaidhoo, although some guests have to do without a complete view of the spectacular sunset in the evening.

Ellaidhoo is not ideal for swimming: the beaches don't extend all around the island, and the little lagoon drops off steeply into the depths of the ocean after just a few meters, at the edge of the house reef. Main reason for the island's fame are the spectacular diving spots throughout the vicinity, foremost among them being the world-renowned shark-sighting spot **Mushimasmingili Thila**, also called **Fish Head** for short. The island's house reef is also very impressive; even the diving schools of the neighboring islands come to visit it.

Diving off Ellaidhoo is an unmitigated experience of rock wall diving. There are fantastic landscapes of hard and soft coral, enchanting overhangs and mysterious caves waiting to be explored. At many points along the house reef, the rock wall drops vertically by more than 30 meters, and there are any number of caves in the 10- to 15-meter range.

Right in front of the island's landing stage, the former director of the diving school, Christian Mietz, sank the *Citomo*, a beat-up banana freighter 30 meters

Right: The Fesdhoo wreck is one of the loveliest artificial reefs in the country.

long, in 1989; the wreck now represents an additional attraction for divers.

The 50 guest units of the **Ellaidhoo Tourist Resort** are situated among coconut palms and bushes, close to the beach, and are designed as self-contained bungalows with open-air showers and toilets. Spacious baths in the inner courtyards of the small huts help to convey a particularly "native" tropical atmosphere. The décor is practical and functional, with a deliberate lack of excessive comfort; for life on this island essentially plays out in the open air or underwater. Each of the bungalows does, however, sport a small terrace looking out over the sea. The large, open restaurant serves both international cuisine and typical Maldivian specialties, with different buffets once a week. Evenings are mostly taken up with diving shop talk in the small but extremely cozy bar.

Ellaidhoo is a divers' paradise. The diving base is very professionally run, boasts a full range of modern equipment, and offers courses in nitrox diving. There are, of course, other activities available, such as ping-pong, windsurfing, soccer and volleyball, as well as a disco once a week, if the guests want it; but in general, the island is a quiet place. Anyone who didn't get her fill of diving during the day can watch slide shows and films about the underwater world in the evening.

Ellaidhoo is about 70 kilometers from Hulhule, and the transfer to the island by speedboat takes about two hours.

Fesdhoo

Fesdhoo, also written as Fesdu, is a central island in the North Ari Atoll, about 9 kilometers to the east of Maalhoss, a well-known inhabited island on the western edge of the atoll. About 200 by 150 meters in size, Fesdhoo is almost round in shape and has fabulous palm trees, which, in conjunction with numerous bushes and a range of colorful

tropical plants, give the island a real South Seas flair. A broad, snow-white sand beach that circles the island only serves to emphasize this effect. The best swimming areas are in the south and southwest. Extending west of the island is a beautiful, long lagoon, while on the eastern side the house reef, which drops off sharply, is an attraction for divers and snorkelers. As it's exposed to strong currents, however, this reef is only really suitable for experienced divers. In the northern part of the island, there are some coral stone breakwaters along the roof of the reef to prevent the island's natural erosion. Especially when seen from the air, Fesdhoo is a typical Maldivian picture-postcard idyll – a visual feast!

The island's name derives from the Dhivehi word *fesko*, denoting a small bush with blue or white blossoms (*Tephrosia tenuis*). Various substances from this plant are used in traditional native medicine; they're supposed to be particularly good for diseases of the urinary tract and the bladder.

Fesdhoo opened as a vacation resort in 1982 under the name of **Fesdhoo Fun Island**. It's not a large island, and there's been a deliberate decision to steer away from mass tourism in the direction of a more friendly, family-like atmosphere. At the moment, there's accommodation for 60 people.

The round bungalows, thatched with palm fronds, integrate harmoniously with the natural environment. Comfort is perfectly adequate here, but the appointments are more functional than luxurious. This isn't necessarily a shortcoming; in fact, it's probably a point in the resort's favor for vacationers weary of civilization and seeking true relaxation. Certainly the resort is heavily trafficked; Fesdhoo is particularly popular with German tourists. A rustic open-air restaurant pampers visitors with tasty local dishes; here, too, guests congregate in the evening before moving on to other evening events on the beach, on the bungalow terraces, in the small disco or at the island's bar.

Scuba diving has a significant following on Fesdhoo. The diving school is particularly proud of a wreck that the diving instructors sank especially for the guests in the vicinity of the island. About 30 meters long, this fishing trawler, lying upright at a depth of 16 to 29 meters on the atoll floor, overgrown with fabulous corals, is widely held to be the most beautiful artificial "wreck" in Maldives at the moment. Apart from the dive to the wreck, there are two diving excursions every day to the most beautiful places in the atoll.

The other recreational facilities available here are in line with the classic range offered on most Maldivian islands: ping-pong, volleyball, windsurfing, sailing and fishing are all on the program. Day trips to the neighboring uninhabited island of **Gaathafushi**, which is located northwest of Fesdhoo, are also popular.

Above: Gangehi from the air. Right: On Halaveli, diesel oil is delivered in a rather unconventional manner.

For those with a penchant for a bird's-eye view, the hotel offers air tours over the fascinating atoll. Shopping tours to the capital of Male or excursions to various native islands are also possible.

From the airport, power boats run to Fesdhoo in about 3.5 hours; the trip goes much faster by helicopter (about 30 minutes).

Gangehi

Gangehi is a small and very exclusive island, and Italian tourists comprise approximately 95% of all the guests. It's also the northernmost resort island in the Ari Atoll. It lies to the northwest at the end of the channel of the same name, Gangehi Kandu, which is very narrow and about 2.5 kilometers long. There are two other resort islands in the immediate vicinity, Nika Hotel and Avi Island.

In the past, Gangehi was always uninhabited, until it was claimed for tourism in 1987. 1995 saw a course of extensive renovation work carried out in the

Gangehi Island Resort, but astonishingly, the complex didn't increase its capacity, and still consists of 25 luxury accommodations.

Over the years, the island's shape has changed as a result of wind erosion (and probably because of human intervention in the natural vegetation). A consequence of extensive sand displacement was that by the beginning of 1996 the pile houses designated "water bungalows" no longer stood over the lagoon, as originally planned, but on dry land. If you observe the Maldive islands carefully over a long period of time, you will find that the monsoon winds often move entire stretches of beach, so that returning visitors may find that an island has changed considerably from season to season. When humans interfere with an island's natural vegetation, especially on the windward sides of an island, this process is often enhanced in unintended ways, as can be seen from Gangehi's example.

Comfortably furnished, the island's 17 self-contained bungalows with air conditioners, fans, a minibar, direct dial telephone, a safe and hair dryer provide visitors with cozy verandas overlooking the sea. In addition, eight luxury stilt bungalows also boast large balconies. Each bungalow is deliberately designed to accommodate two people, with no facilities for a third overnight guest: this island is an adult world, and not tailored for children. Gangehi provides facilities for seminars, film and video shows. A resident Italian doctor is also proof of the island's high standards.

The splendid restaurant has a range of dishes on the menu, from Maldivian-oriental to international specialties, with an emphasis on Italian fare. Breakfast consists of a sumptuous buffet, and lunch is a warm buffet with plenty of variety; there is a sit-down dinner in the evening. A comfortable piano bar is the place for a round of evening drinks, over which you can enjoy the incredible sunset.

Apart from scuba diving, guests can go snorkeling and surfing, take part in night-fishing and deep-sea fishing excursions, or simply join one of the various excursions to other islands. Otherwise, Gangehi is a place where guests can recover from the stresses of daily life, basking in blissful indolence and the pleasures of *la dolce vita*.

Halaveli

Halaveli is located in the eastern area of the North Ari Atoll near the islands of Maayafushi, Bathaala and Ellaidhoo. From the air, the island resembles a half-moon, surrounded by a wide hem reef that stretches away and then drops off sharply at its edge into the depths of the ocean. The name of the island probably comes from the Dhivehi term *hala*, a name for the small-leafed hardwood tree *Suriana maritima*, which probably once grew here in profusion. Measuring about 180 by 300 meters in area, the island is covered with a dense growth of evergreen plants and beautiful, slender coconut palms.

Only about 20% of the island's surface is built up; the rest is a natural idyll populated with tropical birds, lizards, geckos and flying foxes. Walking across the island or strolling along the beach around it is thus a particularly memorable experience. Halaveli is surrounded by a superb beach that invites visitors to swim, sunbathe or simply laze around. A large lagoon attracts surfers, sailors, snorkelers and swimmers.

The island derives its individual flair from the design of the hotel complex and the way its buildings are skillfully integrated into the natural surroundings. Halaveli still has a little of the "pioneer spirit" of the earliest tourist islands, without appearing old-fashioned. The island commenced operations in 1982 as the **Halaveli Holiday Village**. The hotel is

Right: Not for the faint-hearted – a sting ray by the Halaveli wreck.

small and compact, and of practical and contemporary design. Obvious luxuries, such as a swimming pool, sauna or fitness center, would be out of place in this relaxed, intimate, Italianate atmosphere. The 52 self-contained bungalows, each only a few steps from the beach, have air conditioners or fans, hot and cold running water, minibars, telephones, showers, toilets, and small terraces overlooking the sea. Furthermore, the island of Halaveli is an excellent choice for gourmands. Almost 90% of its guests are Italians, and the master chef also hails from this country, known for its high culinary standards. Small wonder, then, that on Halaveli guests can savor not only a range of Maldivian specialties, but also a large complement of delicious Italian dishes. A remarkable selection of Italian wines and spirits, astonishing for Maldives, rounds off the outstanding menu. Apparently, nothing is impossible on Halaveli, from choice vintages of Chianti to the rarer grappas.

Recreational facilities on Halaveli center around water sports. The large lagoon is eminently suitable for surfing, catamaran sailing, waterskiing and jet-skiing, for quiet fishing or for exciting para-sailing. Divers can explore the first-rate reefs of the Ari Atoll and the island's own **Halaveli wreck**, now home to a number of well-fed rays that are happy to eat from your hand.

Maayafushi

Among divers, Maayafushi is as well-known as Ellaidhoo, somewhat further to the southeast. Opened in 1983, the island is, like Ellaidhoo, one of the classic diving destinations in the Maldivian archipelago. Its owes its excellent reputation in part to its wonderful house reef as well as a number of other top-class diving spots in the vicinity. Another reason for its renown is that the name of Maayafushi, like that of Bandos, is

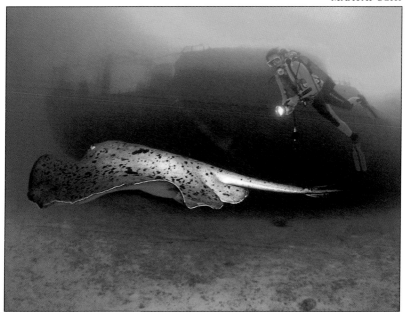

closely associated with the erstwhile director of the diving base here, Herwarth Voigtmann, who was once the grand old man of scuba diving on Maldives. It was he, for instance, who caused a sensation by instituting regular shark feedings; spectacular pictures of these events appeared around the world. Although Voigtmann left Maldives a long time ago, his reputation lives on, and Maayafushi is still a place of pilgrimage for enthusiastic divers.

In 1993, the **Maayafushi Tourist Resort** was completely renovated, but fortunately the island sacrificed none of its old charm in the process. It still has a thick growth of palms and tropical bushes; the dense vegetation extends right up to the lagoon.

Maayafushi is a crescent-shaped island, about 300 by 100 meters in size, with a particularly large lagoon ideal for swimming and popular as a protected anchorage with safari dhonis and excursion boats. Most of the beach is covered in wonderfully fine coral sand, which

mades it especially good for swimmers, particularly along the island's western side. Two large tongues of land projecting out into the lagoon are veritable magnets for vacationing sun-worshippers.

The hotel's 60 rooms are parceled out in row houses of four units each. In designing the appealing but functional amenities, the planners deliberately avoided extra frills without sacrificing comfort. Fans provide fresh air, while guests can peacefully enjoy the day or evening on their small private terraces.

Maayafushi has something rustic about it, and still gives an idea of how Maldives must have been in the early days of the tourist industry. A high occupancy rate attests to the resort's continuing popularity. The Swiss-Maldivian management works very efficiently, and the restaurant's cuisine presents a skillful combination of local and international dishes.

Apart from scuba diving, the other recreational facilities on offer here are waterskiing, windsurfing, deep-sea fishing, para-sailing, catamaran sailing and badminton. Sometimes, there is a disco in the evening. Anyone who wants to expand his or her horizons after a few days can have a look at the Ari Atoll from the air or join an excursion to one of the inhabited islands. Stalwarts can also set off on a trip to Male by plane or helicopter.

Madoogali

Madoogali is located 90 kilometers from the Hulhule airport in the northwest of the Ari Atoll, straight inward at the end of the Madoogalee Kandu, between the resort island of Nika and the inhabited island of Feridhoo. For a long time, Maldivians did live on Madoogali, but, whatever their reasons, they gradually emigrated until, in 1943, the 43 people who were left were finally resettled in Mandhoo, in the southern part of the Ari Atoll. The translation of the name Madoogali, "island formed of coral stones," does not cast any further light on the possible causes of the population's dispersal.

Towards the end of the 1980s, the island was approved as a holiday resort; the first visitors arrived in 1988. Madoogali, an oval island about 500 by 300 meters in size, is thickly wooded with trees and bushes. A wonderful beach that extends around the entire island, with a small lagoon, is a paradise for sun-worshippers and water-rats, while the beautiful house reef comes in very close to the island in some places, and exerts a perpetual fascination on divers and snorkelers.

The 50 self-contained bungalows of the **Madoogali Resort** are thatched with palm fronds and furnished comfortably and tastefully. Hot and cold fresh water, an air conditioner, refrigerator, direct dial telephone and a small veranda with a view of the sea are among the amenities provided.

Right: Moofushi Island Resort is especially popular with Italian visitors.

Most of the visitors here hail from Italy, although about 40% of them are German. In consequence, the first-class cuisine on Madoogali has been tailored to European tastes; enhancing these culinary offerings are a range of local fish specialities.

Sport number one on the island is scuba diving. You can discover superb coral formations even when snorkeling along the house reef; sometimes, you can even spot nurse sharks under the coral blocks. Experienced divers are drawn not only to the house reef, but also to locations in the inner areas of the atoll, where there's a wealth of fish, or to the western outer reef. But Madoogali does offer other types of sport, such as para-sailing, canoeing and kayaking, surfing, water-skiing, volleyball, ping-pong, and badminton. In addition, you can make excursions to the neighboring islands, try your hand at night fishing, or go off on a breathtaking round-trip flight over the atoll. In the evenings, there's dancing in the small but often extremely loud disco.

Madoogali is one of the few islands to have its own doctor, who is responsible for what, in Maldives, is known as "island medicine."

Moofushi

Moofushi is one of the more recent hotel complexes in the Ari Atoll. Tourism didn't come to this oval island at the center of the atoll, which measures about 230 by 160 meters in size, until 1990. In Dhivehi, the syllable *moo* means "root of a tree," perhaps pointing to the lush wealth of trees and bushes that grow like a jungle over the entire island.

From the air, it is easy to see that almost 75% of Moofushi is still virgin land: the island is densely covered with luxuriant tropical vegetation. In fact, the areas of vegetation are protected and cared for like a reserve, a fact that contributes greatly to the island's wonderful,

quasi-primeval atmosphere. The channel of Moofushi Kandu runs to the south of the island, connecting the atoll with the open sea. Most of Moofushi's house reef lies along the outer reef and in the channel. This means that strong currents tend to prevail, and guests should be especially careful when diving and snorkeling. A broad lagoon extends out to the northwest: it is ideal for carefree swimming. Large parts of the island are surrounded by a lovely sand beach that seems to reinforce the image of a quintessential tropical dream island.

The **Moofushi Island Resort** complex consists of 45 self-contained bungalows that are hidden in the greenery. A row of 15 additional bungalows on stilts stands along the island's southern side, in the lagoon; each of these has direct access to the water. Spacious and comfortable, rooms are fitted out with hot and cold showers, air conditioners and fans, modern sanitary facilities, minibars and telephones. Moofushi is mainly frequented by Italian visitors, and the restaurant's culinary specialties are accordingly delicious. In addition, the buffet includes tasty fish dishes and curries, of both Maldivian and Indian origin, once a week, and also features some international dishes for the sake of the German guests (who comprise about 40% of the public). Breakfast and lunch are served buffet-style; while the evening meal is a sit-down affair.

By day, Moofushi offers an unusually varied palette of sporting activities. Apart from the obligatory diving, there's windsurfing, waterskiing, deep-sea fishing and catamaran sailing as well as beach volleyball and water gymnastics. Excursions to inhabited islands and picnic tours to uninhabited islands are also on offer. At night, visitors can hang out in the bar or disco, or simply sit and contemplate the light of the moon on the water.

Nika Hotel (Kudafolhudhoo)

Originally, this island in the northwest of the North Ari Atoll was called Kuda-

145

folhudhoo. Located about 86 kilometers from Hulhule, it can be reached in about 30 minutes by helicopter. When tourists started coming here in 1983, Kudafolhudhoo was rechristened the **Nika Hotel**.

Measuring about 230 by 150 meters, the island boasts a covering of dense vegetation, so that you almost have to search for the bungalows in the greenery. Among other things, Nika is famous for its large, 130-year-old nica or banyan tree (*Ficus benghalensis*), which is located in the middle of the island and obviously played a significant role in establishing the island's new name. Its large, shady branches are strong and flexible, and the Maldivians like to use them for masts for their dhonis. The highly fertile soil, which was specially brought over to the island, is very well suited for the cultivation of various plants.

Above: A diver's dream – encounter with a sea turtle. Right: Turtle breeding has been successful on Nika.

One interesting and positive development on Nika is a project devoted to the breeding of sea turtles. Newly-hatched turtles are reared in a specially built salt-water pool. Later, when they are a little bigger and thus less vulnerable to danger than the very young turtles, they are returned to the freedom of the sea.

Nika is among the most exclusive hotels of Maldives; its Italian management is responsible for the décor and high standards. Exclusivity is reflected in the island's small capacity and the luxurious appointments of the island's 25 large, self-contained bungalows. Each of these was constructed with visible artisan skill and measures more than 70 square meters in area; they're separated from one another by small gardens. Each unit have a large living room, a bedroom and a bathroom, as well as a small terrace with a view of the sea. The architects intentionally designed the houses to be round and used many arc elements in their design. However, the ambience was also designed with an eye to conditions in the early days of Maldivian tourism. Instead of air conditioning, large fans and mosquito nets dominate the rather unusual but undeniably romantic apartments. This isn't to say that the standards of comfort aren't high: all the bungalows also have mini-bars and direct dial telephones.

Nika boasts two restaurants with first-class local and Italian cuisine, as well as an Italian wine cellar. A large and varied buffet breakfast is provided every morning, while the afternoon and evening meals are served at the table. There is also a coffee shop, an excellently equipped bar and a souvenir shop for visitors.

Scuba divers on Nika can explore the house reef, a mere 100 meters away, and some other top diving spots in the vicinity. For other athletes, there's a lawn-tennis court with floodlights for night play, as well as windsurfing, canoeing, sailing and waterskiing. Guests can also play boccie, badminton or ping-pong, sail out for night fishing, or take a look at the neighboring islands. There is a doctor stationed on the island to provide medical care to the guests.

of income of Bodufolhudhoo's 400-odd inhabitants is fishing.

INHABITED ISLANDS AND PICNIC ISLANDS IN THE NORTH ARI ATOLL

Alikoirah

Alikoirah is a tiny little uninhabited island that is situated in the middle of the atoll, northwest of Fish Head.

Bodufolhudhoo

The inhabited island of Bodufolhudhoo is located in the northwest of the atoll, not far from the hotel island of Nika (Kudafolhudhoo). It has a helicopter pad for incoming tourists who are transferring to resort islands in the northern parts of the North Ari Atoll. The main source

Feridhoo

Feridhoo is a large inhabited island on the western border of the North Ari Atoll, which is located exactly between the channels Feridhoo Uthuru Kandu and Feridhoo Dekunu Kandu. Ferihoo is home to about 550 Maldivians.

Settlement on the island dates back to Buddhist times. Many of the island's inhabitants are descendants of former slaves. When he returned from Mecca, Sultan Hassan III (1542-1567) brought about 70 black African slaves to the country; later, Sultan Hassan Nooradhdheen (1779-1799) also returned from his Mecca pilgrimage with a few slaves. When they were liberated, the Africans were resettled on the islands of Kudaf Ari in the Noonu Atoll and on Feridhoo. There, they intermarried with the local population, something that is reflected even today in the strikingly large

147

physiques and dark, curly hair of many of the island's residents.

Gaathafushi

The small island of Gaathafushi lies in the northwest of Fesdhoo and is uninhabited. It is a popular picnic spot with day-trippers from the resort island of Fesdhoo.

Himendhoo

Himdendhoo, a quite sizable inhabited island, is located in the western part of the Ari Atoll, around the midway point of the Himendhoo channel at the eastern end of the *faru* of the same name. About 380 inhabitants presently call it home. Himendhoo is a typical fisherman's island whose historical roots reach back

Above: A place to unwind – a local man relaxes in a traditional Maldivian swing Right: Soft corals in a spectrum of colors grow along the Maalhoss Thila.

into the pre-Islamic epoch, something demonstrated by a number of archaeological finds dating from Buddhist times.

Kandholhudhoo

This island is named after the flower *kandholhudhoo*, a kind of wild lily that grows on the island and sports beautiful blossoms. Kandholhudhoo is situated in the middle of the atoll between Fesdhoo and Ellaidhoo. This uninhabited island was once a popular destination for day excursions or as an ideal spot for a romantic picnic between two dives. Today, however, Kandholhudhoo, along with Bodufoludhoo, is a landing pad for helicopters in the North Ari Atoll. After they land here, guests are then taken by dhoni to their resorts.

Maagaala

This tiny, uninhabited island on the eastern outer edge of the Ari Atoll, near the well-known tourist island of Ellai-

dhoo, is ideally suited for sun-worship-pers. The large lagoon provides superb swimming in its calm waters.

Experienced windsurfers and sailors can reach Maagaala easily from Ellaid-hoo.

Maalhoss

Maalhoss is located on the western side of the atoll between the two channels Maalhohu Kandu and the more southerly Himendhoo Kandu. The syllable *lhoss* denotes the *Morindaefolia* vegetable shrub. One characteristic feature of this island is its dense growth of large trees.

Most of the island's inhabitants are engaged in fishing or dhoni-building. Many of the younger natives, however, have gone off into more lucrative jobs on the resort islands of the Ari Atoll.

One of the most beautiful diving spots in the entire atoll is located near this island: the reef of **Maalhoss Thila**, with its captivating light-blue soft corals.

Madivaru

North of the resort island of Bathaala, on the eastern outer edge of the atoll, is the small, uninhabited island of Madi-varu. *Madi* is a local word for the rays that can often be found in the waters of the Madivaru Kandu and along the outer reef. With a little bit of luck, you can even see them in the still waters of the la-goon. Scattered all around Madivaru are a number of spectacular diving spots, frequented by many of the diving bases in the vicinity. Most impressive are the diving spots along the outer reef, such as Beyru Thila, Beyru Madivaru, Digu Thila and Kari Beyru Thila.

Mathiveri

About 450 people live on Mathiveri, mainly local fisherfolk. The island is situated in the northwest of the Ari Atoll at the end of the extensive reef complex of the Gangehi Maavaru, near the resort island of Nika. *Mathiveri* means "upper

part"; the name is supposed to be an indication of the island's northern position within the Ari Atoll.

As on the neighboring islands of Nika and Bodu Fulhadhoo, there is a large nika or banyan tree on Mathiveri. As these trees can live for several hundred years, this specimen may even have "overseen" the construction of the old mosque on Mathiveri that Sultan Ibrahim Iskandar I (1648-1687) had built during his reign.

Mathiveri Finolhu

Mathiveri's small, uninhabited neighbor is called Mathiveri Finolhu. Both islands are located in the same lagoon and are only a few meters' distant from each other. Just one kilometer to the west is the exclusive resort island of Nika, and Mathiveri Finolhu is popular as a "picnic island" with Nika's guests.

Above: Navigating takes a good eye and a sense of balance. Right: Shredded coconut is an important ingredient in local dishes.

Meerufenfushi

Meerufenfushi, the "namesake" of the resort island in the North Male Atoll, is located quite centrally in the atoll, to the south of the hotel island of Fesdhoo. This small island is uninhabited, and its name means something along the lines of "fresh water island."

Mushimasmingili

Mushimasmingili is a small, uninhabited island in the east of the Ari Atoll with a wonderful beach. The island, located to the southwest of the resort island of Ellaidhoo, is a very popular picnic spot. Near Mushimasmingili is the world-renowned dive site of **Fish Head**, where a continuously growing number of gray reef sharks make their rounds.

Thodhoo

Thodhoo, a remote island 12 kilometers to the north of the Rhasdhoo

Atoll, is located in a miniature atoll a mere 2 kilometers in diameter. The word *Thodhoo* comes from Singhalese and means "island on the large reef." In 1958, Thodhoo gained renown thanks to the excavations of the remains of a large Buddhist temple, where were found a reliquary, a well-preserved statue of the Buddha, and Roman coins from the period around 90 BC. The Buddha's head is on display in the museum in Male. Excavations are ongoing at other burial mounds on the island.

Thodhoo's fertile soil facilitates the cultivation of watermelons, vegetables, betel leaves and chilies. The island's inhabitants are considered very well-educated, and many of them occupy government posts. Another interesting island event are the traditional *bandiya-jehun* dances, performed by young women.

Ukulhass

The fisherman's island of Ukulhass is located in the northeast of the Ari Atoll

and has about 500 inhabitants. On the northeastern edge of the atoll there are two other small islands: Ukulhass Fushi, a sand bar boasting all of three bushes, and Gaagandu ("large stone"), an island that once had a firm stone base, which, however, was washed away many years ago.

Vihamaafaru

This uninhabited island is located on the northwest side of the Ari Atoll to the north of the Madhoogali Kandu. In the local language, its name means "large, poisonous reef," and in fact this island is mainly known for the large reef that surrounds it, although it's more enticing than the "poison" in its name might lead one to believe. Snorkelers, in particular, are fascinated by it because of its magnificent coral formations and the countless fish, some of them poisonous, with their amazing range of colors. These sea creatures present no danger whatsoever, as long they're not hassled.

RASDHOO ATOLL

Almost circular in form, the Rasdhoo Atoll, just northeast of the Ari Atoll, measures about 9 kilometers in diameter. The small atoll consists of three inhabited islands and two uninhabited ones, and all of them, thanks to erosion, are getting smaller all the time. The inhabited islands include the main island of the atoll, Rasdhoo, which also has a helipad, as well as the larger resort island of Veligandhoo in the east, and the elongated Kuramathi, which boasts three hotel complexes, in the south.

RESORT ISLANDS IN THE RASDHOO ATOLL

Kuramathi

Lying in the south of the Rasdhoo Atoll, the island of Kuramathi was settled long ago. This was proven by excavations made in 1988, which indicate the existence of a Buddhist monastery and numerous graves from pre-Islamic times. When the decision was made in 1970 to open the island up to tourism, 124 natives had to be resettled from the island, which measures 2.5 kilometers by 500 meters, in area, to Rasdhoo.

Kuramathi opened in 1977, to start with, in a very modest way, with a small diving camp and 12 simple bungalows that were hardly even noticeable on the island. After a rapid boom, Kuramathi today is a large, modern hotel island with a total of 548 beds. All of this construction, however, has hardly affected the island's exotic appeal. Even today, the island boasts almost untouched areas of land, habitat of a healthy population of flying foxes, herons, pelicans, and various birds of prey.

Left: Proud display of a good day's catch – a huge mackerel.

Longish and sickle-shaped, the island supports no fewer than three independent hotel resorts. The largest, **Kuramathi Village** in the northeast of the island, has been modernized and expanded many times since it opened in 1977. Today, all of its 144 rooms have air conditioners or fans as well as hot and cold showers and individual terraces.

The **Blue Lagoon Beach Resort** has 30 rooms in beach bungalows as well as 20 pile bungalows built out over the waters of the lagoon. All of these are furnished in much the same manner as the accommodations in Kuramathi Village.

The **Blue Lagoon Cottage Club**, with 30 self-contained bungalows and 50 pile bungalows over the water, is probably the most luxurious resort on Kuramathi.

As a fully developed tourist island, Kuramathi offers a richly varied cuisine that caters to the tastes of the island's international visitors, who come mainly from Germany, England and South Africa. There are also Maldivian dishes on the menu, as well as Asian specialties and barbecues, Italian dishes and fresh-caught seafood. Every hotel on Kuramathi operates its own restaurants – there are seven, all told – to provide for the physical well-being of all the island's guests.

Visitors to Kuramathi can avail themselves of the facilities of all three resorts; as a result, there's a strikingly large range of sports and recreational activities on offer. The large lagoon is particularly well-suited for windsurfing, sailing and waterskiing. Other options include various ball sports, such as volleyball, soccer, tennis or badminton. Since 1998, a fitness center, a sauna and swimming pool have also been available to vacationers.

Among divers, Kuramathi is especially popular because of the hammerhead sharks that pass Rasdhoo Madivaru in the early morning hours. Because of the island's relatively exposed position, it's

easy from here to make dives along the outer reef, which is a particularly appealing option for more experienced divers. Between December and May, divers along Thaadhoo Island Reef have a good chance of sighting the fascinating manta rays. Other diving highlights include day-long excursions to the neighboring islands of the Ari Atoll, such as to the world-renowned diving spot known as Fish Head. Kuramathi's diving vessels set out on expeditions to some 35 breathtaking dive sites. There is also a small wreck by the house reef at a depth of about 20 meters.

For the landlubbers among the tourists – if such a creature exists at all on Maldives – the resort offers an excursion to the inhabited island of Rasdhoo not far away, where there are a few places to shop and, at the far end of the village, a dhoni shipyard that tourists can visit,

Above: Bottled drinks are a way to cut down on garbage (Kuramathi). Right: At last, the right souvenir!

where dhonis are still built in the traditional manner.

Veligandhoo

Veligandhoo, the second resort island in the Rasdhoo Atoll, is situated on the eastern outer reef, not far from the large resort island of Kuramathi. It is sometimes confused with an island in the South Male Atoll that bears almost the same name, Veligandhoo Huraa; the latter is now also known as Palm Tree Island.

Veligandhoo, which measures about 600 by 200 meters in size, started its operations as a tourist island as early as 1984. In the summer of 1996, the resort was renovated and upgraded to higher standards of comfort.

Some of the 63 air-conditioned bungalows of the **Veligandhoo Island Resort** have been built on stilts out over the lagoon. All the rooms have hot and cold showers, a mini-bar and a telephone with international direct dialing. The eight

"water bungalows" are somewhat larger and even more comfortably furnished; they also have bathtubs and broad terraces with a view of the sea.

One special feature of Veligandhoo is a large sand bar that projects directly from the island beach into the large lagoon – an ideal base from which to swim in the lagoon's turquoise waters before relaxing in the sun. Even at high tide, the sand bar remains exposed. For more active vacationers, the lagoon is ideal for windsurfing and catamaran sailing.

Because of the island's exposed location on the outer reef, scuba diving has pride of place on the list of sports activities. Beyond the magnificent dives along the house reef, the diving school offers excursions to the same breathtaking diving spots you can visit from Kuramathi. Thanks to the island's north-south alignment, one side of the house reef is usually free of currents and thus presents ideal conditions for snorkelers.

Night life on Veligandhoo centers around a small island disco, where live

bands occasionally perform from time to time. There are also excursions to the nearby inhabited island of Rasdhoo or picnic excursions to small, uninhabited islands.

INHABITED ISLANDS AND PICNIC ISLANDS IN THE RASDHOO ATOLL

Rasdhoo

Today home to 668 people, Rasdhoo can look back upon a long history. It has been settled for centuries; its roots reach all the way back to the days when Buddhism still predominated on Maldives. Rasdhoo is the atoll's main island. Once, it was the site of the administrative center of the entire Ari Atoll; today, the central administration on the island is responsible for the Rasdhoo Atoll as well as some islands of the North Ari Atoll.

Large numbers of tourists from the resorts of Kuramathi and Veligandhoo visit the island to hunt for souvenirs. At the far end of the town, you can visit a shipyard in which dhonis are still built in the traditional manner, according to construction plans which have been passed down by word of mouth through the generations, and which old master craftsmen now dictate to the other workers.

Rasdhoo Madivaru

Rasdhoo Madivaru is not far from the inhabited island of Rasdhoo. Uninhaited today, the island was a really big island in the past, but it's grown smaller and smaller thanks to the influence of the wind, the waves and the currents. In Dhivehi, the word *rasdhoo* means "the start of an island," and the term *madi* stands for "rays."

Between December and May, manta rays frequent the area, especially the channel in the south, the Rasdhoo Kandu; divers are often fascinted by their elegant appearance. The area is also known for its large population of hammerhead sharks. Native fishermen used to go fishing for shark every once in a while, and generally found the hammerhead particularly difficult to capture. Even today, many locals believe that the sharks prefer to hang out in a large cave in the depths of the ocean. Since the ocean floor outside the Rasdhoo Atoll drops precipitously to unknown depths, it will be difficult to determine the truth of this story for a long time to come.

Madivaru Finolhu

Today, this island's name designates nothing more than a small, photogenic sand bar in the southeast of the atoll, which is growing ever smaller because of erosion. On future charts of the region, Madivaru Finolhu will probably not be shown as an island at all, but merely as a shallow area potentially dangerous for ocean-going ships.

NORTH ARI ATOLL

ATHURUGAU
Athurugau Island Resort
Opened in 1990. Male office: M. Veeza, tel. 310489, fax 310370. Island: tel. 450508, fax 450574, E-Mail: athadmin@dhivehinet.net.mv. *BUNGALOWS:* Single and double bungalows, 42 rooms. *AMENITIES:* restaurant, bar, coffee shop. *DIVING BASE:* German, English, French, Italian, PADI, SSI. *CREDIT CARDS:* AE/MC/VC/DC. *AIRPORT* 95 km, 30 min by air taxi, 30 min by helicopter plus 40 min by dhoni.

AVI ISLAND (VELIDHOO)
Avi Island Resort
Opened in 1989, renovated in 1995. Male office: Travel Club Pvt., H. Noouaraha, Roshanee Magu, tel. 313738, fax 326264. Island: tel. 450595, fax 450630, E-Mail: velidhu@dhivehinet.net.mv. *BUNGALOWS:* 80 single bungalows. *AMENITIES:* bar, restaurant, coffee shop. *DIVING BASE:* German, English, French, Italian, PADI, house reef. *CREDIT CARDS:* AE/MC/VC. *AIRPORT:* 76 km, helicopter 20 min plus 30 min by dhoni, 3 hours by motorboat.

BATHALA
Bathala Island Resort
Opened in 1983, renovated in 1991. Male office: B.I.R. Hotel Manag. Ltd., H. Kinolhas, Abadahfehi Magu, tel. 323323, fax 324328. Island: tel. 445960, fax 445960, E-Mail: jtsc7993@dhivehinet.net.mv. *BUNGALOWS:* 38 single bungalows. *AMENITIES:* coffee shop, restaurant, bar. *DIVING BASE:* German, Engl., French, CMAS, PADI. *CREDIT CARDS:* AE/MC/VC. *AIRPORT:* 62 km, 20 min by air taxi, 1.5 hrs by motorboat.

ELLAIDHOO
Ellaidhoo Tourist Resort
Opened 1985. Male office: No. 2 Athereege Aage, H. Boduthakurufaanu Magu, tel. 317717, fax 314977. Island: tel. 450586, fax 450514, E-Mail: travelin@dhivehinet.net.mv. *BUNGALOWS:* 50 single bungalows. *AMENITIES:* bar, coffee shop, restaurant. *DIVING BASE:* (Nitrox), German, Engl., French, CMAS, NAUI, PADI, VIT, house reef, wreck. *CREDIT CARDS:* AE/MC/ VC. *AIRPORT:* 70 km, 2 hrs by motorboat.

FESDHOO
Fesdhoo Fun Island
Opened in 1982, renov. 1995. Male office: Universal Enterprises Pvt., Ltd., tel. 323080, fax 320274. Island: tel. 450541, fax 450547, E-Mail: sales@unisurf.com, Internet: http://www.unisurf.com. *BUNGALOWS:* 60 rooms. *AMENITIES:* bar, coffee shop, restaurant. *DIVING BASE:* German, Engl., French, house reef wreck. *CREDIT CARDS:* AE/MC/VC/DC/JCB. *AIRPORT:* 83 km, 30 min by air taxi, 3.5 hrs by motorboat.

GANGEHI
Gangehi Island Resort
Opened in 1987, renovated in 1995. Maleoffice: 4th

Floor Alia Bldg., Orchid Magu, tel. 313938, fax 313939. Island: tel. 450505, fax 450506, E-Mail: boduvcz@ dhivehinet.net.mv. *BUNGALOWS:* 17 single bungalows, 8 pile bungalows. *AMENITIES:* bar, coffee shop, restaurant. *DIVING BASE:* Italian, English, French. *CREDIT CARDS:* AE/MC/VC. *AIRPORT:* 75 km, 30 min by air taxi, 20 min by motorboat (plus 10 min by motorboat). Exclusive to Club Vacanze.

HALAVELI
Halaveli Holiday Village
Opened in 1982. Male office: Eastinvest Pvt., Ltd., Akiri, Boduthakurufaanu Magu, tel. 322719, fax 323463. Island: tel. 450559, fax 450564, E-Mail: halaveli@dhivehinet.net.mv or dchala@netlink.net.mv. *BUNGALOWS:* 52 single bungalows. *AMENITIES:* bar, coffee shop, restaurant. *DIVING BASE:* Italian, German, English, French, PADI, wreck by house reef. *CREDIT CARDS:* AE/MC/VC/DC. *AIRPORT:* 63 km, 20 min by helicopter, 2 hrs by motorboat.

MAAYAFUSHI
Maayafushi Tourist Resort
Opened in 1983, renovated in 1993. Male office: Luxwood 1, Boduthakurufaanu Magu, tel. 320097, fax 326658. Island: tel. 440588, fax 440568, E-Mail: maaya@dhivehinet.net.mv. *BUNGALOWS:* 60 rooms in row bungalows. *AMENITIES:* bar, coffee shop, restaurant. *DIVING BASE:* German, Engl., French, CMAS, NAUI, PADI. *CREDIT CARDS:* AE/MC/VC, *AIRPORT:* 70 km, 20 min by air taxi.

MADOOGALI
Madoogali Resort
Opened in 1988. Male office: H. Henveyruge, Medhuziyaarai Magu, tel. 317975, fax 317974. Island: tel. 450581, fax. 440554, E-Mail: madugali@dhivehinet. net.mv. *BUNGALOWS:* 50 single bungalows with air conditioning. *AMENITIES:* bar, coffee shop, restaurant. *DIVING BASE:* Italian, English, German, PADI. *CREDIT CARDS:* AE/MC/VC/ DC, *AIRPORT:* 90 km, 30 min by air taxi, 2.5 hours by motorboat.

MOOFUSHI
Moofushi Island Resort
Opened in 1990. Male office: Moofushi Male Office, H. Sun Night, tel. 326141, fax 318237. Island: tel. 450517, fax 450509, E-Mail: moofushi@dhivehinet. net.mv. *BUNGALOWS:* 45 single bungalows, 15 pile bungalows with bathtubs. *AMENITIES:* bar, 2 coffee shops, 2 restaurants, fitness center, *DIVING BASE:* German, English, French. *CREDIT CARDS:* AE/MC/ VC/DC. *AIRPORT:* 90 km, 40 min by air taxi.

NIKA HOTEL (KUDAFOLHUDHOO)
Nika Hotel
Opened in 1983. Male office: 117, Majeedhee Magu, tel. 325091, fax 325097. Island: tel. 450516, fax: 450577, E-Mail: nika@dhivehinet.net.mv. *BUNGALOWS:* 25 single bungalows. *AMENITIES:* bar, coffee shop, 2 restaurants, tennis. *DIVING BASE:* Italian,

German, Engl., French, PADI. *CREDIT CARDS:* AE/MC/VC/DC/JCB. *AIRPORT:* 86 km, 30 min by helicopter (plus 10 min by motorboat) or 2 hrs by motorboat.

RASDHOO ATOLL

KURAMATHI
Opened in 1977. Male office: Universal Enterprises Pvt., Ltd., 39 Orchid Magu, tel. 323080 or 322971, fax: 320274 or 322678, E-Mail: sales@unisurf. com, Internet: http://www.unisurf.com, a total of 274 rooms in 3 hotel complexes. Kuramathi is one of the largest islands in Maldives. Each hotel's *AMENITIES* are at the disposal of all the island's guests.

Kuramathi Village
Tel. 450527, fax 450556. *BUNGALOWS:* 76 rooms in row bungalows, 68 rooms in self-contained bungalows, 33 of them deluxe bungalows. *AMENITIES:* Sung Bar, Atoll Coffee Shop, Haruge Restaurant, Adobe Grill (barbecue 7:30-10:30 pm), desalination plant. *DIVING BASE:* German, Engl., frz., CMAS, PADI, great house reef, wreck at a depth of 19 m, good chances to sight deep-sea fish such as hammerheads. *CREDIT CARDS:* AE/MC/VC/DC/JCB. *AIRPORT:* 60 km, 2 hrs by motorboat.

Blue Lagoon Beach Resort
Tel. 450579, fax 450531. *BUNGALOWS:* 30 self-contained bungalows, 20 pile bungalows over the lagoon, direct dial phones. *AMENITIES:* Island boutique, Lagoona bar, coffee shop, Blue Lagoon main restaurant, La Lagoon Grill, beach barbecue. *DIVING BASE:* German, Engl., French, Spanish, Italian, Dutch, CMAS, NAUI, PADI, house reef (see above). *CREDIT CARDS:* AE/MC/VC/DC/JCB. *AIRPORT:* 60 km, 2 hrs by motorboat.

Blue Lagoon Cottage Club
Tel. 450532, fax 450642. *BUNGALOWS:* 30 self-contained bungalows, 50 pile bungalows out over the lagoon, direct dial phones. *AMENITIES:* Island boutique, Dhoni Bar, Seaweed Coffee Shop, Malaafah Restaurant, Palm Court Restaurant. *DIVING BASE:* located att he Blue Lagoon Beach Resort. House reef: see above. *CREDIT CARDS:* AE/MC/VC/DC/JCB. *AIRPORT:* 60 km, some 2 hours by motorboat.

VELIGANDHOO
Veligandhoo Island Resort
Opened in 1984, renovated in 1996. Male office: Crown Company, PO Box 2034, tel. 322432, fax 324009. Island: tel. 450594, fax 450648, E-Mail: crown@dhivehinet.net.mv. *BUNGALOWS:* 6 standard, 49 superior, 8 deluxe (VIP) bungalows, all with air conditioning. *AMENITIES:* bar, coffee shop, restaurant, desalination plant. *DIVING BASE:* Engl., German, French, Ital., CMAS, PADI, VDST, house reef. *CREDIT CARDS:* AE/MC/VC. *AIRPORT:* 55 km, 2 hrs by motorboat.

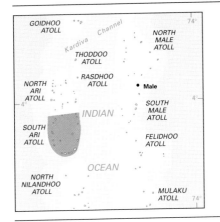

SOUTH ARI ATOLL
(ALIFU ATOLL)

RESORT ISLANDS IN THE SOUTH ARI ATOLL

Angaga (Angaagau)

Located in the middle of the South Ari Atoll, Angaga began operating as a tourist island in 1989 under the name of **Angaga Island Resort**. Before it was opened up for tourism, this beautiful island was known as Angaagau.

Wonderful snow-white sand beaches run around the island; there is an inviting turquoise-blue lagoon for swimming; and the thick, luxuriant vegetation, consisting of coconut palms and screw palms (pandanus), mangroves, Indian almond trees, bougainvillea and hibiscus, lends the place an incredible tropical atmosphere. You can easily walk around the little island – it measures a mere 350 by 150 meters – in 15 to 20 minutes. Angaga changes its appearance according to the season, like many other islands in Maldives. Depending on the direction of the prevailing winds, the beaches wander considerably; they are artificially "restored" as needed.

Preceding pages: Air taxis can reach Angaga Island Resort in a mere 30 minutes. Left: The fruits of the sea, prepared and presented by a pro.

Boasting a wealth of aquatic species, the house reef is best suited for snorkeling and diving, although at the end of the 1980s, an attack by a coral-eating organism known as a crown-of-thorn caused severe damage to the reef. Fortunately, it was able to recover relatively quickly from the effects of the attack.

Each of the hotel's self-contained bungalows is individually furnished. All the 51 rooms have hot and cold running water, air conditioning, a refrigerator, direct dial telephone and a veranda with a view of the sea. Angaga's restaurant provides a good mixture of Maldivian and international cuisine. Meals are usually served buffet-style, and the restaurant has a beautiful view of the lagoon, especially at sunset. In the evenings, guests congregate in the coffee shop or the island bar. For the most part, Angaga is a notably quiet island, free of the blare of a disco, apart from the occasional spontaneous outbreak on the part of a group of visitors.

Sporting highlights on the island are the daily diving trips to the first-class diving sites in the South Ari Atoll. Also popular are snorkeling excursions in the lagoon and the house reef, as well as surfing, waterskiing, sailing, parasailing, darts, volleyball, ping-pong and badminton. People addicted to their daily work-

161

outs can sweat to their hearts' content in the air-conditioned fitness room. Island-hopping and night fishing are other popular recreational activities.

Transfer from the airport, 96 kilometers distant, takes 30 minutes by air taxi and another 45 minutes by dhoni from the seaplane's landing strip.

Ari Beach (Dhidhdhoofinolhu)

Ari Beach is located on the southern outer reef of the Ari Atoll. Further north in the same lagoon are two islands: the longish-shaped native island of Dhigura and to the south, the smaller island of Dhidhdhoo, from which Ari Beach derives its traditional name: Dhidhdhoofinolhu, or "sand bar of Dhidhdhoo." Ari Beach itself is a long, narrow island 1,400 meters long and a mere 35 meters or so wide.

Above: A majestic sunset over Holiday Island. Right: Delicious desserts sweeten the evening mood at Holiday Island Resort.

The island is almost completely surrounded by a beautiful sand beach, while a broad, shallow lagoon tempts would-be swimmers. Since there is hardly any coral growing in the lagoon, it is also ideally suited for surfing and waterskiing. Even children can safely splash about here. For divers and snorkelers, there are free dhoni transfers several times a day to the house reef, located 400 meters away. With some luck, enthusiasts of underwater life will have a chance to experience a special highlight: manta rays and whale sharks often pass by the southern side of the Ari Atoll.

Visitors can also take excursions to the inhabited island of Dhigura to shop for souvenirs and get acquainted with some facets of the Maldivians' daily life.

Dhidhdhoofinolhu, as it once was known, was the first tourist island in the South Ari Atoll and, at that time, also the most remote and isolated hotel complex of Maldives. The island was rechristened **Ari Beach Resort** when it was opened to tourists in 1987. Since its thorough reno-

vation in 1994, it's had a total of 120 bright double bungalows with modern décor and appointments. The standard rooms have air conditioning, fans, hot and cold showers, private toilets, telephones, and a veranda; in the superior rooms, which have classier amenities, there are also mini-bars and IDD telephones. The family bungalows are furnished like the superior rooms, but have more beds. Apart from the coffee shop and the boutique, guests can hang out in the island's restaurant, which has an extensive and varied menu that includes tasty local dishes. Breakfast is served as a buffet, lunch is a sit-down affair, and dinner is again a hot buffet with all kinds of delicacies. There is a landing strip on the island for helicopters and air taxis, which cover the 97 kilometers to Hulhule airport in about 30 minutes.

Holiday Island (Dhiffushi)

The island originally called Dhiffushi is located in the south of the Ari Atoll; it opened for tourists in 1994, after it was taken over by the LTI group, as the **Holiday Island Resort**. Together with the inhabited island of Maamigili, which has a landing pad for helicopters, and the uninhabited island of Ariyadhoo, which is used for agricultural purposes, it forms the southern border of the Ari Atoll. Longish in form, Dhiffushi extends from east to west, measuring 800 by 100 meters. The island has a wonderful sand beach and lush tropical vegetation with many palms and colorful plants. Helicopters cover the 109 kilometers from the airport to the neighboring island of Maamigili in just 30 minutes; from the landing strip on Maamigili, it's only 10 minutes by dhoni to the island. Another option is to cover the entire distance in about 2.5 hours by speedboat.

Holiday Island, designed along the most modern lines for the discriminating guest and therefore right in tune with the times, is certainly one of the most luxurious hotel complexes in Maldives. All the single and double bungalows, which

163

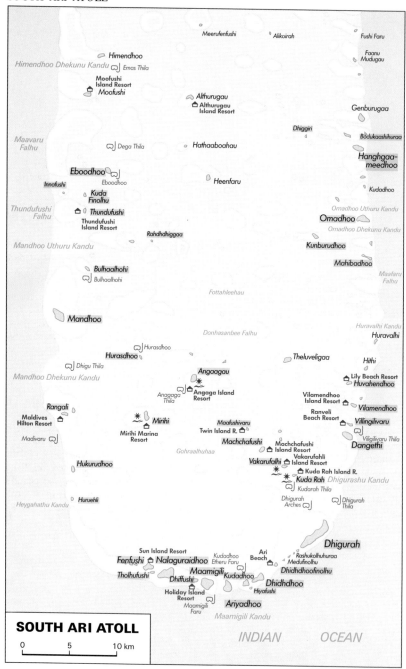

Meerufenfushi · Alikoirah · Fushi Faru

Faanu Mudugau

⌒ **Himendhoo**

Himendhoo Dhekunu Kandu ⌒ *Emas Thila*

Moofushi Island Resort
Moofushi

⌒ **Althurugau**
⌒ **Althurugau Island Resort**

Genburugaa

Dhiggiri

Bodukaashihuraa

Maavaru Falhu

⌒ *Dega Thila* · ⌒ **Hathaaboahau**

Hanghgaa-meedhoo

Eboodhoo ⌒
Eboodhoo

Heenfaru

Innafushi

Kuda Finolhu

Kudadhoo

Thundufushi Falhu
⌒ **Thundufushi**
Thundufushi Island Resort

Omadhoo Uthuru Kandu

Omadhoo ⌒

Mandhoo Uthuru Kandu

Rahdhdhiggaa

Omadhoo Dhekunu Kandu

Kunburudhoo

Mahibadhoo

⌒ **Bulhaalhohi**
⌒ *Bulhaalhohi*

Maafaru Falhu

Fottahleehau

Mandhoo

Huravalhi Kandu

Donhasanbee Falhu

Huravalhi

⌒ *Hurasdhoo*

Hurasdhoo

⌒ **Theluveligaa**

Hithi

⌒ *Dhigu Thila*

⌒ **Angaagau**

⌒ **Lily Beach Resort**
Huvahendhoo

Mandhoo Dhekunu Kandu

Anagaga Thila ⌒ **Angaga Island Resort**

Vilamendhoo Island Resort ⌒ **Vilamendhoo**

Ranveli Beach Resort ⌒ **Villingilivaru**

Rangali ⌒

Maldives Hilton Resort ⌒

⌒ **Mirihi**

Mirihi Marina Resort

Maafushivaru
Twin Island R. ⌒

Viligilivaru Thila

Dangethi

Madivaru ⌒

Machchafushi ⌒ **Machchafushi Island Resort**

Gohraalhuhaa

Vakarufalhi ⌒ **Vakarufalhi Island Resort**

Hukurudhoo

⌒ **Kuda Rah Island R.**
Kuda Rah *Dhigurashu Kandu*

⌒ *Kudarah Thila*

Huruehli

Heygahathu Kandu

Dhigurah Arches ⌒

⌒ *Dhigurah Thila*

Dhigurah

Rashukolhuhuraa
Medufinolhu

Sun Island Resort

Kudadhoo Etheru Faru

Ari Beach ⌒

Fenfushi ⌒ **Nalaguraidhoo**

Maamigili

Tholhufushi

Dhiffushi

Kudadhoo

Dhidhdhoofinolhu

Dhidhdhoo

Holiday Island Resort

Hiyafushi

Maamigili Faru

Ariyadhoo

Maamigili Kandu

INDIAN OCEAN

SOUTH ARI ATOLL

0   5   10 km

are located right by the beach, have air conditioning, hot and cold water, a bath, shower, toilet and bidet, as well as a hair dryer, television set with video channels, music system, mini-bar, safe and IDD telephone in the room. Although the number of beds is relatively high (284), guests are never made to feel that they're just one of the crowd. The island provides every visitor with his own private "hideaway."

Four bars serve refreshing drinks, the open-air restaurant pampers diners with first-class international cuisine, and the coffee shop is open to visitors 'round the clock. And those who are really tireless can dance away their evenings in the island's disco. Other entertainment options include various shows and live performances of music or Maldivian folklore to transport you into another world.

By day, of course, sports head the program on Holiday Island, from the ubiquitous scuba diving, to surfing, sailing, waterskiing, tennis (illuminated at night), ping-pong, billiards and volleyball. In an air-conditioned fitness center, you can tone up your biceps, and if the island isn't warm enough for you – which would be hard to believe – you can even sweat it out in a sauna with a steam bath.

In addition, there are also excursions to the neighboring islands, flights over the beautiful atoll, or shopping trips to Male. All in all, Holiday Island has been successful in providing just the right mixture of exclusive ambience, a tropical flair, and a vast range of recreational facilities.

Kuda Rah

This oval island, about 300 meters long and 130 meters wide, was opened in 1991 as the **Kuda Rah Island Resort**. It lies in the southeastern part of the Ari Atoll, near the neighboring tourist island of Vakarufalhi. The island has beautiful tropical vegetation and a superb sand

beach with an inviting lagoon for swimming. The house reef, which lures divers with the prospect of exploring its steep rock walls, is just 15 meters from the island and is easy to reach via two entrances. And the area around Kuda Rah, with its many *thilas* and *giris*, boasts a number of other spectacular diving spots.

The resort has 25 single bungalows and 5 bungalows on stilts, each measuring 60 square meters, with tastefully elegant furnishings. All the rooms have fans, air conditioning, a refrigerator, a mini-bar, a safe, a music system, television and video, a beautiful bathroom, a separate bedroom and a living room with a terrace that faces the sea.

The Italian management is responsible for the first-class facilities on Kuda Rah. Nor do the recreational facilities leave anything to be desired. Scuba diving is, as one might expect, sport number one on the island. Snorkeling, surfing, billiards, ping-pong, volleyball, aerobics and canoeing are also available. In the evening, the tennis courts are brightly lit with floodlights. Guests less inclined towards physical exertion can go off island-hopping or take a flight over the enchanting world of the atoll. After the day's activities, there is a disco and a piano bar, as well as entertaining cabaret performances, to enliven the evening.

The hotel management has an island doctor permanently stationed on Kuda Rah, who can also operate the island's own decompression chamber in case of a diving accident. The airport is 100 kilometers away; an air taxi transfer takes 30 minutes of flight time followed by 20 minutes in a dhoni.

Lily Beach (Huvahendhoo)

Lily Beach, a long, oval island, is located in the southeast of the Ari Atoll at the end of the Huvahendhoo Kandu channel. Until 1994, when it was opened up to tourism, the island, which measures about 550 meters long and 100 wide, went by the name of Huvahendhoo. Dense foliage covers the island's northern and western sides; there are, however, no large coconut trees, a "shortcoming" which the management is attempting to redress by planting a number of young saplings. About 20% of the area of the island has been left untouched; the remaining 80% is built up.

To the east, as an extension of the pool bar, there is a marvelous beach with excellent swimming. Other stretches of beach extend in the island's north and west. Small walls erected on the roof of the reef protect the island from any further erosion by the strong currents of the Huvahendhoo channel.

Runnning around the entire island, the house reef has the character of an outer reef and is therefore an especially noteworthy area for diving and snorkeling, with magnificent coral formations on the northern and southern sides.

These sides of the island also sport the accommodations of the **Lily Beach Resort**. The 16 larger pile bungalows on the southern side have their own access directly into the lagoon; there are another 34 double bungalows on the northern beach.

All the accommodation has modern sanitary facilities, hot and cold running water, an open-air bath as well as a small garden. Further, all rooms have mini-bars and air conditioning. The reception area, the restaurant and the two bars are also in the open, and laid out along generous lines. The cuisine of the island is predominantly oriented towards the tastes of the international visitors, who hail for the most part from Germany, Great Britain, Austria and Switzerland. However, the menu also features excellent Maldivian and Indian delicacies, with a range of fresh-caught seafood.

Right: A dhoni approaches Machchafushi through the arrow-straight lagoon entrance.

A full complement of sports facilities is available (surfing, fishing, aerobics, body-building, and a tennis court with floodlights), while scuba divers can choose between a number of coral reefs with a wealth of different species. There is a swimming pool for a refreshing dip, and guests can go "island-hopping" for further variety; while a disco once a week provides evening entertainment. There is a separate small pool for children.

Visitors to Lily Beach can book an all-inclusive package for their stay which includes, apart from accommodation and full board, use of all sports facilities, one day excursion and unlimited consumption of such drinks as tea, coffee, water, beer, wine, gin, whiskey and vodka. Only diving and fishing have to be paid for extra.

Machchafushi

Machchafushi is located in the southeastern part of the Ari Atoll, near the resort islands of Twin Island, Vakarufalhi and Kuda Rah. Its name means something along the lines of "the island that is being created," and was perhaps a forecast of the development of tourism that's been taking place here since Machchafushi opened in 1993.

Today, the **Machchafushi Island Resort** looks like a typical Maldivian picture-book island. Almost triangular in form, it measures about 300 by 200 meters and has a terrific lagoon for swimming as well as a beautiful house reef running in close to the beach. One feature particularly enchanting for visitors is the noticeably dense stand of majestic coconut palms. Happily, about 80% of the island's surface has been left virgin and untouched.

There is a helicopter landing pad not far from the island, on the small islet of Dhe Hasanu Lonuboa Huraaein, so that visitors can reach the Machchafushi Island Resort and the neighboring Twin Is-

land Resort (Maafushivaru) from the airport at Hulhule in a matter of around 25 minutes.

Accommodations consist of 24 double bungalows with 48 rooms, all of which have air conditioning and ceiling fans. Further, they also have hot and cold fresh water, showers, a bath and toilet, as well as a mini-bar, telephone and a terrace with a view of the sea. Twelve pile bungalows with the same furnishings and facilities are built out over the lagoon. Machchafushi's cuisine includes international dishes as well as Maldivian delicacies.

In terms of sports, Machchafushi's guests have a wide range of options. Diving has pride of place, because the island's proximity to the top spots in the South Ari Atoll guarantees exciting experiences underwater. Snorkeling excursions, surfing, sailing and canoeing also add spice to a day of vacation. Ping-pong, badminton, volleyball, darts, and even round-trip air tours and island-hopping round off the daily program. In the evening, guests not infrequently participate in a spontaneous "disco."

Mirihi

A tiny spot in the middle of the South Ari Atoll, the island of Mirihi is just about 300 meters by 100 meters in size, with a longish oval shape. The resort opened in 1990 under the impressive-sounding name of **Mirihi Marina Resort**.

The island's name comes from the local mirihi plant (*Wedelia calendulacea biflora*), a bush-like creeper with small yellow blossoms, which is often used in the islanders' traditional medicine. In addition to its healing properties, so Maldivian folklore claims, the plant also drives away poisonous snakes; therefore, assert the Maldivians, there can be no snakes on an island if mirihi plants grow there. Apparently snakes die immediately if they come into physical contact with a mirihi branch. But in any case, there are very few snakes on Maldives.

167

Buildings on the island have been tastefully integrated in the luxuriant tropical vegetation and manage to meet the standards of modern tourism without sacrificing any of the island's original earthy charm. Beautiful sand beaches and a magnificent emerald-green lagoon make for excellent swimming. With its population of well-fed and very trusting rays, the intact house reef promises eventful, interesting dives. The rays prefer the southern side of the house reef, whereas the northern side has enchantingly lovely coral formations that are really worth seeing.

On land, Mirihi has 40 rooms in double bungalows and pile bungalows. All of them have air conditioning or a ceiling fan, a mini-bar, telephone, hot and cold running fresh water as well as a small terrace with a view of the sea. Furnished with more or less identical amenities, the rooms are distributed between 8 conventional bungalows and 32 pile bungalows. Rather than terraces, the pile bungalows have verandas out over the lagoon, so that you can observe the most beautiful reef fish from your own veranda.

The cuisine of Mirihi has been geared to the palates of international visitors. Since the head chef is of Austrian origin, it is hardly surprising that in addition to many fish dishes, the menu has all kinds of tasty delicacies from that Alpine land. For between-meals snacks, visitors can repair to the coffee shop. In the evenings, the cozy layout of the island bar makes for a relaxing atmosphere, and those who prefer to work off more energy can go dancing in the disco that is organized sporadically.

Recreational facilities on the island include windsurfing, snorkeling, diving, sailing and waterskiing as well as fishing, volleyball and ping-pong. If you really want to tone up your muscles, Mirihi also has a fitness center available to guests. In the evenings, the entertainment can include anything from folk dances to beach parties, discos and beach buffets.

Rangali

Not to be confused with the hotel island of Rannahli in the South Male Atoll, Rangali is situated to the southwest, on the outer edge of the South Ari Atoll. The hotel resort's bungalows, 130 in number, were completed in the summer of 1993.

The name Rangali is derived from the Dhivehi words *ran*, "gold," and *gaa*, "coral stone." The name could have come from the bright coral stone on the reef around the island, which gleams particularly brightly, almost like gold, when the sun shines on it.

Right next to the resort island, there is a small, uninhabited island that's always been called Rangali. The larger island, which used to be nameless, was eventually also called Rangali after it. Today, the smaller Rangali serves as a helicopter pad for the larger Rangali and other surrounding hotel islands.

Oval in form, Rangali measures about 800 by 400 meters. A wonderful sand beach, 15 to 40 meters wide, surrounds the entire island, a guarantee of terrific beach fun. Together with its two neighboring islets – tiny, uninhabited picnic islands – Rangali forms a sort of a mini-atoll within the larger Ari Atoll. The vegetation on the island is typical of Maldives and luxuriant, as is the fauna: you can often see geckos, flying foxes and various kinds of birds.

The **Maldives Hilton Resort** is among the most modern hotel complexes on Maldives, and has an excellent reputation internationally. Since 1998, it has been under the management of the Hilton International hotel chain. Each of the 130 bungalows (measuring from 72.5 to 115

Right: You can see geckoe on a number of the islands.

square meters), air-conditioned, tasteful and individually furnished, has a large bedroom with a banquette, a dressing room, and a mini-bar as well as a bathroom with shower, bathtub and hot and cold running water. Verandas in front of each room ensure that every guest has a wonderful view of the sea. Since its renovation, Rangali also boasts a small freshwater pool and a tennis court that's illuminated with floodlights for night play.

The restaurant's chefs aim, and succeed, at creating a delicious mixture of or balance between the cuisines of Maldives and Europe, with all kinds of tasty fish and meat dishes.

After the hotel opened, Rangali's proximity to the outer reef and its fantastic, intact house reef quickly made the island a top address for divers and snorkelers. Other recreational options are surfing, sailing, fishing, volleyball or ping-pong. There are no organized performances or programs as such for guests on Rangali, but there are sometimes informal darts or volleyball tournaments, crab races, and video presentations.

Ranveli (Villingilivaru)

Small and shaped like an elongated oval, the island of Ranveli, also known under its old name of Villingilivaru, is located in the southeast of the Ari Atoll in the middle of the Dhangethi Kandu channel. To the south is the inhabited island of Dhangethi with a heliport; this, however, is becoming less and less important because of the increasing use of air taxis. The tourist resort **Ranveli Beach Resort** opened in the year 1991; some 95% of its visitors are Italians.

The island boasts a dense growth of tropical vegetation, with plenty of lovely coconut palms, and a remarkably large, protected lagoon. Small wonder, then, that even in the past, long before the island was opened up to tourism, safari dhonis often used to anchor in the north bay. The breathtaking house reef, only 20 meters from the beach, entrances

169

divers and snorkelers in equal measure.

Not least because of the shortage of space on the island, the 56 rooms on Ranveli are distributed over seven two-storey four-unit bungalows, built as complex units on stilts in front of the lagoon. All the rooms have hot and cold running fresh water, refrigerators, music systems, mini-bars, IDD telephones and small terraces or balconies with views of the sea. Other amenities on Ranveli include an island boutique, a diving base and a water sports center.

The island's excellent cuisine essentially caters to the tastes of its Italian clientele. Large, varied buffets are served in the morning and afternoon, and there's a sit-down dinner in the evening.

There's no time for boredom on Ranveli. Activities of preference include scuba diving, snorkeling, canoeing, surfing and night fishing as well as ping-pong, volleyball or even island-hopping.

In the evenings, guests can unwind in the piano bar, in the cozy lounge, at video shows or in the fresh-water swimming pool. In addition, the island's own disco tempts fans of dancing with a show of southern temperament and, sometimes, pretty loud music.

Sun Island (Nalaguraidhoo)

After its takeover by the LTI group, Nalaguraidhoo was renamed LTI-Villa Sun Island. The island is located on the southern border of the Ari Atoll, right next to the LTI-Villa Holiday Island (formerly known as Dhiffushi). The complex officially opened for business in the fall of 1998. Sun Island was the last island in the South Ari Atoll that got permission to build. The elongated island is quite big, and surrounded by a beach. *Nala* means "pretty," and *guraa* is a kind of parrot.

Above: A classy picnic. Right: Sailing into the setting sun.

170

The **Sun Island Resort** corresponds fully to the most up-to-date standards of comfort. The air-conditioned rooms have lovely views of the sea. All the accommodations have hot and cold water in both tub and shower; and guests coming in from the beach can rinse off in a second, open-air shower to prevent them from tracking sand into the rooms. Within, the rooms boast televisions with video channels, hair dryers, music systems, mini-bars and IDD telephones.

No fewer than five restaurants offer dishes from all over the world. Apart from the obligatory coffee shop, bars on the beach, on the sun porch and by the pool serve a range of refreshing drinks. There's even a shopping arcade with stores offering souvenirs, jewelry and clothes.

As far as sports and recreation are concerned, Sun Island offers a diving base that's been completely done over, and two tennis courts with floodlights. In addition, there is volleyball, surfing and sailing. Particularly athletic or energetic guests can use the sauna, the fitness center and the massage facilities and then cool off in the swimming pool, while children can splash about safely in a separate children's pool.

Thundufushi

Thundufushi, a small tropical island with luxuriant vegetation, is located on the western side of the Ari Atoll at the end of the large reef complex Thundufushi Falhu. Thundu means "corner" or "point," and indicates the position of the island on the eastern border of the Thundufushi Falhu. The oval island, which measures about 300 by 150 meters, started tourist operations in 1990 as the **Thundufushi Island Resort**. The majestic coconut trees and the large lagoon around the island are distinctive characterisitcs of Thundufushi. Even from the air, you can make out the distinctive

house reef which has plenty to offer for both diving and snorkeling.

Not far from Thundufushi, in the northeast, is the tiny, uninhabited island of **Eboodhoo** with luxuriantly green, dense vegetation. Often visited by picnickers, it also serves as a heliport for the neighboring tourist resorts.

Thundufushi's guests, of which about 10% are from Germany, are accommodated in 44 self-contained bungalows, all of them meeting high standards of comfort. Air conditioning, a mini-bar, telephone and a music system are as much a matter of course as hot and cold running water in the shower and the bath. The restaurant serves mainly international dishes, but also delicious specialties of fresh-caught fish. In addition, Thundufushi sports a small island boutique stocked with typical local souvenirs, a hairdresser, and a video room. In the bar, you can wind down after the day's activities with a sophisticated drink.

In addition to diving school's program, the water sports center offers snorkeling,

surfing, waterskiing, canoeing and sailing. Other activities are night fishing, ping-pong and volleyball, as well as a disco for night owls. If you wish to explore the area, you can take an island-hopping tour to visit inhabited islands such as Innafushi or uninhabited picnic islands.

Twin Island (Maafushivaru)

Maafushivaru, as this island used to be known in Dhivehi, means "island covered with vegetation." Since it was opened to tourism in 1991, the oval island, which really does boast a cover of dense foliage, has been called Twin Island. Measuring 350 by 250 meters in size, it has an enchantingly lovely beach facing the lagoon side. Located in the southeast of the Ari Atoll, this island, together with the well-known tourist re-

Above: Picnic excursion with barbecue.
Right: Many resorts now have their own de-salination plants.

sorts of Machchafushi and Vakarufalhi, forms a triangle in the middle of which there is another hotel island, Kuda Rah. This region is especially known for its large number of top-class diving sites, popular destinations even with hotel islands that are considerably further away. Hard by Twin Island is the tiny island of Dhe Hasanu Lonuboa Huraa, which serves as a heliport for the surrounding islands.

Twin Island Resort, which is frequented almost exclusively by German-speaking guests, immediately catches the eye because of the distinctive blue-tiled roofs of its 37 bungalows. The accommodation falls into two categories: five double bungalows on pilings are built out over the waters of the pretty lagoon near the house reef, which is excellent for diving; and there are self-contained bungalows near the beach. High standards prevail in all the rooms, which are equipped with air conditioning or ceiling fans, a mini-bar, and IDD telephones. Every bungalow has hot and cold running fresh

water from the island's own desalination plant, an additional open-air shower at the side entrance, as well as a terrace with a view of the sea.

In the restaurant, the varied, tasty cuisine has a very Italian flavor, but the menu also has international dishes with lots of fish. There is a cozy bar and a small coffee shop at this rather quiet, restful island.

Twin Island offers an extensive roster of sports and recreational activities, with diving and snorkeling in the lead. Windsurfing, sailing, ping-pong, canoeing, volleyball and night fishing, as well as airplane tours over the unique island world of Maldives, are all popular. "Island-hopping" is a good way to explore the neighboring resorts and inhabited islands. At night, guests can strut their stuff in the island's small disco.

Vakarufalhi

Vakarufalhi is a pretty, almost triangular island in the southeast of the Ari Atoll. Some 220 by 240 meters in area, with dense, varied vegetation and a number of coconut palms, it's an enchanting place. It was opened in the summer of 1994. Many travelers find this island paradise, which is surrounded by a magnificent beach, to be among the most beautiful resort islands in Maldives.

The **Vakarufalhi Island Resort** has 50 air-conditioned self-contained bungalows with spacious rooms, making for a total of 100 beds. Hot and cold running fresh water is sourced from the hotel's own sea-water desalination plant. One original idea implemented in the hotel are the covered open-air toilets in the enclosed inner gardens of the bungalows. A mini-bar is also among the standard facilities in the well-kept rooms; the restaurant, too, has the same elegant atmosphere. Very good and varied, the cuisine is tailored to European tastes; at least 40% of the guests here are from Germany. Breakfast and lunch are served in large, opulent buffets, while there is an elegant sit-down dinner in the evenings,

173

and, once a week, a beach barbecue. Those who wish can sit in the coffee shop during the day or withdraw to the small bar in the evening.

It will come as no surprise that scuba diving is the main recreational activity on Vakarufalhi. The intact house reef, linked to the island by two jetties, is an inner reef and therefore excellent for easy dives. A diving dhoni runs out on excursions to the many beautiful reefs in the vicinity. Snorkeling excursions, night fishing, windsurfing and sailing are also very popular. Badminton, aerobics, ping-pong and volleyball can also serve to vary the program. Other diversions include the hotel's organized excursions to the neighboring islands or shopping trips to Male, or gaining a bird's-eye perspective of Vakarufalhi from an airplane. In the evenings, you can go to the small disco or dance at beach parties.

Above: Divers set out for the house reef. Right: In-depth advice in Vilamendhoo's diving school.

Vilamendhoo

Vilamendhoo is among the newer hotel islands in Maldives. The **Vilamendhoo Island Resort** didn't open until 1994 on this elongated island, 900 meters long and about 300 meters wide, whch stretches from east to west and is surrounded by a sand beach. The island is located on the southeastern outer side of the Ari Atoll.

Since the Ari Atoll doesn't have a long, continuous outer reef, there are narrow channels all around the atoll. The atoll's eastern and southeastern side are not subjected to the same kind of intense pounding from the surf that its western side regularly deals with; hence, they have a wealth of smaller reef formations with numerous channels and delicate coral structures – advantages that divers can fully appreciate. In the past, fishing boats used to anchor off Vilamendhoo regularly to take on fresh water.

Almost 90% of this relatively large island is covered by dense vegetation.

Small, shadowy footpaths trodden out long ago by coconut gatherers and wood-cutters lead through the interior of the island. A notable wealth and variety of fauna, including lizards, non-poisonous snakes, herons, flying foxes and butter-flies of all kinds, complete the picture of this quasi-primeval and eminently beautiful island.

When designing the resort complex, the hotel management deliberately sought environmentally sound solutions with an eye to the natural ecology, and attempted to integrate the buildings harmoniously into the natural landscape.

Each of the island's 81 bungalows is spacious, modern and comfortably furnished. All the rooms have mini-bars and direct-dial telephones as well as half-open bathrooms with desalinated cold and hot water. A small shop offers hand-made souvenirs and there is even a jewelry store on the island.

In view of the predominantly European clientele, the cuisine is oriented to-ward the Western palate, but Maldivian dishes are also offered. The restaurant's reputation is excellent all over the country. Apart from diving, which is virtually always the sport of preference, recreational activities include surfing, sailing, fishing and various ball sports. Regular disco evenings also help keep you fit. If you'd rather just watch, there are occasional shows of *bodu-beru* dancers, magicians, or fire-dancers from Sri Lanka.

INHABITED ISLANDS AND PICNIC ISLANDS IN THE SOUTH ARI ATOLL

Ariyadhoo

The atoll's southernmost island, Ariyadhoo divides the passage from the inner atoll to the open sea into the two channels of Ariyadhoo Kandu and Maamigili Kandu.

Uninhabited, thickly wooded with palms and fruit trees, this is the island

175

which gave the Ari Atoll its name. It is privately rented and mainly used for agricultural purposes.

In the recent past, Ariyadhoo made headlines all over the world: in the year 1959, archaeological excavations carried out here uncovered significant parts of a Buddhist monastery. Among the artifacts is a Shiva-linga (phallic statue) 38 centimeters in length, 30 centimenters around at the base. Subsequent excavations in 1988 brought up other Buddhist and Hindu artifacts.

Bodukaashihuraa

This tiny island is uninhabited and is located on the eastern hem of the atoll, near the *kandu* or channel of the same name. In Dhivehi, the island's name means something along the lines of "coconut island."

Above: Hard to photograph – dancing shrimps. Right: Some uninhabited islands serve as heliports.

Bulhaalhohi

Located on the western side of the atoll, this island is just a dwarf among the Ari Atoll's uninhabited islands. It is situated about four kilometers north of the large inhabited island of Mandhoo. Only a few coconut palms and bushes grow on Bulhaalhohi.

The Dhivehi word *bulhaa* means "cat," but the island's name must be a reminder of times long past, since there are clearly no cats on the island today.

Bulhaalhohi has a lovely, sandy bay that provides a safe approach and a secure anchorage. This is just one of the reasons Bulhaalhohi is so extremely popular with picnickers from the surrounding resort islands. In the southwest, the island has excellent snorkeling and diving.

Dangethi

Dangethi, located on the outer edge of the atoll in its southeastern reaches, is

home to a population of 554, and is fairly typical of inhabited islands on Maldives.

There is a massive *nika* or banyan tree in the middle of the island; a distinctive landmark, it can be seen even from very far away. Nobody seems to be able to give accurate information as to how old this tree is; but some of the local inhabitants opine that it is more than two centuries old. The tree's remarkably long roots, which have grown to extend over a large area, would seem to add credence to this hypothesis, even if no one can prove it.

Fishing is the islanders' main source of income. The younger generation, however, prefers to work in the more lucrative jobs on the neighboring resort islands.

A heliport on Dangethi allows helicopters to land; also located here is a landing facility for the air taxis (or seaplanes) which bring guests from the airport on their way to the neighboring resort islands.

Dhiggiri

This tiny island is situated in the central area of the eastern South Ari Atoll. Dhiggiri is uninhabited, but safari ships come here often because it has a strikingly long reef with wonderful coral formations.

Dhidhdhoo

The native island of Dhidhdhoo is home to just 97 inhabitants. It's located in the southeastern part of the atoll, in the immediate vicinity of the tourist resort of Ari Beach.

According to Maldivian tradition, the inhabitants of Dhidhdhoo are said to be particularly strong and are admired because of their very beautiful skin. This fact could perhaps stem from the local legend that a French ship once ran aground on the nearby reef, and the seamen who were stranded there remained on Dhidhdhoo and intermarried with the local population.

177

Dhigurah

Dhigurah lies to the north of the resort island of Ari Beach, on the southeastern border of the atoll. The island really lives up to its Dhivehi name, which means "the long island": at 3,000 meters, it is the longest island in the whole Ari Atoll. Dhigurah has an enchanting long beach, a protected lagoon and straw-thatched huts that appear to merge into the thick foliage. During the period of the northeast monsoon, the lagoon provides good protected anchorage for safari boats. There are a few sand bars on the southern side of the lagoon. 349 Maldivians live on this picturesque island.

Eboodhoo

Small and almost invisible, this uninhabited island is located on the western side in the central section of the atoll, about 3 kilometers northeast of the inhabited island of Innafushi. The name Eboodhoo includes the Dhivehi term *emboo*, which means a small fruit that grows on a certain wild bush (*Glochidion littorale*). Eboodhoo has beautiful trees and a very pretty bay with excellent snorkeling and diving along the southern reef. The island is popular as a picnic spot with guests from the neighboring resorts. It already has a long landing stage at which excursion boats can anchor, and a heliport for helicopters.

Fenfushi

Fenfushi is located in the south of the Ari Atoll near the tourist island LTI-Villa Sun and Holiday Island. Its name means something along the lines of "island of good water." Fenfushi's 429 inhabitants mainly catch fish for their livelihood; they also engage in artisan work. The na-

tives are known for their coral sculpting, stonecarving, particularly of gravestones, and mosque-building. The Friday mosque of Fenfushi is very similar to the large mosque in Male, and is an excellent example of the artisan skills of the local inhabitants. It was constructed during the reign of Sultan Mohammed Ibn al-Haj Ali (1692-1701).

Unfortunately, the traditional stonecutting skills are dying out; only a few craftsmen still keep them alive today. Modern gravestones of concrete have already begun to make an appearance on Fenfushi.

Hanghgaameedhoo

The island, whose name seems almost unpronounceable at first sight (Han-ja-me-du), has 328 inhabitants and is in the middle of the atoll's eastern edge. A special sight that is worth seeing on Hanghgaameedhoo is the grave of Sultan Ibrahim III (1585-1609). He was murdered in 1609 by Malabar pirates after they attacked Male.

Hiyafushi

Uninhabited Hiyafushi is located in the southeast of the atoll, in a line with Kudahoo and Dhidhdhoo. *Hiya* means 69, possibly an indication of the fact that Hiyafushi was once the 69th island counted in the Ari Atoll.

Hukurudhoo

Hukurudhoo is situated in the southwest of the atoll near the resort island of Rangali. It lies like an obstacle in the channel that shares its name, Hukurudhoo Kandu, dividing it into a northern and a southern section.

Uninhabited, this island is covered with a growth of lush vegetation. In days gone by, when it was still inhabited, the island was called Hukuruehli, a name

Right: Full of curiosity, Hanghgaameedhoo's children wait for a boatload of tourists.

that derives from the word *hukuru*, "Friday."

In the southwest of the island, attentive observers can note a large rocky hillock. For centuries now, the inhabitants of the islands have been telling a story about this hill and how it was created, which is offered as an explanation of why the island is uninhabited today.

Once, in the period of the main fishing season, the fishermen of Hukurudhoo set out to fish on a Friday rather than praying in the mosque. This could not go unpunished by Allah. From land, observers saw a whale following the boats to the sea. When the fishermen were so far out that they could no longer return to the island, their friends and relatives at home erected this hillock from which they could keep watch and wait for the boats. After the fishermen had vanished completely, and showed no signs of returning, the inhabitants grew increasingly uneasy and sceptical, until they ultimately decided to move to another island.

However attractive this tale, the theory that this pile of stones may have been the work of cyclones appears more plausible, as the island's offshore reef extends a long way out in a southwesterly direction, which is exactly where the cyclones come from.

Hurasdhoo

Hurasdhoo, which is used as a resting point by many frigate birds, lies in the southernmost third of the atoll, on an imaginary line between the hotel resort of Angaga and the inhabited island of Mandhoo. Hurasdhoo is called the "pineapple island" because in the past this uninhabited patch of land proved to be the most fertile island in the vicinity. Pineapples were therefore cultivated on the island for some time. Since then, the plants have grown wilder and wilder, and today, their sweet smell attracts innumerable crabs which gnaw on the pineapples. It's easy to recognize the island from a distance because of the distinctive coco-

179

nut palms at its center. Since the entry into the lagoon is easy to navigate, Hurasdhoo is a popular destination for tourists on trips from the nearby resort islands.

Huruehli

Lying to the north of the Heygahathu Kandu channel in the southwest of the atoll, the tiny island of Huruehli is uninhabited, with sparse vegetation. Because of the lack of shade, adequate sun-tan lotion and headgear are very important if you go visiting!

Innafushi

There is little vegetation on the uninhabited island of Innafushi. The island is located at the midpoint of the atoll on its western side, north of the resort island of Thundhufushi.

Above: Lacquerwork is produced on a number of the inhabited islands.

Kudadhoo

A small, uninhabited island, Kudadhoo is situated in the southern part of the Ari Atoll, very close to the outer reef; its southern side abuts on the channel of Ariyadhoo Kandu.

Kuda Finolhu

Kuda Finolhu, the "small island," is a treeless island with bushes located about 8 kilometers east of Eboodhoo. On the western outer side of the atoll is the large reef of **Maavaru Falhu**, presenting a wealth of unique coral landscapes and good anchorages.

Kunburudhoo

This island is a long, uninhabited island in the central eastern area of the atoll. The name is derived from the Dhivehi word *kunburu*, the name of a local creeper that grows in the sandy soil.

On its western side, Kunburudhoo has a very long reef which is a splendid spot for diving.

Maamigili

Maamigili is a large island located at the southern end of the Ari Atoll, and is home to 970 inhabitants. It lies on the Maamigil Kandu, which is of interest to divers, and marks the southernmost endpoint of the Fenfushi Faru, which, at 15 kilometers in length, is said to be the longest reef in the atoll. The inhabitants of the island are known for the production of stone blocks of limestone and the extraction of coral and sand. A mosque from the 17th century stands on the island, which also boasts a heliport on the western side.

Mahibadhoo

Mahibadhoo, which lies at the midpoint of the outer reef's eastern edge, is the main island of the South Ari Atoll, home to the atoll's administration. Main sources of revenue are artisan work and fishing; there is a fish processing center on the island, as well as some large refrigeration units. Mahibadhoo's population is 1,199.

Mandhoo

A fairly large inhabited island, Mandhoo, situated in the south of the atoll on its western side, is home to 249 Maldivians. Characteristic of the island is its varied vegetation, with a number of large trees. Vegetables are the main crop cultivated on Mandhoo because of the island's highly fertile soil. The inhabitants are known as good fishermen even beyond the atoll's borders.

Mandhoo was settled a very long time ago, and Buddhist relics were found here in the course of archaeological excavations. The large rock piles that the archaeologists explored were probably *hawittas*, comprised of coral debris. The British colonial officer H. C. P. Bell studied Buddhist influences on Maldives from 1879 on. During his investigations, he discovered the *hawittas*, which he thought to be remains of *stupas*, since they were similar to the Buddhist *dagoba* temples in Sri Lanka. Based on these finds, he hypothesized that Buddhism came to Maldives with the first settlers, arriving after 500 BC.

Omadhoo

The longish island of Omadhoo lies at the center of the eastern edge of the South Ari Atoll. Omadhoo divides the channel of the same name into the Omaadhoo Dhekunu and the Omadhoo Uthuru Kandu. It is a very old inhabited island; its residents, 523 in number, live mainly from fishing.

Rahdhdhiggaa

Raddhdhigga lies within the atoll, about 5 kilometers to the northeast of Bulhaalhohi. The island is small, uninhabited, and has little in the way of vegetation. It does, however, offer good anchorage within the lagoon, and easy access to the sand beach.

Rangali

This tiny, uninhabited island is situated at the southwestern outer reef of the Ari Atoll. Rangali is used as a helipad for the surrounding islands.

Tholhufushi

The small island of Tholhufushi is situated all the way in the south of the Ari Atoll, right next to the resort island of LTI-Villa Sun Island, which is, for the time being, the last holiday island that will be allowed in the South Ari Atoll.

ANGAGA (ANGAAGAU)
Angaga Island Resort
Opened in 1989. Male office: STO Koshi 9, Ameenee Magu, tel. 318136, fax 323115. Island tel. 450520, fax 450520. BUNGALOWS: 51 self-contained bungalows, air conditioning, mini-bar, refrigerators, open-air bath, hot & cold fresh-water showers, terraces with Maldivian porch swings. AMENITIES: bar, coffee shop, island boutique, open-air restaurant, water sports center. DIVING BASE: German, Engl., NAUI, PADI, house reef. CREDIT CARDS: AE/MC/VC/DCI. AIRPORT: 96 kilometers, 30 min by air taxi, 30 min by helicopter plus an additional 45 min by dhoni.

ARI BEACH (DHIDHDHOOFINOLHU)
Ari Beach Resort
Opened in 1987, renovated in 1994. Male office: 1st floor, 35 Boduthakurufaanu Magu, tel. 321930, fax 327355. Island tel. 450513, fax 450512, E-Mail: aribeach@dhivehinet.net.mv, internet: http://www. aribeach.com. BUNGALOWS: 56 standard bungalows with cold showers, 50 superior bungalows with warm showers, 14 family bungalows, all with air conditioning and telephone, superior also with mini-bar. AMENITIES: 2 bars, coffee shop, 3 souvenir shops, 2 restaurants, desalinification plant, boutique, tennis court, soccer field, canoe rental and parasailing (extra charge). DIVING BASE: German, Engl., French, Italian, PADI, house reef 400 m away. CREDIT CARDS: AE/MC/VC/EC. AIRPORT: 97 kilometers, 30 min by helicopter or air taxi, 3 hours by speedboat.

LTI-VILLA HOLIDAY ISLAND (Dhiffushi)
Holiday Island Resort
Opened in 1994 Male office: Villa Hotels, 3rd floor, STO Trade Center, tel. 316161, fax 314565. Island tel. 450011, fax 450022, E-Mail: holiday@dhivehinet.mv. BUNGALOWS: 106 self-contained bungalows, 18 double bungalows with air conditioning, minibar, TV, bath with tub, bidet, outside shower. AMENITIES: 4 bars, coffee shop, 2 restaurants, fitness room, sauna, steam bath, tennis court, jewelry shop, karaoke, billiards, parasailing on request. DIVING BASE: German, Engl., PADI, no house reef. CREDIT CARDS: AE/MC/VC. AIRPORT: 109 kilometers, 30 min by helicopter plus 10 min by dhoni, 2.5 hours by speedboat.

KUDA RAH
Kuda Rah Island Resort
Opened in 1991, Male office: 4th Floor Alia Bldg. Orchid Magu, tel. 310129, fax 313939. Island tel. 450549, fax 450550. BUNGALOWS: 25 deluxe single bungalows (60 m^2), 5 deluxe pile bungalows, with air conditioning, safe, mini-bar, telephone, TV, bath with tub, bidet, outside shower, roofed terrace.

AMENITIES: 2 bars, coffee shop, restaurant, island boutique, hard tennis court, pool, desalination plant. DIVE BASE: Ital., French, Engl., PADI, SSI, decompression chamber, diving doctor, house reef. CREDIT CARDS: AE/MC/VC/ DC. AIRPORT: 100 kilometers, 30 min by helicopter or air taxi with an additional 20 min by dhoni, 2.5 hours by speedboat. Exclusive to Club Vacanze, 95% of the guests are Italian. On-island doctor.

LILY BEACH (HUVAHENDHOO)
Lily Beach Resort
Opened in 1994. Male office: Lily Hotels Pte. Ltd., No. 1 Orchid Magu, tel. 317464, fax 317466. Island tel. 450013/-15, fax 450646, E-Mail: lilybeach@ dhivehinet.net.mv. BUNGALOWS: 68 rooms in double bungalows, 16 pile bungalows with air conditioning, mini-bar, bathtub, bidet, hair dryer and direct dial telephone, outside shower. AMENITIES: 2 bars, coffee shop, restaurant, 2 fresh-water pools (one for children), tennis court, sports and fitness room, boutique. DIVE BASE: German, Engl., French, Italian, PADI, house reef. CREDIT CARDS: AE/MC/VC. AIRPORT: 85 kilometers, 35 min by helicopter plus 30 min by dhoni.

MACHCHAFUSHI
Machchafushi Island Resort
Opened in 1993, Male office: Luxwood 1, Boduthakurufaanu Magu, tel. 327849, fax 327277. Island tel. 454545, fax 454546. BUNGALOWS: 60 rooms, 48 in double and 12 in single bungalows over the lagoon, air conditioning, mini-bar, telephone, fresh-water showers (hot/cold), bath with tub, terrace. AMENITIES: 2 bars, coffee shop, open-air restaurant, tennis court (illuminated), salt-water pool, island boutique, disco. DIVE BASE: German, Engl., French, Italian, NAUI, PADI, noteworthy house reef 40 m from the dive base. CREDIT CARDS: AE/MC/VC/EC/JCB. AIRPORT: 90 kilometers, 25 min by air taxi, 25 min by helicopter plus 10 min by dhoni.

MIRIHI
Mirihi Marina Resort
Opened in 1990. Male office: H. Silver Star 3, Haveeree Higun, tel. 325448, fax 325448. Island tel. 450500, fax 450501, E-Mail: reservation@com.mv. BUNGALOWS: 40 rooms, 8 in double bungalows, 32 in pile bungalows, 6 suites, air conditioning, telephone, mini-bar, fresh-water shower (warm/kalt). AMENITIES: 2 bars, coffee shop, fitness center, souvenir shop. DIVE BASE: German, Engl., French, Italian, CMAS, PADI, house reef (inner reef) 40 m from the dive base, small wreck. CREDIT CARDS: AE/MC/VC. AIRPORT: 103 kilometers, 30 min by air taxi, 30 min by helicopter plus an additional 20 min by speedboat.

RANGALI
Maldives Hilton Resort

Opened in 1993. Maldives office: PO Box 2034, South Ari Atoll. Island tel. 450520, fax 450520, E-Mail: hilton@dhivehinet.net.mv. *BUNGALOWS:* 100 villas (72.5 m², 28 water bungalows (74.5 m²), 2 honeymoon water bungalows (115 m²), air conditioning, bath with tub, mini-bar, telephone, water bungalows with outdoor showers. *AMENITIES:* bar, lobby lounge, 2 restaurants, island boutique, jewelry shop, swimming pool, windsurfing school, relaxation center, pool with warm water (spa), tennis court (illuminated), disco, karaoke. *DIVE BASE:* German, Engl., French, NAUI, PADI, VIT, CMAS, house reef 80-100 m from the dive base. *CREDIT CARDS:* AE/MC/VC. *AIRPORT:* 96 kilometers, 30 min by air taxi, 30 min by helicopter plus 45 min by dhoni.

RANVELI (VILLINGILIVARU)
Ranveli Beach Resort

Opened in 1991, renovated in 1997, Male office: Ranveli Holiday Pvt., Ltd., 4th Floor Alia Bldg., tel. 313938, fax 313939. Island tel. 450570, fax 450523. *BUNGALOWS:* 56 rooms in two-story double bungalows with air conditioning, bathtubs, mini-bar, IDD telephone. *AMENITIES:* bar, coffee shop, restaurant on pilings in the lagoon, fresh-water pool, kids' pool, desalination plant, doctor. *DIVE BASE:* Italian, Engl., PADI, house reef. *CREDIT CARDS:* AE/MC/VC. *AIRPORT:* 95 km, 30 min by helicopter plus 20 min by dhoni, 2.5 hours by speedboat. Exclusive to Club Vacanze; 95% of guests are Italian.

LTI-VILLA SUN ISLAND
(NALAGURAIDHOO)
Sun Island Resort

Opened in 1998, Male office: 3 Silver Star, Haveeree Higun, tel. 318136, fax 323115. Island tel. 450520, fax 450520, E-Mail: Vilahtls@netlink.net.mv. *BUNGALOWS:* 218 super-deluxe bungalows, 60 deluxe beach bungalows, 72 water bungalows, 64 super deluxe water bungalows, 4 Presidential suites, air conditioning, mini-bar, TV, hair dryer, fresh-water showers (hot/cold), bathtub. *AMENITIES:* 5 restaurants, 4 bars, karaoke, fresh-water pool, childrens' pool, sauna, spa, massage rooms, fitness center, tennis court (illuminated). *DIVE BASE:* German, Engl., PADI, house reef. *CREDIT CARDS:* AE/MC/VC/EC. *AIRPORT:* 109 kilometers, 30 min by air taxi, 30 min by helicopter plus 10 min by dhoni, 2.5 hrs by motorboat.

THUNDUFUSHI
Thundufushi Island Resort

Opened in 1990. Male office: M. Veeza, Dhambu Goalhi, tel. 310489, fax 310390. Island tel. 450583, fax 450515, E-Mail: thundmin@dhivehinet.net.mv. *BUNGALOWS:* 44 self-contained bungalows with air conditioning, music system, telephone, mini-bar, bath, hot showers (fresh water). *AMENITIES:* bar, coffee shop, restaurant, island boutique, water sports center, hairdresser, video room. *DIVE BASE:* German, English, PADI, house reef. *CREDIT CARDS:* AE/MC/ VC. *AIRPORT:* 85 km, 20 min by air taxi, 2.5 hours by speedboat.

TWIN ISLAND (MAAFUSHIVARU)
Twin Island Resort

Opened in 1991, Male office: Universal Enterprises Ltd., 38 Orchid Magu, tel. 323512, fax 322678. Island tel. 450596, fax 450524, E-Mail: sales@unisurf.com, Internet: http://www.unisurf.com. *BUNGALOWS:* 22 self-contained bungalows, 5 double pile bungalows, air conditioning, fresh-water showers (hot/cold), mini-bar, telephone, terrace. *AMENITIES:* bar, coffee shop, disco. *DIVE BASE:* Italian, Engl., PADI, house reef. *CREDIT CARDS:* AE/MC/VC/DC. *AIRPORT:* 95 km, 30 min by air taxi or helicopter, 2.5 hours by speedboat. 95% of the guests are from the German-speaking world.

VAKARUFALHI
Vakarufalhi Island Resort

Opened in 1994, Male office: 3rd floor, Champa Building, Ahmadhee Baazar, tel. 314154, fax 314150. Island tel. 450004, fax 450007, E-Mail: vakaru@dhivehinet.net.mv. *BUNGALOWS:* 50 single bungalows, air conditioning, fresh-water showers (hot/cold), bath with bathtub, open-air toilets in an inner courtyard, refrigerator, TV. *AMENITIES:* bar, coffee shop, restaurant, island boutique, disco, water sports center, beach barbecues once a week. *DIVE BASE:* German, Engl., Italian, PADI, house reef (inner reef) 20 m from the beach. *CREDIT CARDS:* AE/MC/ VC. *AIRPORT:* 97 km, 30 min by air taxi or helicopter.

VILAMENDHOO
Vilamendhoo Island Resort

Opened in 1994, renovated and expanded in 1997. Male office: STO Trade Center, 3rd Floor, tel. 324933, fax 324943. Island tel. 450637, fax 450639. *BUNGALOWS:* 121 rooms in double bungalows with fans, mini-bar, partially exposed bathrooms, fresh-water showers (hot/cold), telephone; 10 additional self-contained bungalows, also with air conditioning. *AMENITIES:* 2 bars, coffee shop, restaurant, souvenir shop, jewelry shop, disco, tennis court. *DIVE BASE:* German, English, CMAS, PADI, VIT, VDST, house reef (inner reef) 10 meters from the dive base. *CREDIT CARDS:* AE/MC/VC. *AIRPORT:* 96 kilometers, 30 min by air taxi, 30 min by helicopter plus 45 min by dhoni.

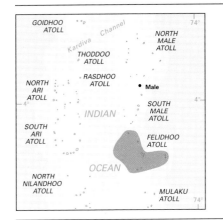

FELIDHOO ATOLL (VAAVU ATOLL)

THE FELIDHOO ATOLL

The Felidhoo Atoll, officially known as the Vaavu Atoll for administrative purposes, is located to the south of the South Male Atoll on the eastern side of the Maldivian archipelago. Separating it from the South Male Atoll is the Fulidhoo Kandu channel, which is about 14 kilometers wide. With a little imagination, you could describe the Felidhoo Atoll as being shaped like a boot, with the toe pointing to the east. It is 42 kilometers long and 55 kilometers wide, and therefore the broadest atoll in Maldives. Its easternmost point is Fotteyo Muli, a noticeably sharp extension of the eastern reef complex of Fotteyo Falhu. This unbroken reef system more than 60 kilometers long, which runs right around the atoll's southern side, starts at the last channel in the east, the Hurras Kandu, and extends all the way to the Rakeedhoo Dhekunu Kandu, the first channel on the south side. As is also the case with other atolls, there are a number of channels in the atoll's eastern and western sides, giving ships easy access to the inner atoll's shallower waters.

Preceding pages: Fishermen clean up their dhonis at twilight. Left: A very small businessman on Felidhoo.

There are five inhabited islands in the Felidhoo Atoll: Rakeedhoo, Thinadhoo, Fulidhoo, Felidhoo and Keyodhoo. In addition, the 1996 Statistical Yearbook of the Maldives mentions ten uninhabited islands, of which two, Dhiggiri and Alimatha, are used as resorts. This number doesn't include the atoll's numerous sand bars and small sand islets with limited but appreciable vegetation.

Lying 4.5 kilometers south of the Felidhoo Atoll is Vattaru Falhu, another atoll. Miniature in scale, it measures a mere 9 kilometers in diameter, and has only a single barrier reef, which boasts beautiful coral gardens on the south side. Another 4.5 kilometers further south is the Mulaku Atoll, which became well-known the world over because of the historically significant excavation work carried out there by the famous researcher Thor Heyerdahl.

RESORT ISLANDS IN THE FELIDHOO ATOLL

Alimatha

At present, Alimatha and Dhiggiri are the only resort islands in the Felidhoo Atoll. Having started operations in 1975, Alimatha is among Maldives' very first hotel islands. Almost perfectly round in

187

form, the island lies in the northeast of the atoll, not far from the outer reef at the end of the Dhiggiri Kandu, and measures about 280 meters in diameter. It takes a speedboat about 2 hours to cover the 65 kilometers from the Hulhule airport to the island. The 122 double rooms of the **Alimatha Aquatic Resort**, all with air conditioners, refrigerators, and small terraces, are distributed in 55 double bungalows and 6 water bungalows. Alimatha is extremely popular with Italian tourists, something reflected in the excellent food; the menu has a large selection of tasty preparations.

Alimatha offers good snorkeling as well as lovely dives on the south side of the house reef, a mere 100 meters away. There are also attractive diving spots along the outer reef, near the island, a short boat ride away. However, since the outer reef channels often have strong cur-

rents, diving here requires a certain amount of prior experience. Right around Alimatha, on the nearby reefs of Kudadhiggaru Falhu and Kolhudhiffushi Falhu, there once used to be two other islands, but the ocean swallowed them up long ago.

Other recreational options include sailing, surfing, waterskiing, and fishing as well as volleyball and soccer on the broad beach. However clear its waters, however, the offshore lagoon is not ideal for swimming, since some of its sharp stone corals jut up to just beneath the surface of the water.

Dhiggiri

The word Dhiggiri translates as "a long coral patch," but this is in fact a small, round island, a mere 350 by 250 meters in size. It lies just a few kilometers north of Alimatha, near the northeastern outer reef, a position divers appreciate because it gives them a chance to sight the large fish that pass by. The island has a beauti-

Above: No need to fear boredom – volleyball teams can be formed in a matter of minutes.

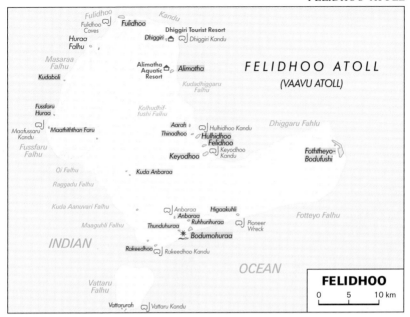

ful sand beach that slopes down gradually into the sea, and its luxuriant vegetation, with many palms and bushes, makes for a real tropical holiday atmosphere. The **Dhiggiri Tourist Resort** opened in 1982. 15 of its 45 air-conditioned self-contained bungalows are built on stilts over the lagoon and provide direct access to the sea. Dhiggiri is another island that's very popular with Italians. It has two restaurants that serve excellent food.

Dhiggiri has a beautiful house reef that drops off to a depth of 20 meters, and is great for snorkelers. Four entrances make for easy access. With a little luck, divers can sometimes see a rare manta ray "winging" past. Since there are only two resort islands in the Felidhoo Atoll, you hardly encounter any other divers, and feel you're exploring virgin diving territory. The dive sites along the outer reef, in particular, have a fascinating range and variety of aquatic species. During the southwest monsoon, divers can sometimes sight whale sharks, who are drawn

by the increased amount of plankton. Other sports on Dhiggiri include surfing, sailing, waterskiing, volleyball, darts and ping-pong. A power boat can cover the 60 kilometers between Dhiggiri and Hulhule in 2 hours; you can cut this down to just 30 minutes by taking an air taxi.

INHABITED ISLANDS AND PICNIC ISLANDS IN THE FELIDHOO ATOLL

Anbaraa

This medium-sized, uninhabited island is located in the southwest, within the Felidhoo Atoll, at the Anbaraa Kandu, about 15 minutes by boat from Rakedhoo, an inhabited island further to the south. Anbaraa is a picture-book specimen of a typical Maldives island, with a few coconut trees and an enchanting beach that's the embodiment of tropical holiday dreams come true. Small wonder that it's a popular place for picnics and beach barbecues. It also has good, protected anchorage for boats. The island's name derives from the word *ambra*. Ambra, or ambergris, is a valuable organic excretion of the sperm whale, which sometimes washes up on the beach and means sudden riches for anyone lucky enough to find it (see p. 238).

Aarah

This island is situated on the eastern edge of the atoll, somewhat further north than the neighboring isle of Hulhidhoo and separated from it by the Hulhidhoo Kandu, which boasts some spectacular diving spots. Aarah is uninhabited; in fact, it was created only recently by a whim of the sea, and thus doesn't yet have much vegetation. It is surrounded by a barrier reef that's a big obstacle to easy access for boats and visitors.

Bodumohuraa

Bodumohuraa is located in the south of the atoll, east of Rakeedhoo, the southernmost island in the atoll. It is about 7 kilometers west of the island of Higaahuraa on the Fotteyo Falhu reef. Bodumohuraa, too, is uninhabited, but sports lush vegetation. The island has a beautiful beach on its south side, with a shallow bathing lagoon that works like a magnet on visitors.

Felidhoo

Felidhoo, an inhabited island in the eastern part of the atoll on the Felidhoo Kandu, which gave the atoll its name, is also the atoll's administrative hub, with a population of 388. The natives are famous for their *bodu-beru* dances. During the day, they go fishing. Towering over the island is a radio antenna, a useful navigational aid for passing ships.

Right: Young women on Fulidhoo perform a bandiyaa (pot dance).

Foththeyo-Bodufushi

Foththeyo-Bodufushi, a large, uninhabited island, is located on the eastern border of the Felidhoo Atoll. The distinctive landmark of Foththeyo-Bodufushi, visible from miles around, is a large radio antenna. The hyphenated name reflects the fact that there were originally two islands, Foththeyo and the neighboring Bodufushi, which, as happens so often in Maldives, merged into one owing to the effects of the wind, the waves and the currents.

Fulidhoo

Lying at the atoll's northern tip, the inhabited island of Fulidhoo has 258 inhabitants. It is a typical Maldivian island with pretty coral stone houses and peaceful village life. Nestled in the shade of the coconut palms are fishermen's huts thatched with palm fronds, scattered all along the beach. Fulidhoo has a very accessible harbor, which safari boat captains are happy to use as overnight anchorage for their vessels. Native fishermen knew about this harbor even in the distant past, and they used to stop off here on their way from Male to the southern atolls.

Fulidhoo is known locally for the *bandiyaa* dance or "pot dance" performed by the island's young women. In contrast, the *bodu-beru* dances are traditionally the domain of the men; they, too, are a popular evening recreation. In the east of the island, a tall lighthouse marks the beginning of the atoll.

According to legend, the war-like Redin people once arrived on the island at a time when the inhabitants were in the mosque for Friday prayers. In Maldivian tales and legends, the Redin are a threatening tribe that worshipped fire and idols. They set the mosque on fire, and all the inhabitants of the island were burned alive, except for one single person. The

gravestone of this supposed survivor, who is said to have died a few years after the tragedy, is still visible today.

Fussfaru Huraa

This small, uninhabited island is situated on the northwestern side of the atoll near the large, west-reaching reef complex of Fussfaru Falhu.

In the local language, *fussfaru* means "invisible reef." Even experienced dhoni captains approaching from the west find it almost impossible to say exactly where the atoll starts, since there are no distinctive islands in this area that indicate the way and enable one to pinpoint one's location.

Higaakuhli

Higaakuhli is a small, uninhabited island in the south of the atoll on the long reef of Fotteyo Falhu. The name Higaakuhli means something like "turbulent lake."

Quite near the island is the wreck of the *Pioneer*, a freighter laden with general cargo that was making its way from Colombo to Male on May 13, 1958, when it rammed the reef, ran aground and subsequently went to the bottom.

Hulhidhoo

Hulhidhoo is an island in the eastern part of the atoll, north of Felidhoo. Narrow and uninhabited, densely overgrown with trees and bushes, the island is surrounded by a barrier reef that makes for excellent snorkeling on the northern and southern sides. The channel of Hulhidhoo Kandu, which leads in toward the atoll, also enchants divers with its breathtaking coral formations.

Hulhi means "coconut" or "fruit that has nothing to eat inside it."

An unlikely but true feature of the island of late is a small man who sometimes climbs out of the trees to greet arriving visitors with a sign bearing the in-

191

telligence "Deserted Island – two dollars!"

Keyodhoo

Keyodhoo, an immediate neighbor of Felidhoo, is an inhabited island. Located in the eastern part of the atoll, it is home to 528 inhabitants; its offshore lagoon is a safe anchorage, and safari boats often come here to tank up on water. Officially, tourists are not permitted to set foot on the inhabited islands after 6:00 p.m., but the safari boats' crews and passengers often take the opportunity to mingle with the natives and chat or even share a hookah or water-pipe.

Kuda Anbaraa

This tiny islet is located within the atoll, about 6 kilometers north of Anbaraa. A few coconut palms grow on the is-

Above: It takes a lot of skill and know-how to spin a rope.

land. Kuda Anbaraa is no more than a picturesque, uninhabited picnic spot.

Kudaboli

Kudaboli, another uninhabited island, is located in the northwest of the atoll on the reef of Masaraa Falhu. The name of this popular picnic island in Dhivehi means something like the "island of small shells," and indeed, beachcombers can discover shells here in an astounding variety of shapes and colors. Worth an underwater visit is a striking reef right off the island, in the Diggaluvashee Kuda Kandu.

Maathiththan Faru

Maathiththan Faru is a reef on the western side of the Felidhoo Atoll. A nameless island floats above the sea here, bearing, in lieu of trees, a tall radio antenna. Nearby Maafussaru Kandu is said to have one of the most beautiful coral landscapes in this part of the atoll.

Rakeedhoo

Rakeedhoo lies at the atoll's southern tip, on the channel of the same name, Rakeedhoo Kandu, which is also a well-known dive site. With a population of 269, the island has an atmosphere typical of a native island. In the evenings, safari boats often seek anchorage on the island's protected northern side, so that its passengers can set out bright and early for dives in the Rakeedhoo Kandu.

Ruhhurihuraa

Not particularly striking, the island of Ruhhurihuraa is located in the atoll's southern reaches, about 2 kilometers north of Thunduhuraa. Small and uninhabited, Ruhhurihuraa boasts a few coconut palms, something indicated by the island's name: *Ruh huri* means "There are coconut trees here."

Thinadhoo

Thinadhoo lies on the eastern side of the atoll and has 136 inhabitants. Also known as Mas Thinadhoo, it is, along with Felidhoo, Fulidhoo, Keyodhoo and Rakeedhoo, the atoll's fifth inhabited island. In the southern atolls, the word *thina* stands for a woman's breast, while *mas* means "fish"; the name is an indication of the wealth of fish available here.

There are well-known and attractive diving sites near the island, such as the breathtakingly beautiful overhangs and caves in the Hulhidhoo Kandu channel.

Thunduhuraa

The island of Thunduhuraa lies to the south, on the inner side of the reef of Fotteyo Falhu. Thunduhuraa is basically a small sand bar that invites you to laze around and soak up the sun. Since the few bushes here cast hardly any shade, visitors should bring plenty of sun block.

ALIMATHA

Alimatha Aquatic Resort

Opened in 1975, renovated in 1997. Male office: Safari Tours Ltd., Opera 2, Chandani Magu, 20-02 Male, tel. 323524, fax 322516 and 322510. Island: tel. 450544, fax 450575, Telex 0896 66030 SAFARI MF. *BUNGALOWS:* 122 rooms in double bungalows and six water bungalows, with air conditioning, fans, cold and hot showers (fresh water), refrigerator, small terrace on the ocean side with two deck chairs. *AMENITIES:* bar with disco (featuring live music once a week) and sun deck, restaurant, island boutique, coffee shop, water sports center (with canoe rental; deep-sea fishing by arrangement), desalination plant. *DIVING SCHOOL:* German, English, French, PADI, house reef (outer reef) 50 meters from the dive base, nearest decompression chamber on Bandos (North Male Atoll), 70 kilometers away. *CREDIT CARDS:* AE/MC/VC/ DC/EC. *AIRPORT:* 65 kilometers, 2 hours by speedboat.

Alimatha has gorgeous beaches and marvelous palm trees. For divers, there are more than 40 different dive sites, virtually untouched, in the vicinity.

Most of the guests to this island come from Italy; however, about a quarter of them come from the German-speaking world.

DHIGGIRI

Dhiggiri Tourist Resort

Opened in 1982, renovated in 1994. Male office: Safari Tours Ltd., Opera 2, Chandani Magu, 20-02 Male, tel. 323524, fax 322516 or 322510. Island: tel. 450593, fax 450592, Telex 0896 66030 SAFARI MF. *BUNGALOWS:* 30 self-contained bungalows with air conditioning or fans, cold and hot showers (fresh water), small terrace with ocean view, 15 pile bungalows out over the water, all with air conditioning and direct access to the water. *AMENITIES:* bar (featuring live music once a week), 2 restaurants, island boutique, windsurfing base, deep-sea fishing by arrangement, desalination plant, rainwater collection. *DIVE BASE:* German, English, French, Italian, PADI, house reef (inner reef) 30 meters from the dive base with four marked points of entry, nearest decompression chamber on Bandos (North Male Atoll), 60 kilometers away. *CREDIT CARDS:* AE/MC/VC. *AIRPORT:* 60 kilometers, 2 hours by speedboat, 25 minutes by air taxi.

Dhiggiri is a picture-book Maldive island with lush tropical vegetation. Divers can find incomparably beautiful diving terrain with more than 30 breathtaking dive sites around the island, and chances of sighting manta rays and whale sharks. Some 85% of the clientele hails from Germany.

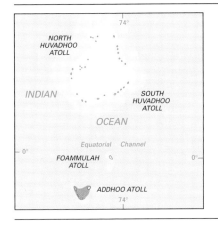

ADDHOO ATOLL
(SEENU ATOLL)

THE ADDHOO ATOLL

This atoll is officially known as Seenu Atoll and is the most southerly of the Maldives islands, lying below the equator in the southern hemisphere. Gan (0°42 S) is the southernmost island. The atoll has four inhabited islands and around 20 uninhabited ones, as well as a few sand bars. It measures 18 kilometers wide and 15 kilometers long, and resembles a heart in shape.

The atoll's relatively large islands form a kind of protective barrier along the east and west sides. In the west are the four inhabited islands, Gan, Feydhoo, Maradhoo and Hithadhoo. These four islands are linked by a causeway, which is broad and sturdy enough to bear the weight of vehicles; in fact, it represents the only opportunity visitors will find of cycling from one island to another. This artificial barrier also forms effective protection against the tides. Bordering the atoll to the east are the islands of Hulhumeedhoo, Mulikolhu and Viligili.

All of the islands in this atoll boast dense growths of coconut palms. The vil-

Preceding pages: Optimistic look into the future – young boys on Gan. Lefts: Reddish plumage indicates a heron's youth.

lages are very clean and well looked-after. They are so small that house names suffice as mailing addresses. Lush gardens with flourishing banana trees surround the houses, which are built out of coral stone.

British Influence in the Addhoo Atoll

Apart from the period of Portuguese occupation, Maldives long remained a sovereign state, managing to avoid colonial status. In 1887, the archipelago became a British protectorate, retaining only limited autonomy: questions of defense and foreign policy were now regarded as British responsibilities. Britain continued to hold sway until the country gained complete independence in 1965.

In World War II, the archipelago played an important strategic role in the Allies' Indian Ocean defense operations against the Japanese.

When the British took up their position in the Addhoo Atoll in 1941, the atoll had around 5,600 inhabitants (today, the population has swollen to around 21,000). Most of the local residents got jobs working for the British Army. Gan, renamed with characteristic military secrecy "Port T," became Britain's most important base in the Indian Ocean. Brit-

197

ish command built a military administration center here, a sturdier, land-based replacement for a more vulnerable, mobile command center that had operated from the decks of a warship. Later, the British stationed all their advance troops on the island.

Six months after Whitehall decided to establish a military presence on Maldives, regiments from Bengal and India arrived and construction work started on an air base that would allow seaplanes to land in Hithadhoo's lagoon. This new development extended Gan's logistical support as far as Singapore and Trincomalee, on Sri Lanka. On the island of Maradhoo, underground bunkers, camouflaged with trees, were built to store ammunition and other military supplies, and a short airstrip, the first on land in Maldives, was built on Gan itself. During the war years, the runway consisted of steel plates. Nearly all of Gan's villages and all of its

Above: Muslims at prayer in a quiet mosque on Gan.

198

trees were flattened to make room for the runway, which extended the entire length of the island. The population was forcibly relocated to the neighboring island of Feydhoo, while quays and buildings were put up on the island which they had once called home. The atoll's defensive installations were reinforced: submarine nets and mine fields were laid across access channels into the inner atoll. This construction program may have been excellent for military purposes, but unfortunately it also destroyed the historical ruins that had represented the last legacy of the island's Buddhist past.

In 1944, a Japanese submarine attacked the British oil tanker *HMS British Loyalty*, which was anchored near Viligili, in Addhoo's harbor. About a week before the attack, lookouts reported an unidentified and very high-flying plane over Addhoo harbor, where the tanker was anchored. Fighter planes were immediately sent out in pursuit, but were unable to find the enemy plane; and the

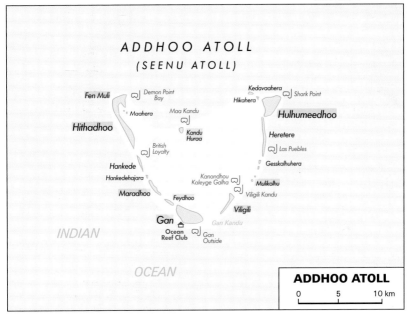

entire base was promptly placed on red alert. Sure enough, a week later, on the night of March 9, 1944, a Japanese submarine appeared outside the atoll under cover of night and fired a torpedo diagonally through the Gan Channel and all of the anti-submarine defenses to score a direct hit on the hapless tanker. One consequence of this loss was that the British moved all their fueling facilities south to the island of Diego Garcia in the Chagos Archipelago. The *British Loyalty* itself was badly damaged, but did not actually sink. Not until after the war was the ship, which was beyond repair, sent to its watery grave southeast of Hithadhoo, within the atoll. Today, the wreck stands upright on the sea bed at a depth of between 12 and 33 meters, a mute testimony to past conflict, and a favorite sight for generations of Maldives divers.

After the war, British troops pulled out of Gan, but when India and Sri Lanka both gained their independence, Britain started to worry about maintaining its military presence in Southeast Asia. In 1952, therefore, the British Air Ministry had Gan surveyed for the construction of a modern air base. When Sri Lanka declared, in 1956, that it would no longer allow the British to use the navy harbor in Trincomalee and the air force base at Katunayake for military purposes, Maldives were the only remaining acceptable alternative as a strategic base to maintain military links between Britain, the Far East and Australia. A treaty with the Maldivian government affirmed Britain's right to use Gan as an air base and Hithadhoo as a military communications center, and construction work began on expanding the base, which was to become a replacement for the facilities relinquished on Sri Lanka, in 1957.

In the period of their military presence on this island, the British on Gan monitored the largest area of air space in the world, and were able to provide facilities for the most modern military aircraft of the time. The island was busy: 630 planes landed, and 12,500 passengers passed through the terminal, in

1960-61 alone. At the beginning of 1976, the British decided to withdraw from Maldives, a process which was not completely effected until 1986. The former Soviet Union made a million-dollar offer for the use of Gan as a base for its fishing fleets, but President Nasir rejected it. Later, textile production began on the island. Today, the hope is that tourism will provide the atoll with a stable economic future.

ADDHOO ATOLL'S RESORT ISLAND

Gan

Gan, which measures 5 kilometers by 3 kilometers in area, is currently the only resort island in the Addhoo Atoll. It lies about 695 kilometers south of

Above: The rare fairy sea swallow only breeds in the southern atolls. Right: Working in Gan's textile mills brings a family useful extra income.

Male. Maldives Airlines planes from Hulhule reach the island about 75 minutes; passengers are only allowed 15 kilos of baggage.

Gan is markedly different from other resort islands on Maldives in that there's plenty of contact with the locals; tourists and residents are not separated at all. Foreign visitors can cycle over to the neighboring islands, which are home to around 20,000 people.

The **Ocean Reef Club Resort** opened in 1995 within the buildings of the former Royal Air Force base, which have now been attractively renovated and converted into comfortable tourist facilities. The officers' mess is now the hotel restaurant. The complex consists of 17 buildings containing four to six units each, for a total of 82 rooms available to visitors. A former Anglican church on the grounds has been converted into a mosque, and there's also an old British post office, both testimony to the days when the islands were a British protectorate. The spacious bar

and the reception area are both new constructions. Some of the former officers' quarters are now used to put up government representatives when they come to visit.

Near the resort, the cannons of a former gun battery, originally located on the east coast, have been converted into a war memorial.

It goes almost without saying that diving is the recreational pastime of preference on Gan. The wreck of the *British Loyalty*, 140 meters long, is one special highlight, while the many large fish which pass close to the atoll delight the eyes of visiting divers.

The neighboring island of Viligili is particularly good for swimming and surfing. There are plans to enlarge and reopen the nine-hole golf course, another relic of the days of the British, along with the tennis court and soccer field.

There are daily flights between Gan and Hulhule, and a high-speed ferry travels between Male and Gan once a week.

INHABITED ISLANDS IN THE ADDHOO ATOLL

Feydhoo

Feydhoo, an inhabited island, has a population of 2,467. In 1970, a causeway was built linking the island to Maradhoo and Gan, which means that today people can drive or cycle along the longest road in Maldives (all of 9 kilometers!) from Gan via Feydhoo and Maradhoo to Hithadhoo in the north of the atoll. Small sand bars lie off of Feydhoo's western coast.

Hithadhoo

Hithadhoo, the atoll's main island, has 7,090 inhabitants, and boasts a number of attractive historical relics. By Koattey there is the ruin of an old fort. The archaeologist H.C.P. Bell visited the island as long ago as 1922 and examined the ruin, yet its origins and purpose are still unknown. One legend has it that the fort

was the base for Maldivian rebels led by Muhammad Thakurufaan, who drove the Portuguese out of the country in 1557. Other historians believe that the fort was built by Kunhali Marakkar of Malabar, the ruler of Maldives, who carried on an active business in trade in the southern parts of the archipelago during the Portuguese occupation. Kunhali possessed 200 ships, with which he sailed the Indian Ocean and went out marauding and plundering with his men. The Koattey fort, which offers good anchorage, was a safe refuge to which he could withdraw when the Portuguese were after him or when ships damaged in battle had to be repaired.

By Fen Muli, on the island's west coast, there are still some concrete remains of a British coastal battery that was constructed at the beginning of World War II. It originally represented a part of

the defenses protecting the atoll's northwest side.

The wreck of the *HMS British Royalty* lies off the southwest tip of the island. Approximately 4 kilometers south of Fen Muli, on the west coast of Hithadhoo, are the last remains of another old fort, which has almost completely disappeared, and whose original function has been obscured by the mists of time. By Thakurufaanu Miskiy is the grave of Sultan Hassan X (born in 1701) who died there in 1765 after 60 years in exile.

Today, Hithadhoo is a thriving island. New buildings, an Islamic center, cars, businesses, shops, educational institutions, and even a hospital combine to demonstrate that even here, on the remotest, southernmost islands of Maldives, things are changing with the times.

Hulhumeedhoo

On Hulhumeedhoo, in the northeast of the atoll, there are two villages which were split up in 1975: Hulhudhoo, popu-

Above: Traditional patterns, woven on Gan's beach. Right: Hookahs, or water pipes, are enjoyed by men and women alike.

202

GAN
Ocean Reef Club
Opened in 1995. Male office: Crossworld Maledives Pvt., Ltd., No. 8 Marine Drive, 20-05 Male, tel. 320912 and 323181, fax 320913, telex 0896 66301 CWORLD MF. Island: tel. 575019, fax 575020. *BUNGALOWS:* 82 rooms in row houses, each equipped with air conditioning, hot and cold showers, mini-bar. *AMENITIES:* 2 bars (one a pool bar), restaurant, swimming pool, children's pool, golf course, 2 tennis courts, squash court, billiards, bike rental. *DIVING BASE:* German, English; PADI 5 Star IDC Center, email: edmaldop@dhivehinet.net.mv, Internet: http://www.euro-divers.com, house reef 50 m away; the nearest decompression chamber is on Bandos (can only be reached by plane; the nearest doctor is on Feedhoo (10 min by car). *CREDIT CARDS:* MC/VC, up to sums of US $1,000. *AIRPORT:* 695 kilometers away, 75 minutes by plane; 15 kg of luggage is the maximum allowed. Because of flight times, passengers have to plan an overnight stay in Male on the return trip. This island is ideal for nature-lovers. The five islands around Gan have 20,000 inhabitants. Divers can find magnificent, unspoiled diving areas and an impressive wreck from World War II.

lation 1,828, and Meedhoo, with 1,489 inhabitants. Visitors are still a rarity here. On the island's east coast, you can inspect the concrete remains of a gun emplacement from World War II. According to a memorial plaque, it was erected by the 8th Indian Coastal Battery. The inhabitants used to live mainly from the production and sale of dried fish; today, many of the men have opted for better-paying jobs on the resort islands, or gone off to sea.

The inhabitants of Hulhumeedhoo are devout Moslems; they even maintain that they were converted 281 years before the rest of Maldives, when a sailor named Youssuff Naib Kalheihaara Thakurufaanu, whose ship had strayed off course, landed on the island and converted the population to Islam.

Kandu Huraa

This tiny island, also known as Bushy Island, is located at the midpoint of the northern edge of the Addhoo Atoll. During World War II, it housed the central administration responsible for controlling the mine fields.

East of the island is the Maa Kandu channel, a wonderful place to go diving, where you can sometimes spot a manta ray, always an impressive sight.

Maradhoo

Long and narrow, the island of Maradhoo supports two villages: one is called Maradhoo, with 1,492 inhabitants, and the other is Maaradhoofeydhoo, at the island's southern end, with a population of 811.

To make room for the British air force base on Gan during World War II, Gan's erstwhile residents were resettled to neighboring Feydhoo, while Feydhoo's inhabitants were moved over to Maradhoo, a rather questionable example of military logic.

Today, the causeway, built in 1970, links Maradhoo with Hankede Island, not far away.

DIVING IN THE CORAL BELTS

The Maldives offer some of the finest diving in the world. Since the opening of the first islands to tourism in 1972, the atoll state has been a favorite destination for European visitors.

Anyone who has been fortunate enough to see the Maldives' underwater glories talks in glowing terms about the beauty of the varied coral landscapes for long afterwards. Even after 25 years of diving tourism, the stream of visitors has yet to diminish. In fact, the number of tourists is growing steadily, and there is an astonishingly high rate of return visitors.

Scuba diving in the Maldives is like being inside a tropical aquarium. The variety of corals and tropical fish is practically endless. Everywhere you look you see small brightly colored fish and, with a bit of luck, you may spot larger ones as well. Equally astonishing is the world of corals, which extends in a seemingly endless variety of shapes and colors. Although they barely move, the corals are nevertheless, hard as it is to believe, representatives of the animal world.

Anyone visiting the Maldives simply cannot leave without venturing below the sea's surface, even if only with no more than a snorkel, mask and flippers (the ABC equipment, as it were). Leaving the Maldives without having done at least that much would truly be a sin of omission!

To go scuba diving in the Maldives, you need an internationally valid certificate from a recognized diving association in your home country. These include various diving clubs in individual countries as well as the major international associations, such as PADI, NAUI, DIWA,

Preceding pages: First diving lesson in the lagoon's shallows – communication through sign language. Left: A dive in the Halaveli wreck.

SSI and CMAS. The "certificate" usually takes the form of a plastic card, which has to be presented to the head of the diving school at the beginning of your stay, along with your log book, which documents the precise extent of your prior experience. If you have never gone diving before, every resort island on the Maldives has a diving school where you can take your first underwater "steps" and get a certificate. To demonstrate that you're physically fit for diving, you also need a certification of fitness from a qualified doctor in your own country.

As a rule, diving courses on the islands last at least four days and end with the Open Water Diver test or with one for a sport diver's certificate. After that you can begin to descend into the new, fascinating, silent world underwater. In diving, the first two commandments are "Always dive on the safe side" and "Never dive alone." To make sure that things go smoothly, most schools in the Maldives require beginners to do at least 30 dives with an instructor first. After that, a new diver has established a certain routine, and is experienced enough to set off without a trained guide, in the company of a dive partner, on submarine explorations.

Nearly all the diving schools in the Maldives offer two dives a day, and some offer night dives, as well. In general, the first dive takes place in the morning, and another goes down in the afternoon. Special traditional "divers' dhonis" ferry you to the most beautiful coral reefs around the islands. On some islands, such as Ellaidhoo in the Ari Atoll, there are now dhonis fitted with extra-powerful motors that enable them to travel twice as fast as the traditional ones. The journey to the dive site seldom takes more than an hour; often enough, it is over in a matter of five minutes or so.

Every diving base has a full complement of scuba diving and snorkeling equipment. For snorkeling, you need at

least the bare minimum of the three essential pieces of diving equipment: a mask, snorkel, and flippers, the so-called ABC outfit. These three items are the basic pieces of equipment for all kinds of diving, including scuba diving, and should be worn as a matter of principle whenever you go anywhere where the water is too deep to stand. A swimmer without flippers can run into serious trouble in the ocean. Even a scuba diver in full gear can't make headway against a current of more than 1.5 knots; and in the Maldives, there are many currents, and many of them easily move at speeds of three knots or more.

When you're on an organized snorkeling excursion, however, fast currents aren't too great a problem. If the current gets too strong, you can simply let it carry you along the reef until the dhoni can "fish" you out. It is important, how-

ever, to talk to the personnel on the boat before you go off, and to keep both the dhoni and the reef in clear view at all times. Anyone who wants to go off snorkeling at the so-called "house reef" has to take better precautions: being swept along by a current there can have fatal consequences. For this reason, you should always make sure there's someone on the island who knows where you want to go snorkeling, and about how long you plan to stay. And in snorkeling as in scuba diving, the iron rule is "Never go out alone!"

Scuba diving requires not only the snorkeling equipment described above but also additional pieces of equipment, some of which are even required by Maldivian law. Every diver, for example, has to have a weight vest or jacket; these garments can also be inflated, allowing the diver to float comfortably on the water's surface and conserve his or her energy. Every aqualung, the gadget which enables the diver to breathe from the oxygen tanks, is required to have a sec-

Above: A T-shirt protects snorkelers against sunburn. Right: Check equipment carefully before every dive!

ond respirator, known as the octopus attachment, which enables a diver to provide his or her dive partner with air in case of emergency underwater. Further requirements in every diver's kit are a diver's watch; a diving table, which shows how long you can stay underwater and at what depths; a pressure gauge, which indicates how much pressure (and hence air) is left in the aqualung and tanks, and a depth gauge. A diving computer may make diving procedures easier, but it can't replace these essential pieces of gear. A diver's decision whether or not to wear a diving suit depends on individual sensitivity to cold. As water temperatures in the Maldives lie between 28°C and 30°C, cold is hardly a major problem; a suit is, however, good protection against stinging anemones or the knife-like edges of sharp corals.

Well-equipped and prepared along the lines described above, you can now explore the fantastic realm of the corals. As a final measure before a day's diving, conscientious diving schools will carry out a check or practice dive with their students to make sure they have mastered the basics and are really ready to venture out into the water.

No one is sure exactly how many reefs there are, in total, in the Maldives, and the number will doubtless continue to be elusive for many years to come. Even the latest charts aren't specific as to precise figures. But basically, you can jump into the water just about anywhere in this region, and the beauty of this underwater world will be yours to see.

Every resort island has some 30 to 40 preferred diving locations. Apart from the house reef that girdles nearly every island, there are a range of other reef types. *Giris* are reefs that lie close to an island's shore and rise to just below the water's surface; while a *thila*, while it also lies just beneath the water, lies somewhere out in an atoll, not necessarily close to an island, and often in areas exposed to strong currents. For this reason, many *thilas* are particularly popular with divers because the current's influence helps creates breathtakingly beautiful corals. A *faru* denotes a long reef extending along a lagoon. A channel between two reefs is known as a *kandu*. Most of these channels flow to the outer reef, the *maa kandu*. For many divers, dives at the outer reef or in these channels are particular favorites. Large fish frequently swim past the outer reef, so it's worth keeping an eye out at the edge of the open sea: divers have been known to spot whales, such as orcas or "killer whales," off the Maldives.

There are usually strong currents in the channels. At flood tide, water shoots like a jet through the narrow passages into the inner atoll, filling it up like a swimming pool. Because of the water's velocity at ebb tide, and the sediment it whirls up from the atoll floor as it retreats, visibility is generally poor as the tide goes out. The best and easiest diving conditions prevail in the hour of high tide, when the water is still; the atoll is full of "clean" water from the sea, and there aren't any currents to worry about.

Apart from the periods of full ebb and full flood, it's not easy to predict the direction of the current at certain locations. Although the main currents in the Maldives all run East - West, the currents at each reef have their own particular changing patterns. Only when you actually get to a dive spot can you really say much about the current there, and even then they can easily change directions during a dive. Usually, divers are set down at places from which they can easily drift to the reef with the current and then ride the current along the reef (a process known as drift diving). On dives like this, the boat does not anchor, but also drifts with the current, and later picks the divers up.

Around two million dives a year are made in the Maldives, many of them at

Right: Gray reef shark in the Vaadhoo Kandu – a special highlight for divers.

locations particularly attractive to visitors. For example, the wreck of the *Maldive Victory* is now known to divers the world over. This freighter, which sank in 1981, sits upright, as if deliberately parked, at a depth of 40 meters, resting on the ocean floor of the North Male Atoll at a spot southwest of Hulhule, the airport island. The ship, 82 meters long, is now heavily overgrown; the tip of its 10-meter long mast extends to just 12 meters below the water's surface. Its bridge and superstructure are intact and provide much adventurous diving at an average depth of 25 meters in the safe zones. As the wreck lies right in the channel between Male and Hulhule, there are often very powerful currents.

Another excellent place for diving is the nearby Vaadhoo Kandu in the northern reaches of the South Male Atoll. Large fish such as eagle rays, various types of shark and barracudas often make their way through the channel, which is some 4.5 meters wide. At Lion's Head, where people used to go to feed the sharks, you can still sometimes spot gray reef sharks at close proximity; these aquatic denizens prefer to hang out at depths of around 30 meters. At slightly shallower levels, between 20 and 25 meters, there are impressive overhangs and caves, a feature also found at the neighboring locality to the east, Old Shark Point, which, as the name implies, is also a reliable place for shark-sighting. The sheer walls of the Vaadhoo Kandu fascinate every diver, thanks in part to their many wonderful overhangs and caves, with names such as Velassaru Caves, Vaadhoo Caves, Emboodhoo Canyon, and Cathedral.

Another site with sheer, cliff-like walls is a diving location at the southern end of Gulhi Falhu which is named after Hans Hass, the diving pioneer. When the water is clear, you can see directly from here into the deep blue of the Vaadhoo channel.

A short way further north, between the islands of Kurumba and Furana (Full Moon), is the Banana Reef. At its northeastern corner, there's an impressive landscape reminiscent of an open-air theater: the reef descends in large overhangs, like terraces, for more than 30 meters. Large shoals of fish congregate at the outlying coral blocks; particularly attractive are the colorful banner fish, which can gather here in schools of more than 1,000. Banana Reef also has fabulous growths of coral and large table corals on the roof of the reef, which lies some 3 to 5 meters underwater. There are other splendid diving spots along the outer reef by Furana and Farukolhufushi, including Club Med Corner, Furnana North and South, Chicken Island and Maagiri Caves.

Between June and October, large manta rays, which can reach a span of as much as 7 meters, can be spotted along the outer reef's southwestern rim (especially at Manta Point and by the Lankan Caves). During this period the rays take advantage of the large plankton supply and also their symbiosis with the small cleaner wrasse, who free them of their skin parasites. The sight of mantas elegantly winging their way through the water is unforgettable; for many divers, it's the highlight of their experiences in Maldivian waters.

A further spectacular reef, the Girifusi Thila or HP reef, lies in the Himmafushi Channel close to the island of Girifushi. Its roof, which lies at a depth of 10 to 12 meters, is covered in a carpet of soft corals in a seemingly endless range of colors. Off its west side there are impressive blocks of coral, occasionally circumnavigated by passing sharks and barracudas.

Further north, Kani Corner and Aquarium in the Lhohifushi Channel and Coliseum in the Thulusdhoo Channel rank among the top dive sites near the outer reef. In addition, the resort island of Helengeli offers diving excursions to magnificent spots along the outer reef. These sites, such as the fabulous Helengeli

Thila, also benefit from their relatively isolated position in the north of the North Male Atoll; only seldom are they visited by tourist divers.

Wreck fans can get their money's worth around the neighboring reef of Gaafaru Falhu. On its north side there are no fewer than three sunken ships lying on the sea bed: the *Lady Christine*, which went down in 1974, the *SS Sea Gull* (sunk in 1879), and the *SS Crusader*, which broke up on the reef in 1905. The east side of the North Male Atoll also offers an impressive wreck near Hembadhoo. Sunk in 1988, the ship now sits upright at a depth of 15 to 22 meters. Along the outer reef, divers at Eriyadhoo, Makunudhoo, Ziyaaraifushi, Reethi Rah, Hembadhoo and Nakatchchaafushi can find superb reefs with magnificent corals, which especially flourish near the channels into the atoll.

Distinguishing characteristics of the western part of the South Male Atoll are the shallow channels, which frequently house beautiful overgrown *thilas*, such as Emboodhoo Thila, Dhigu Thila (with Manta Point), Kandoom Thila and Guraidhoo Thila. Due to the stimulating influence of the currents, the reef roofs, which lie at depths of around 10 meters, have particularly colorful soft corals. One world-famous current – among divers, at least – is the so-called Emboodhoo Express: divers can let it propel them for more than 2 kilometers along the reef at the south side of the Emboodhoo Channel, which is an unforgettable experience. In the south, the islands of Kandooma, Biyadhoo, Villivaru, Rihiveli, Fihalhohi and Rannahli share the diving spots. Biyadhoo and Villivaru offer the largest number of different reefs: 119 in all.

More world-famous reefs are located in the Ari Atoll, to the west, above all

Right: Giant morays can reach lengths of as much as 2.5 meters.

Fish Head, Mushimasmingili Thila and Maaya Thila. Here, divers have excellent chances of encountering a gray reef shark. At Fish Head, which is exposed to currents, you can also sight large shoals of gold stripe snappers and batfish. Local divers are also on familiar terms with a giant napoleon fish and an eagle ray which have made this locality their home. South of the reef Maaya Thila, large schools of soldier fish and barracudas gather around the impressive blocks of coral. Divers can expect to encounter the largest number of fish at the point where the current meets the reef; such places are also popular with sharks.

The islands of Ellaidhoo, Halaveli and Fesdhoo each boast their own wreck. You can swim down to the one at Ellaidhoo, which lies at between 18 and 33 meters, right from the house reef. The Halaveli wreck has a large population of sting rays, which are so tame you can almost touch them. The specimen at Fesdhoo sits upright on the sandy ocean floor, 29 meters down. Its machine room is now home to giant moray eels. The most beautiful "natural" diving sites in this area include the entire outer reef, Maagaala Thila, which boasts breathtaking overhangs along its southern side and whose roof is covered in a vast field of anemones; and Kandholhudhoo Thila, where small manta rays often swim between the *thila* and the nearby *faru*.

At Bodu Thila, a large population of conger eels lives at a depth of around 15 meters. This particular species was discovered by Hans Hass and Irenäus Eibl-Eibelsfeldt, and thus bears Hass's name: *Heteroconger hassi*.

The diving areas off Rasdhoo Madivaru in the neighboring Rasdhoo Atoll are not for the faint-hearted. There, you can encounter hammerhead sharks (*Sphyrna leweni*) in the early morning and late afternoon. If you are lucky, a school of several hundred of them may suddenly emerge from the blue depths.

This unforgettable sight is, however, generally reserved for divers who are staying on Kuramathi and Veligandhoo, as the hammerheads are usually already in open sea and out of sight by the time diving dhonis arrive from the Ari Atoll. The spellbinding reef landscapes around Rasdhoo are concentrated along the outer reef and in the Rasdhoo Kandu. Due to the current, some diving experience and a good sense of direction are required in this area. The bizarre reef landscapes are spread like a labyrinth across an area of several hundred meters. Manta rays, white-tipped reef sharks, barracudas and other deep-sea fish often visit this spectacular area.

Another highlight for experienced divers is the isolated Ukulhass Thila, approximately 300 meters long, in the northern region of the Ari Atoll. This *thila*, which lies in the current, boasts three large coral banks that come to within 14 meters of the surface; on the side, it drops down to a depth of more than 30 meters. Between December and April, the reef is heavily frequented by manta rays who come in search of a "makeover." Eagle rays too, can often be found in the reef's shallow water.

There's more excellent diving to be had on the east side of this atoll: above all at the Miyaruga Thila, southwest of the resort island of Nika, and at the Maalhoss Thila near the island of the same name, which has no tourist facilities. Both reefs lie in channels and are therefore more suitable for advanced divers. Exquisite overhangs and reef landscapes characterize these sites. In the south of the Ari Atoll, which is being increasingly opened up to tourism, the locations around Kuda Rah (Kudarah Thila, Broken Rock, Dhigura Thila), Sun Island (Maamigili Faru) and Thundufushi (Thundufushi Thila, Panettone) offer the biggest variety in the region.

In fact, it hardly matters where you jump into the water in the Maldives. Everywhere you look there are countless rare, unusual and bizarre kinds of marine life to gaze at in wonder.

MARINE LIFE

The waters of the Maldives offer some of the most varied and attractive diving in the world. The incomparable underwater coral landscapes are a paradise for scuba divers and snorkelers alike. A glance below the surface is like looking into a richly-stocked aquarium. The colors and forms of the countless reefs seem endless in their variety.

It is estimated that there are around 200,000 kinds of saltwater fish on earth, which have all to a greater or lesser extent adapted to an immense range of environments and living conditions. Sharks, which are among the most primitive species of fish, existed as long as 350 million years ago and have barely changed since the Devonian period. Rays, on the other hand, who are related to sharks, have slowly evolved a flat

Above: Stone corals fascinate with their bizarre array of forms (Discus coral). Right: A rare sight – a manta ray:

body that's ideally suited to a life close to the ocean bed.

Many tropical invertebrates, zoologically classified as lower animals, evolved early in the earth's history. Jellyfish (*Scyphozoa*) for example, have inhabited the world's seas for around 600 million years.

There is almost no plant life in the Indian ocean, except for a few kinds of algae. Even the seemingly lifeless Maldivian stone corals, of which there are more than 200 different kinds, consist of colonies of minute animals, whose calcified waste products have created the underwater reef landscapes that make such an impression on visitors to the islands.

Tropical Saltwater Fish

Diving sites in the Maldives are mainly characterized by the colorful comings and goings of small and medium-sized coral fish, but larger ocean denizens occasionally pass by the reefs, as well. Most frequently observed of the larger fish are

gray reef sharks (*Carcharhinus amblyrhinchos*), white-tipped reef sharks (*Triaenodon obesus*), and nurse sharks (*Ginglynostoma cirratum*). On occasions divers sight a deep-sea shark, such as the white-tipped cousin of the reef shark (*Carcharhinus longimanus*), or a hammerhead (*Sphyrna spec*). Rarest of all is a sighting of the whale shark (*Rhincodon typus*), the largest fish in the world. These can grow to lengths of up to 18 meters, and seeing one is one of the most impressive experiences you can have in tropical seas.

Mantas or devil rays (*Manta birostris*), too, are marvelous to watch as they elegantly "wing" their way through the water. They can reach a span of 7 meters, and come to the reefs to be cleaned by the little cleaner wrasse (*Labroidus dimidiatus*). The latter never stray far from their home turf, and free other fish from skin parasites which they themselves cannot reach. To do this, they perform a distinctive "seesaw dance" to attract and literally entrance larger fish, who then even allow the little cleaners into their open mouths to take care of their teeth. The "customer" signals the end of this cleaning process with a brief jerk of his body, a sign for the cleaner to depart its oral orifice as swiftly as possible and move on to the next in line. These clean-up points, which get as many as 250 fish a day, are spectacular places for divers to visit.

Particularly colorful denizens of the coral reefs are butterfly fish (*Chaetodontidae*), imperial angelfish (*Pomacanthidae*), sweetlips (*Plectorhynchidae*) and banner fish (*Zanclidae*). Their colorful exteriors identify them to fellow members of their species on the one hand and signal their defensive territorial behavior on the other. Imperial angelfish live either alone or in pairs, and defend their space vigorously against others of their species with similar markings. For this reason, young fish have different markings in the early phase of their life, so that they can survive without being attacked until they're big enough to stand up for

themselves. Many butterfly fish (to whom they are related) sport a dark "eye" at the back of their bodies, which is supposed to confuse pursuing attackers should the fish turn to flee.

The damselfish family (*Pomacentridae*), well-represented at every reef, embraces more than 200 different types. One of these is the gaudily-colored clownfish (*Amphiprioninae*), a breed that lives in symbiosis with sea anemones, mainly by defending them from imperial angelfish and butterfly fish, both of which are very fond of sea-anemone tentacles as a snack. The energetic clownfish, about 10 centimeters long, are repaid in that they're able to take refuge from predators amidst the anemones, protected from the latter's sting by a layer of secretion. If you take a close look, you can often discover other lodgers, such as tiny shrimps and crabs, nestled among an

Above: The clownfish lives symbiotically with sea anemones. Right: "Napoleon" fish dwell by one reef for many years.

anemone's tentacles. Anemones also settle in shallow waters, so that snorkelers in lagoons often come across them, as well.

Another sight well worth watching is the courtship of the damselfish. With its body the male "sweeps" clean a site for the female to lay her eggs, after which he attracts her attention by making rapid swimming movements.

In the afternoon, large schools of parrotfish (*Scaridae*), so called because of their beak-like mouths, frequently do the rounds of reefs in shallow waters to graze on the coral's algae. Parrotfish are conspicuous for their luminous colors and the amusing rocking motion they make when swimming, thanks to their use of their breast fins. At night they envelop themselves in a "sleeping bag" of secretions to protect themselves from moray eels, which have a very good sense of smell. The "sleeping bag" then makes a good breakfast in the morning.

Like the parrotfish, hawkfish (*Cirrhitidae*) prefer shallower areas of the reef.

They are poor swimmers and guard their territory by hanging out motionless at judicious vantage points, suddenly erupting to dart off at lightning speed to catch their prey. The reptilian-looking lizard fish (*Synodontidae*) also prefers such vantage points among the reefs. Most common of the lizard fish is *Synodus veriegatus*, but divers can also occasionally spot a marble lizard fish (*Saurida gracilis*).

Wrasse (*Labridae*) are present in great numbers at every reef. Constantly scouring the reef and shallow sandbanks for food, they like to follow other fish who are also looking for food, in order to pick up easily digested leftovers. Wrasse come in all colors and sizes, from the 8-centimeter-long cleaner fish already mentioned (*Labroides dimidiatus*) to the impressive two-and-a-half meter giant wrasse (*Cheilinus undulatus*), known to scuba divers as "Napoleon." Many types of wrasse are able to change their gender, a feature they have in common with the damselfish.

There are approximately 300 kinds of blennies (*Blenniidae* and *Salaridae*) and around 2,000 types of gobies (*Gobiidae*); both are present in massive numbers and difficult to define exactly. Averaging between 4 and 10 centimeters in size, they are accounted among the small fry of the reefs. As gobies generally inhabit sand bars which afford little natural cover, some of them have evolved fascinating survival strategies. Species such as *Cryptocentrus*, *Lotilia*, *Obortiophagus* and *Vanderhorstia*, for example, live symbiotically with alpha crabs in little holes. While the crabs, which are nearly blind, tirelessly try to keep the entrances of their caves from sanding up, the gobies keep an eye out for possible predators. If danger approaches, they alert the crabs with the tips of their tails, which are in constant contact with the crabs' feelers, and both animals then beat a hasty retreat to safety. The tireless crabs do not resume their "sweeping" work again until the gobies have surveyed the premises and given the all-clear.

217

Among the schools of fish that are found at almost every reef include snappers (*Lutjanidae*) and fusilier fish (*Caesiodidae*); the streamlined bodies of the latter make them easy to pick out. For small fish, a school serves two natural protective functions. A school appears larger and more dangerous to predators, almost like one giant fish; and the same predators have trouble focusing on a single potential victim in all of the school's movement and sparkle.

In their early phases of development, surgeon fish (*Acanthuridae*) also form schools and live near reefs. The adults of this species, however, generally live in pairs. The name comes from the scalpel-like "thorns" on their tails which stand out from the rest of their bodies by virtue of their color and are meant to scare off predators. If harassed, surgeon fish can also inflict unpleasant knife-like slash wounds on divers.

Puffer fish (*Tetradontidae*) have become world famous as a Japanese delicacy called *fugu*. These yellow or blue fish, which grow to lengths of about 20 centimeters, live mainly off snails and little crabs, which they break open with their powerful jaws. Their relatives the porcupine fish (*Diodontidae*) are easy to recognize thanks to their distinctive prickly coats (whence their name). They can pump themselves up with water if need be, which makes them rather unwieldy and unmanoeuverable, but also unapproachable, as they appear as a large, thorny ball to potential enemies.

The scorpion fish family (*Scorpaenidae*) is one of the most formidable in the reefs, with poisonous fin tips on their backs. The latter are particularly evident in the colorful zebra fish, one of the largest members of this family, measuring around 30 centimeters long. Far from co-lorful, on the other hand, are scorpion fish and stonefish, which prefer to keep a low profile, lying motionless and well-camouflaged by the reef. Divers should therefore look carefully and think twice before reaching out to touch any part of the reef: not only because human intervention can disturb the delicate underwater environment, but also because stonefish are among the most poisonous in the world, and their sting can be fatal to humans. If you are stung, clean the wound and immerse it in water heated to 50-70°C, as the proteins in the poison cannot survive heat. Then seek medical aid as fast as possible.

Moray eels (*Muraenidae*) generally stay well-concealed in their safe hideouts during the daytime and are neither poisonous nor aggressive – as long as they're left in peace. By day, they lie in wait for any prey that may happen to chance by; they come out for real hunting at night. Most morays range from about 80 to 100 centimeters long, but two species, the honeycomb moray eel (*Gymnothorax favagineus*) and the giant moray (*Gymnothorax javanicus*), can grow to lengths of up to 2.5 meters.

Groupers (*Serranidae*) prefer to live alone in deeper waters (15-30 meters), preferably well-camouflaged under overhangs or in small caves. In the underwater twilight, their dark, speckled bodies become almost invisible, so that divers have trouble making them out, as do small food fish, which swim in blissful ignorance toward their concealed predators.

Invertebrates

It has been estimated that there are more than one million different kinds of tropical invertebrates. Interest in these creatures is increasing among divers, whether because of the incredible variety of species or the fact that, although quite a bit is known about them, scientific re-

Right: The giant clam is large, colorful, and – harmless.

search in this field is still in its relative infancy.

Often bizarre in appearance, these reef inhabitants are always good for a surprise, even in the realms visible to the naked eye. Believe it or not, even common sponges (*Porifera*), be they round, branched, or tube-shaped, are animals which filter plankton out of the water.

The world's oceans are home to approximately 200 different kinds of jellyfish. Most of the ones belonging to the *Cnideria* family are too small to be visible to the naked eye; you can only feel them. Larger jellyfish, such as Rhizostoma, generally frequent the open seas.

Anthozoa corals, also known as "flower creatures" because of their variety of colors, are divided into six- and eight-branched families (*hectacorallia* and *octocorallia*). There are more than 4,000 kinds of six-branched corals, ranging from stone corals (*Scleractinia* or *Madreporaria*) through tube anemones (*Ceriantaria*) and sea anemones (*Acti-*

niaria) to *zoantharia*. Some of the zoantharia polyps are easily visible and very beautiful at night. Of the eight-branched corals, the richly-colored soft ones are particularly enchanting. There are more than 2,500 kinds of eight-branched corals in existence, including soft or leather corals (*Alcyonacea*), horn coral or gorgonians (*Gorgonacea*), feather coral (*pennatularea*), and a species of blue coral called *Heliopora coerulea* which is similar to stone corals.

Flatworms (*Plathelminthes*) closely resemble sea slugs, of which there are around 5,000 kinds; however, they lack the gill cluster that's typical of the latter. Their extensible mouths are located on their lower bodies.

Large and varied, the mollusk family embraces around 105,000 types of snail (gastropods), polyplacophora or chitons, mussels or *bivalvia* (of which there are some 20,000 different kinds), and octopi (*cephalopoda*), of which there are 730 kinds. Cepalopods are subdivided into two families: the 8-armed octopus and

219

10-armed cuttlefish or sepia. Calcified cuttlefish valves are used in birdseed in our northern climes. Cowries, the shells of which are a kind of Maldivian specialty, are actually snails, zoologically speaking, rather than bivalves such as clams or mussels, which consist of two identical halves.

Crustaceans such as crabs, langouste, lobster, shrimps and prawns belong to the arthropods, the biggest group in the animal kingdom, with more than one million different kinds. Sea lilies and featherstars (*Crinoidea*), sea urchins (*Echinoidea*) and starfish (*Asteroidea*), along with the somewhat less poetically-named sea cucumbers (*Holothuroidea*), are among the 6,000-odd different kinds of *Echinodermata*. Tunicates are classified into two groups: *Ascidiacea* or sea squirts, which are rooted to the sea bed, and Thaliacea, which move through the water. Both types have openings in their "tunics," which are comprised of celluslose; one opening for intake and explusion as well as a breathing organ with which they also filter plankton out of the water. It is interesting to note that these "simple" tunicates are zoologically closer to us than one might think. They are members of the chordate phylum, which, in addition to tunicates (Urochordata), consists of lancelets (Cephalochordata) and vertebrates. The vertebrate family also includes mammals, which of course means humans, among others.

Endangered Fauna

The complex ecosystem of the coral reefs reacts very sensitively to climatic changes. Even slight temperature changes or a gentle warming of the water can adversely affect the growth of entire coral landscapes – and corals are at best

Right: The tentacles of Spirobranchus giganteus waft in the current with a filigree beauty.

slow growers, gaining only a few centimeters a year. Fortunately, there have so far been few signs of coral death in the Maldives; it's easy to spot when it does occur, as the corals turn white. One threat to the fish population are the large fishing fleets which catch sharks and wrasse for export and throw off the natural population balance in the sea. The aquarium fish trade is also a source of disruption to the ecosystem, causing long-term damage to the coral reefs, in particular. To catch these timid fish, poison is poured over a large area of reef, forcing them out into the open. Being stationary, the coral polyps are unable either to avoid or to withstand the poison, and die.

The sea is also being burdened by increasing amounts of waste. The association Professional Association of Diving Instructors (PADI) has formed a program called AWARE (Aquatic World Awareness, Responsibility and Education) to help further measures to preserve and protect oceans around the world. During the International Year of the Oceans in 1998, divers from more than 70 countries, including representatives of more than 30 Maldivian diving schools, took part in clean-up programs both above and below the surface. In addition, reefs heavily frequented by divers are now protected by buoys, to prevent boats from dropping anchor, which destroys sections of the fragile coral each time it occurs.

A campaign against the slaughter of the rare sea turtle is also underway throughout the Maldives. Until recently, these animals, which have swum the world's oceans for more than 200 million years, were still being cut up alive so that their valuable meat could be processed into soup and their shells turned into various souvenirs for the tourists. Turtles are very sensitive to changes in temperature. If the eggs are laid in sand warmer than 30°C, noticeably more females are born when the eggs hatch after around 50 days. At lower temperatures, male babies

predominate. On average, 3 out of every 1,000 young turtles survive to reach adulthood.

In the Maldives, some two million dives are made every year into the underwater paradise full of wonders and beauty in endless forms and colors. As visitors to this marvelous, silent world, we are obliged to behave as guests and help protect nature's fragile miracles. Every one of us can help in this respect by observing the following recommendations:

– Learn to dive at a recognized association or club which respects the environment and teaches how to use weights properly.
– Make sure to use the proper weights to avoid breaking coral. It's helpful in this regard to keep the weights to the minimum one actually needs.
– Kick up as little sand as possible with your flippers, as this covers small coral polyps and suffocates them.
– Walk into the sea only as far as you have to until it's deep enough to swim.

Even the sandy shallows are home to a range of creatures, even if it doesn't look that way at first sight.
– Don't capture or kill any invertebrates or "lower creatures" to feed to the fish.
– Do not feed, touch or otherwise harass the "natives" in their natural environment.
– Adjust weights correctly so that you remain well above reefs when filming or taking photos; don't sit on the corals or try to get a firm footrest on them.
– Do not take anything out of the water. Even empty shells are often re-used as housing by many species.
– Do not catch or harpoon animals. Harpoons are strictly prohibited on the Maldives, and violators are fined!
– Whenever possible, do not throw any kind of rubbish into the water; if you do feel compelled to do so, at least make sure it's biodegradable.
– Do not buy any ocean creatures or products made out of them. Only demand dictates whether protected species will continue to be hunted.

THE FLORA OF THE MALDIVES

Where the Maldives boast an almost immeasurable variety of aquatic life forms and colors beneath the water, the islands can't claim the same range of species and contrasts on land. For one thing, the islands are generally small in size; for another, fresh water is available only in very limited supply. Most of the plant and animal life on the Maldives originally came from the Indian subcontinent or Sri Lanka by way of the Laccadives to the islands of this atoll country. Later, human settlers introduced additional species.

The sparse landscapes of the Maldivian islands are home to about 600 different kinds of plants, of which approximately 260 grow wild. The others came with seafarers or were imported in recent years to beautify the tourist islands. Many of the indigenous plants are related to ones on Pacific Ocean islands 8,000 to 16,000 kilometers away. It is believed that seeds which were resistant to salt water were borne by the ocean's major currents to the Maldives and took root there. Some may also have come by "air mail," as it were, nestling in the feathers of migratory birds.

Geologically speaking, the Maldives are relatively young islands, and so far only five forms of domestic pandanus, or screw palm, have taken hold. They are immediately noticeable by virtue of their bizarre roots, which grow above ground, and their bright red fruit, the size of a child's head. The Maldivians used to weave the leaves into sails for their dhonis; today, they are mainly used for screens, mats and roof coverings.

For many tourists from colder climes, coconut palms (*Cocos nucifera*) are the

Right: Screw palms (pandanus) are easy to recognize from their bright red lumpy fruit, as big as a child's head.

quintessential symbol of tropical vegetation. They probably originated in Polynesia, where the trees, which can grow up to 30 meters high, have been used for more than 4,000 years. Salt evidently poses no problem for coconuts; it has been demonstrated that they can travel more than 4,500 kilometers in salt water and still germinate afterwards. The palm trees generally grow vertically and straight, their trunks maintaining even diameters from top to toe; the famous "photographers' palms," which grow virtually horizontally on some beaches, are an exception. Coconuts themselves, the trees' fruit, are very well packaged. Beneath the outer shell lies a layer of fiber known as bast, which envelops the hard shell and the kernel. The unripe white meat of the lining, known as endosperm, and the coconut milk provide nourishment as well as refreshment. The milk could even be used for transfusions, as it has the same isotonic electrolyte concentration as blood. Dried and grated, the meat of the kernel, called *copra*, is used as an ingredient to refine curries and salads. The sweet sap of the coconut blossom, known as *toddy*, is used to make palm wine, a beverage which enjoys something of a reputation all over the world. Nor does the rest of the plant get thrown away: boats are made out of the trees' trunks, the leaves are woven into various products, the shells become kitchen implements and containers, and if after all this there is anything left over, it is welcome fuel for the fire.

The breadfruit tree (*Artocarpus altilis*) is another useful cultivated plant. The species on the Maldives is a domesticated version of a type called *Artocarpus champeden* that grows wild in Malaysia. The trees can grow up to 30 meters tall and are usually to be found at humid locations in an island's interior, as they cannot tolerate salt water. They first bear fruit at the age of 5, after which they can continue to be harvested for another 70

years. Three times a year a tree produces as many as 50 ball-shaped bunches of fruit, around 20 to 30 centimeters in size. The fresh fruit is stewed to a pulp and eaten or roasted and processed into flour. As in the case of the coconut palm, the breadfruit tree trunk is used in boat-building, and the trunk fibers are useful for weaving and tying things up.

The betel or areca palm (*Areca catechu*) is best known for its nuts. Locals chew micro-thin slivers of these nuts, together with the leaves, which colors their saliva a vivid blood-red.

Mightiest tree on the Maldives is the nica or banyan (*Ficus benghalensis*), which too grows to about 30 meters in height. Its generous canopy of foliage can reach a diameter of up to 90 meters, which makes it popular as a source of shade. This tree is also known as the strangle fig because its roots, which are above ground, wind around and "strangle" other nearby trees.

On populated islands the inhabitants have cultivated other plants which are useful or decorative and provide shade. Among these are the magnificent, shining red flame tree (*Delonix regia*); the horseradish tree (*Moringa oleifera*); the Indian almond (*Terminalia catappa*) and the holy fig tree (*Ficus religiosa*), which is revered by both Buddhists and Hindus. If you are lucky you can even find a species of orchids called *Eulophia* in the undergrowth.

Arable soil on the Maldives is poor and represents less than 5% of the available land. It is used for cultivating several types of millet, such as Italian millet, black finger or sorghum. Although millet is very nutritious, it is regarded as poor people's food. Taro, yams and cassava (manioc or tapioca) are among the most widespread tubers and are particularly common on the southern islands. Maldivians like to plant paprikas, peppers and onions in their small gardens. Popular fruits are pineapples, bananas, watermelons and lemons. On the island of Fua Mulaku, in the south, there are even a few orange trees.

223

THE FAUNA OF MALDIVES

The islands of Maldives are not particularly rich in fauna. The creatures visitors will encounter most are hermit crabs doggedly making their way across the sand, dragging their houses behind them. These animals, which originated in the sea, would drown in water today: in the course of time they swapped their gills for lungs. Only the larvae still grow in the water. To lay her eggs, a female waits for the tide to go out and buries the eggs in the shallows that are covered at high water. When they're disturbed, these little 10-footers close their shells at lightning speed, using a pincer and one of their legs.

Of all animal lovers, it's bird-watchers who are likely to have the most fun on Maldives. At least 113 different species are known on the islands, and around 20 of them brood there. The other kinds stray there or are migratory visitors during the winters in the northern or southern hemispheres.

Of the local avian denizens of the islands, the most common, after the seagull, is the black-necked tern (*Sterna sumtrana methewsi*). This bird prefers open coastal regions, and lays its eggs on lonely cliff ledges. Snow-white fairy terns (*Gygis alba monte*) are most active in the early morning and late evening. Each pair produces a chick several times a year. The brooding habits of these delicate birds are particularly interesting. Rather than building nests, they carefully balance their single egg in the fork of a tree branch. For this reason, they prefer to brood on the southern islands, away from egg-stealing birds of prey such as the Indian raven (*Corvus splendens*) or its Maldivian cousin, a local kind of crow (*C. splendens maledivicus*). The northern

Right: Land hermit crabs need to find new accommodation every time they have a growth spurt.

atolls are home to the koel (*Eudynamis scolopacea*) a species of cuckoo, which of course lays its eggs in other birds' nests, preferably those of crows and ravens, which are roughly its own size. The koel seizes its opportunity while the other birds are off scavenging fruits or dried fish from human communities.

A bright green species of parrot called the small Alexander budgerigar (*Psittacula krameri*), is mainly found on Male, just like the imported house sparrow, which has yet to extend its territory beyond the lanes and alleys of the island capital.

When it's winter in the northern hemisphere, a lot of migratory birds come to Maldives: teal and garganeys; desert, Mongolian, and lapwing plovers, dwarf sandpipers, turnstones, river terns, snipes and curlews. A number of birds of prey also seek out these warmer southern climes: short-eared owls, Montagu's harriers, and kestrels. When it's winter in the southern hemisphere, on the other hand, a number of birds come north, inlcuding Wilson's stormy petrels, wedgetails and flash-footed sheerwaters.

Mammals are few and far between on Maldives. The Maldivian flying fox (*Pteropus giganteus ariel*) and its rarer cousin, *Pteropus hypomelanus maris*, rest hanging head-down from the shaded branches of evergreens during the day. In the early evening, these bat-like creatures emerge in impressively large swarms and search for sustenance.

The musk shrew (*Suncus murinus caerulescens*) was accidentally "imported" to Maldives on ships from Sri Lankan harbors. These useful creatures, which come out to hunt around twilight, wipe out cockroaches and other vermin. A threat to all types of agricultural products are the two types of rat that live on the islands, *Rattus rattus ceylonus* and *R. rattus kandidus*. Surprisingly, mice are relatively rare on Maldives; their numbers are presumably kept in check by the

rats and shrews. Sometimes, you can spot a wild rabbit, *Oryctolagus cuniculus*, descended from domestic animals that escaped long ago.

Nor is the range and number of amphibians and reptiles on Maldives particularly large. There is one species of toad, *Bufo melanosticus*, and one of frog (*Rana breviceps*). House geckos (*Hemidactylus frenatus*), on the other hand, are almost everywhere. These sweet little lizard-like creatures, approximately 10 centimeters long, often reside in hotel bungalows and catch mosquitoes, who swarm around any light which is on. You can also find the agama or bloodsucker lizard (*Calotes versicolor*) on almost all the islands. They get this rather misleading name from the red color their head assumes when they are aroused.

Snakes are as rare in Maldives as are scorpions and spiders. The so-called flowerpot snake (*Ramphotyphlops braminus*), a non-poisonous example of the species, with vestigial eyes, feeds mainly on soft-skinned insects. Rather more am-

bitious in its appetites, the cowled wolf snake (*Lycodon aulicus capuzinus*), preys on geckos. It, too, is non-poisonous.

A memorable but infrequent experience is an encounter with a sea turtle. Lumbering and clumsy on land, these creatures become speed demons in the water, swimming at speeds of up to 70 kilometers an hour. Five species come to the beaches of Maldives' islands to lay their eggs. Largest of these, the leatherback turtle (*Dermochelys coriacea*) can attain a flipper span of 2 meters and weigh as much as 865 kilos. Loggerhead turtles (*Caretta caretta*), who, like their larger cousins, eat meat, weigh in at up to 408 kilos. Their powerful jaws crack open mussels and snails. Most common turtles in Maldives are the hawksbill turtles (*Eretmochelys imbricata*). Sadly, their numbers have declined noticeably in recent years. Rarer turtles include the green turtle, a vegetarian; and the bastard turtle, *Lepidochelys olivacea*, some 60 centimeters in size.

TOURISM AND THE ENVIRONMENT

Tourism has been booming in the Maldives for the past 25 years. Ever-increasing numbers of people are coming to the islands to experience the incomparable beauty of their snow-white beaches and turquoise lagoons. In 1997 there were 365,000 tourists, far outnumbering the country's population, which numbers 263,000. What this means is that an average of 1,000 people arrive and leave every day, an increase of 7.9% over 1996. Most of the tourists come from Germany (22%), followed by Italy, Great Britain and Japan. At present, the 74 resort islands average 160 beds per facility. The Ministry of Tourism's new "master plan" involves increasing this number of beds by 10,000, to a total of 22,000, by 2004. As early as the end of 1999, 14 new resort islands are expected to open with 3,170 new beds.

Tourism on the Maldives was allowed to develop haphazardly and completely unchecked until President Gayoom instigated the first laws to regulate it in 1978. The following year saw Parliament's introduction of a "bed tax" which guests have to pay for every night they stay. In 1982, the Office of Tourism was created in order to bring some structure into the industry, which is an important source of foreign currency and now accounts for 20% of the gross national product. In 1988, the President gave this office the status of a ministry. The same year saw the creation of another new ministry, the Ministry of Planning and the Environment, which was established to analyze and deal with the unexpected problems that the rapid growth of tourism had brought. Apart from the omnipresent,

Right: More than 300,000 tourists a year can leave a lot of garbage. LTU encourages guests to collect their own garbage and turn it in when they check in for their return flight.

lowering threat of global warming caused by damage to the ozone layer, there are also the problems caused by continually increasing amounts of waste and rubbish. If the earth's atmosphere warms enough to raise the surface of the ocean by just a few centimeters as a result of global warming, the Maldives will disappear beneath the waves of the Indian Ocean. While the problem of CFCs and the dwindling ozone layer can only be tackled by means of global solutions, the more local task of effective waste disposal can at least be dealt with and regulated on a national level.

The Maldivians used to just get rid of their rubbish in the sea, which was perfectly acceptable, since their garbage consisted mainly of organic substances. The rise of tourism meant that not only was there more and more garbage, but that garbage was of new and different kinds. A drastic rise in non-organic products, such as cans, plastic containers and used batteries, placed a new burden on the fragile ecosystems of the ocean and the coral reefs. An environmental plan drawn up by the government in 1989 stipulated that all tourist islands should have waste compactors for tins and cans, so that these would at least sink. Since 1995, all hotel complexes have had to burn their waste in furnaces, although this solution is itself questionable from an ecological standpoint.

One thing that every visitor can do is to take all used plastic containers and used batteries back home with him; after all, it's the tourists who brought them in the first place, and they can generally be disposed of much more effectively in visitors' native countries than on the islands.

In 1993, the German airline LTU began a praiseworthy initiative when it started handing out "LTU eco-bags" to its passengers on flights to the Maldives. It is good to note that more than 70% of the tourists do hand over their collected garbage at the airport when they come

back for their return flights. Every year around 200 tons of refuse leaves the islands this way. The Swiss airline BA-LAIR runs a similar operation to help deal with the Maldives' garbage problem. In co-operation with the diving organization PADI, LTU has also been carrying out garbage collection operations in conjunction with island diving bases since 1994.

Things have also been changing with regard to the coral reefs, the Maldives' greatest attraction. The Ministry of the Environment has banned harpoons and any kind of anchoring at corals, and has also declared 15 diving zones as underwater conservation areas where fishing is prohibited. Nevertheless, large fishing fleets are a threat to the shark population, as shark-fin soup is a delicacy in some Asian countries. Shark-liver oil, which was once used as a protective coating for the dhonis, is nowadays sold for good money to the pharmaceutical and cosmetic industries. Tropical aquarium fish are also much in demand. Around 90% of

these timid fish, which are caught with the aid of poison that damages the reefs, die during transport. A further 70% of those who manage to survive then come to an unhappy end due to incorrect handling. Thus, it's really not a good idea to buy these colorful creatures, nor, indeed, to purchase any product that falls within the stipulations of the Washington Treaty on Endangered Species. The Maldivian government has banned the buying and selling of protected corals and tortoise-shell, but many stores and souvenir shops still offer stuffed or otherwise preserved sea creatures.

The environmental problems on the Maldives and, indeed, throughout the world can basically be attributed to human egotism and lack of understanding for habitats which have evolved naturally over millions of years. However, this kind of understanding will be necessary to protect the precious natural environment of this island world, and, indeed, nature around the globe, in the years ahead.

DIVING SAFARIS AND CRUISES

A so-called diving safari on board a large dhoni or cruise ship is one of the best ways to get to know the islands of Maldives. The number of operators who offer these exclusive tours through the atolls is steadily increasing: a sign that the demand continues to rise. The allure of seeking out isolated spots, sleeping out under the stars, or wandering on an uninhabited, truly "desert" island clearly exerts a powerful pull on many visitors. Furthermore, nothing can match the carefree pace of life on board a ship.

Most of the safaris pick up their passengers directly at the arrivals terminal of the airport on Hulhule or at Male's new harbor in the southwest of the island, and conclude at the sites from which they started. The capital's new harbor, built

Above: Moving from reef to reef is the special allure of a diving safari. Right: Back from Neptune's realm.

228

with Japanese financial aid, was finished in 1992; today, it offers protected anchorage to more than 100 ships, relieving the pressure on the old harbor.

Many of the larger safari dhonis have beautifully decorated bowsprits and carvings on the stern. They lie moored cheek by jowl at the new concrete landing stage. When the tourists show up, the atmosphere of peace and quiet that has surrounded the ships disappears, replaced by a commotion of activity. Compressors, aqualungs and luggage are loaded on board from the transport pick-up trucks, while water and fuel are pumped into the ships from barrels.

At other times, when there aren't any tourists around, work at the harbor is generally carried out in the early morning hours, when the temperatures are more pleasant. Unusual sounds rise into the air, and a passing stroller can see remarkable things. A workman makes his rudder fast to his ship with a robe of coconut fiber; at another pier, someone is taking the motor out of his dhoni, attracting a buzzing crowd of onlookers. In the morning sun, the shadows of large wooden ships from India envelop smaller vessels, while workers hammer, drill, and stain wood. Wooden masts thrust up into the sky, and the faint movement of the ships' anchor ropes creates ever-changing patterns on the surface of the harbor's water, smooth as a mirror, over which the dhonis glide with swan-like ease. Despite all the activity there is a kind of calm in the air, a peaceful, relaxed atmosphere that's typical of Maldives. In their free time, the crews of fishing dhonis play cards, while tourists sip fresh tea on the front decks of their safari boats and wait for their departure. Most safari passengers have a chance to absorb this kind of local color until, filled with these exotic, unfamiliar and yet enchanting impressions, they set off in their boats for their various destinations in the fascinating world of the Maldivian atolls.

Most of the diving safaris follow either a northern or a southern route, which, depending on the length of time (cruises generally last between 4 and 10 days), include the Ari Atoll in the west and the Rasdhoo Atoll. Although the routes are usually charted out in advance, tour guides are often ready to change them in accordance with visitors' wishes.

The classic north route first takes in the North Male Atoll and its best-known diving sites in the inner atoll and along the outer reef. Of these, the areas officially designated as underwater conservation areas are the most interesting: these include Hans Hass Place, Lion's Head and Kuda Haa in the south, or HP reef and Banana Reef in the southeast of the atoll. Along the atoll's western outer reef there are breathtaking coral landscapes, such as Rasfari or the passages in the Makunudhoo Kandu channel.

North of the atoll is a particular treat for divers in the form of Maldives' biggest single reef, Gaafaru Falhu, with its four well-known wrecks. In the Faadhipholu Atoll, further to the north, there is also a small "ships' graveyard" and a unique underwater park at Fushifaru Thila. If time allows, safari boats run up to the South Maalhosmadulu Atoll, which lies in the northwest; this atoll has countless reefs which have yet to be explored by divers. Alternately, the ship can also make for the northern Ari and Rasdhoo Atolls. Located here are the world-famous reefs Maaya Thila and Fish Head, where you can more or less count on seeing sharks, as well as the dive site of Orimas Thila, famous for its variety of species. In addition, there are three "wrecks," actually deliberately sunken ships, off the islands of Fesdhoo, Halaveli and Ellaidhoo respectively. At the Halaveli wreck, divers can observe tame sting rays at close range.

Cruises along the southern route also include, whether at the beginning or the end of the trip, the best-known dive sites at the southern end of the North Male Atoll. In addition, the wreck that must count as the best-known in Maldives, the

Maldive Victory, awaits divers in the Vaadhoo Channel. It stands upright on the sea bed at a depth of between 15 and 40 meters. After this, the journey goes on to the South Male Atoll, where divers can take the world-famous "Emboodhoo Express," as the Emboodhoo Channel is known thanks to its strong currents. To the southeast, near the island of Guraidhoo, there are more wonderful places for diving, which are particularly notable for the beauty of their landscapes of soft coral. After these highlights, safari ships take a number of different routes. Some boats steer to the Felidhoo Atoll, down to the reef of Vattaru Falhu, and then go on to the Maluku Atoll, where to date relatively few divers have explored the unspoilt beauties of the world under water. Others head westwards to the southern part of the Ari Atoll. In the southeast of this atoll, there's magnificent diving at

the Dhigura Arches and, nearby, at the "wreck" *Rand 11*, sunken deliberately, and such other sites as Kudarah Thila, Broken Rock, Lucky Hell or at Vila-mendhoo Thila. In the southern part of the atoll, near Holiday Island, divers often encounter whale sharks and mantas, who pass throughout The Madivaru dive site in the southwest is famous as "Manta Point."

Other cruises restrict themselves to the Ari Atoll, which alone has more than enough fantastic dive sites for any diver. Divers can combine various safari routes and packages with sojourns on a single resort island.

These days, divers have also begun to seek out the remote and seemingly completely deserted locations in the Haa-Alifu Atoll, only recently opened to tourism. All the other atolls not mentioned here, except the Addhoo Atoll, are still closed to tourists. However, it is likely that they too will be opened up, providing divers with a whole new range of sights and discoveries.

Above: In the morning, the day's dive is planned out over breakfast.

SAFARI BOATS

The number of boats in service is increasing all the time. Travel agencies and tourist offices can give information as to current routes and trip dates. *ATOLL EXPLORER*, motor yacht, 20 cabins, 8 with balcony, air conditioning. Diving base: Eurodivers. Operator: Universal Enterprises, Male, fax 322678, E-Mail: sales@unisurf.com. *ALI PASHAH*, motor dhoni, 19 m, 3 cabins, diving dhoni. Operator: S. Beyer, D-74177 Bad Friedrichshall, fax +49 7136 23051, E-Mail: stopover@malediven.de. *ARK*, sailing dhoni, 19 m, 5 cabins, air conditioning, diving dhoni. *BAARA BARU*, motor dhoni, 18 m, 2 double and 3 triple cabins, diving dhoni. *BARUTHEELA*, historic motor-sailer, 25 m, 6 double cabins, air conditioning. Operator: Nino Holm, A-Graz, fax +43 316 810149, E-Mail: holmaustria@ styria.com. *BLUE DOLPHIN*, motor yacht, 24 m, 5 cabins, equipment dhoni. *BLUE SHARK*, motor yacht, 26 m, 9 double cabins, air conditioning, equipment dhoni. *BODUMAHURA*, 21 m, 6 double cabins. Operator: Cross World Maldives, Male, tel. 320884. *CASSIOPAIA*, motor yacht, 22 m, 7 double cabins, equipment dhoni. *CORAL PRINCESS*, motor yacht, 41 m, 6 suites, 12 double cabins, air conditioning, each cabin with private bath, diving dhoni, nitrox. Operator: Sea Island Cruises Maldives, fax 323463, E-Mail: halaveli@ dhivehinet.net.mv. *FI-EYRA*, 22 m, 4 double cabins, 1 four-man cabin. *FLY-ING FISH*, motor-sailer, 27 m, 10 cabins, equipment dhoni. *GAHAA*, yacht dhoni, 18 m, 6 double cabins, equipment dhoni. Operator: Voyages Maldives, Male, fax 325336. *GET WET 1*, motor yacht, 31 m, 8 double cabins, diving dhoni. Operator: D-Get Wet Adventure, fax +49 6227 891136. *GOMA*, sailing yacht, 22 m, 3 double cabins, air conditioning. Operator: Champa Brothers, Male, fax 314150. *GOMAFULHU*, motor-sailer, 23 m, 6 double cabins, air conditioning, diving dhoni. Operator: Champa Brothers, Male, fax 314150. *GREEN PEACE*, yacht dhoni, 16 m, 8 beds in a common cabin. Operator: Voyages Maldives, Male, fax 322019. *GULFAAM*, yacht dhoni, 19 m, 6 double cabins. Operator: Voyages Maldives, Male, fax 325336. *HAGERN*, sailing yacht, 25 m, 4 double cabins. Operator: Champa Brothers, Male, fax 314150. *HAMMERHEAD I.*, motor yacht, 24 m, 7 double cabins, diving dhoni. *HAMMERHEAD II.*, motor yacht, 27 m, 7 double cabins, diving dhoni. *HA-VEYLI*, motor yacht, 30 m, 11 double cabins, diving dhoni. *IRUVAI*, sailing yacht, 19 m, 4 double cabins. Operator: GSA South Asian Charter, Belgium, fax +32 3 2329887, E-Mail: info@sacharter.com. *ISLAND EX-PLORER*, motor yacht, 84 m, 4 suites, 14 deluxe cabins facing in, 56 facing out, air conditioning, pool, 2 sun decks, dive base: Eurodivers, diving dhoni. Operator: Universal Enterprises, Male, fax 322678, E-Mail: sales@unisurf.com. *JAARIA*, motor-sailing yacht, 32

m, 10 double cabins, air conditioning, diving dhoni. *KAMANA*, two-masted wooden sailboat, 28 m, 6 double cabins, air conditioning, equipment dhoni. *KETHI*, yacht dhoni, 20 m, 6 double cabins, air conditioning, equipment dhoni. Operator: Voyages Maldives, Male, fax 325336. *KOIMALA*, yacht dhoni, 23 m, 2 suites, 5 double cabins, equipment dhoni. Operator: Voyages Maldives, Male, fax 325336. *MAN-THIRI*, motor yacht, 24 m, 6 double cabins, air conditioning, diving dhoni. *MOONIMA*, motor yacht, 26 m, 6 double cabins, 2 triple cabins, diving dhoni. *MUNA*, sailing yacht, 23 m, 5 double cabins. Operator: Champa Brothers, Male, fax 314150. *NASRUALI*, motor dhoni, 23 m, 6 double cabins, no accompanying dhoni. Operator: Fun Dive Malediven, D-82377 Penzberg, fax +49 8856 932979, E-Mail: info@fun-dive.com. *NASRUMANU*, motor dhoni, 25 m, 4 double cabins, air conditioning, diving dhoni. Operator: Fun Dive Malediven, E-Mail: info@fundive.com. *NASRUVELI*, motor dhoni, 20 m, 6 double cabins. Operator: Fun Dive Malediven, D-82377 Penzberg, fax +49 8856 932979, E-Mail: info@fundive.com. *NIRU*, yacht dhoni, 17 m, 2 double cabins, 1 four-man cabin, D-Tauchsport Hans Hein, tel. +49 89 74793311. *OCEAN PARADISE*, motor yacht, 74 m, 1 honeymoon suite, 12 superior and 28 standard cabins with A/C, diving dhoni. Operator: Travelin Maldives, Male, fax 314977, E-Mail: travelin@ netlink.net.mv. *OCEAN SAFARI*, motor-sailer, 30 m, 10 double cabins, air conditioning, diving dhoni. Operator: Travelin Maldives, Male, fax 314977, E-Mail: travelin@ netlink.net.mv. *ORCA*, motor yacht, 24 m, 9 double cabins. *PANORAMA*, motor-sailer, 17 m, 4 double cabins, diving dhoni. *POLLUX*, motor yacht, 50 m, 8 outer cabins with fresh-air fans, 2 inner cabins with air conditioning, 2 diving dhonis. *RANI*, motor-boat, 24 m, 6 double cabins, diving dhoni. *SARAH 1*, motor yacht, 24 m, 6 double cabins. Operator: Champa Brothers, Male, fax 314150. *SEA CORAL*, yacht dhoni, 18 m, 6 double cabins, equipment dhoni. Operator: Voyages Maldives, Male, fax: 325336. *SEA-FARER*, yacht dhoni, 17 m, 4 double cabins, Voyages Maldives, Male, fax 325336. *SEA PLEASURE*, yacht dhoni, 17 m, 4 double cabins, diving dhoni. Operator: Sea Pleasure, Male, fax 316783, E-Mail: seaexplo@dhivehinet.net.mv. *SEA RANGER*, yacht dhoni, 15 m, 3 double cabins. Operator: Voyages Maldives, Male, fax 325 336. *SPICE ISLANDER*, motor yacht, 37 m, 21 double cabins. Operator: Worldlink, Male, tel. 316516. *SUWASA*, motor yacht, 16 m, 2 four-man, 2 double cabins. Operator: Crossworld Maldives, tel. 320884. *TRITON*, yacht dhoni, 21 m, 5 double cabins, diving dhoni. Operator: D-Blue Fin Cruises, tel. +49 8036 2395. *VAAREDHUNI*, motor dhoni, 21 m, 5 doubles, diving dhoni. Operator: AKIRI Sub Aqua Maldives, tel. 320856, fax 316272, e-mail: holidays@dhivehinet.net.mv

SHIPBUILDING ON MALDIVES

Since the islands of Maldives were first settled, the lives of their inhabitants have been inextricably bound up with the sea and with their boats. Through centuries of experience, tradition, and the skilful mastery of relatively simple techniques evolved the vessel that's characteristic of the Maldives' islands: the dhoni. Large or small, all dhonis are constructed according to the same principles. They are extremely manoeuvrable, which is exactly what is required in the narrow reef passages in the atolls. In the past, dhonis not only performed an essential service in transporting the fishing catch, they also played a significant role in uniting all the Maldivian atolls into a single

Above: For centuries, sailing dhonis have ensured contact between the atolls. Right: A dhoni's shallow draft enables the vessel to pass over the coral reefs (traditional boatyard on Maalhoss).

state. By establishing and maintaining contact between the various atolls and their countless islands, the boats helped the communities slowly to develop into a single society. They facilated trading and, over the centuries, contact with other peoples and cultures.

The dhoni's origins reach far back into past history. The vessel is probably a specifically Maldivian variation on the Arab dhow, developed and adapted to local conditions. Long ago, the dhow dominated the waters from Persia and the Arab Peninsula to East Africa and Asia. A connection can even be seen in the word "dhoni," which is closely related to "dhow." Although some modern dhonis have departed fairly decisively from the original pattern, the traditional models continue to dominate in the harbors of Maldives, as they have for hundreds of years.

The original dhoni, called the *mas dhoni*, was initially created and further developed by Maldivian fishermen. The simplest form of dhoni was used for fish-

ing and made sailing through the island world of Maldives both easy and effective. These earliest dhonis consisted mainly of planks bound together, a construction technique found in the Indian and Arab worlds, as well as in other regions, in centuries gone by; in fact, it is still in use in some areas. Later, more stable wooden plugs and copper nails replaced ropes and cord as a means of keeping the planks together. Dhonis, robust little open ships, have a shallow draft, which is a great advantage in navigating the region's tricky coral reefs, some of which reach to just below the water's surface. Under sail, the boats can attain speeds of six to seven knots, enabling them to cover great distances, something demonstrated by Maldives' longstanding trade links with India, Sri Lanka, Sumatra and other distant countries. When seas are rough and the waves are high, the excellent manoeuvrability of these boats is an added advantage.

Maldivian boatbuilders generally use the wood of the coconut palm for the ribs and lower hull of their dhonis, as this material is easily available and, furthermore, has proven to be extremely durable in tropical waters. Another additional advantage of this type of wood is that it's heavier than other kinds of wood, which confers better stability upon the boat. The planks are usually made of wood from the inner core of the lower part of the trunk, which is especially hard. Experienced shipbuilders on the islands can tell just by looking at a tree trunk which sections are hard enough to serve for boatbuilding.

On the boat's upper deck there are two particularly light and especially buoyant beams, which serve to right the ship if it capsizes; after that, the water can be bailed out, and the ship goes on its way. Rising high above the rest of the vessel, the bowsprit is purely decorative, and its upper part can even be removed. The boat tapers toward the stern, culminating in the aft stem, which holds the rudder in place; this form is part of the reason that this ship is such an excellent sailing

233

vessel. The dhoni's hull is varnished with fish oil, preferably shark oil, which boths facilitates launching of the vessel and preserves the wood once it's in the water, as well as cutting down on the dhoni's resistance as it glides through the water. In recent years, builders have begun sheathing dhonis with a thin layer of copper plating, which is supposed to prevent damage from the woodworms which are so prevalent in tropical climes.

The men who build dhonis are boatbuilders with many years' experience; there are not many of these people left. They hardly use any tools in the boat's construction, much less any blueprints. They are protective of their skills and knowledge, a store of wisdom that's passed on by word of mouth from generation to generation. In the language of Maldives, the word for such boatbuilders is *kissaru vadin*, which

Above: A family with its own dhonis is proud of its possession. Right: A souvenir created with a loving eye to detail.

234

means something along the lines of "carpenter who can build shaped things." The *kissaru vadin* are well-paid specialists, and figures of high regard in their communities.

As a rule, dhonis, which are usually around 12 to 14 meters long and 4 meters wide, are assembled in a simple open-air "boatyard" under the palms, near the beach. The entire process from beginning to launch, when the workers join forces to drag the finished boat across the beach to the waters of the lagoon, takes a mere two to three months. Only the simplest tools are employed in the dhoni's construction. The *kissaru vadin* use only wooden mallets and two-hand hammers, an adze for stripping bark, planes, chisels, axes, and a hand drill operated by means of a cord. The dhonis which modern tourists see and use have evolved from the original *mas dhoni*.

In addition to the basic form of dhoni, there are other variants which differ in size and sail. One type is the *baththeli*, which also used to move under sail, and

is larger than the traditional dhoni. These vessels have small removable hut-like constructions on board, and the sail is supplemented by a second, central fore-sail; they also lack the stern platform typical of other dhonis. These boats were once used for transport between atolls. Two other variations on the dhoni theme are *baggalas* and *odis*. These have the same rigging as the *baththeli*, but are larger, and their "hut" sits aft and is a permanent part of the boat. Before the advent of motors, *baggalas* were frequently used as cargo boats to ferry goods to the Indian subcontinent. They were also once employed as "passenger ships" for pilgrims on the way to Mecca. *Odis* are rare nowadays; in fact, they're no longer seen at all as pure sailing boats.

The late 1960s saw the rise of the maschine, and boats with light diesel motors became increasingly widespread. This development necessitated a few alterations in a dhoni's basic design. Furthermore, as dhonis were used more often to transport tourists or to ferry scuba divers from reef to reef, the ships, which had thereto been open, started to sport built-in upper decks with awnings as protection against the sun.

From the mid-1980s on, improved technical knowledge resulted in the construction of modified, shallower boats, which are easier to load and unload. At first, Maldivians tended to regard these new vessels with amusement; however, more and more dhonis today are being built along these modern lines. Nowadays dhoni hulls are often made of fiberglass, which makes construction of the boats easier and cheaper; it also means the boats can carry more cargo while using less fuel.

Tourism is one factor that will help determine whether the old boatbuilding skills and traditions in Maldives slowly die out in the face of modern technology and methods. Even today, a breath of sweet nostalgia wafts from every traditional *mas dhoni* that glides silently through the waves of the Maldives archipelago.

THE SPIRIT WORLD OF
MALDIVES

While the presence of satellite TV and the Internet may indicate that Maldives is no stranger to global communications and technological advancement, many older Maldivians have retained the superstitions and rites of older, occult traditions. Supernatural powers, palmistry, alchemy, astrology, magic and spirits continue to play a significant role on the atolls' more isolated islands. Many superstitions are deeply rooted in long-distant local history and tradition. A close empathy with nature, as well as religious influences from Hinduism and Buddhism, are as decisive to peoples' beliefs and actions as are the teachings of the ubiquitous Islam.

Maldivians believe that there are two worlds. One of these is the world of human beings, who originally came from the water. The other world belongs to the so-called *jinnis*, or spirits, which were created out of fire. Just as there are good and bad people in the material world of the senses, so too are there good and bad characters in the spirit world. The archipelago's inhabitants are convinced that *jinnis* don't simply stay in their own world but also exist in our material one, flitting around and influencing the lives of mortals for good and ill. Maldivians also believe that the spirits both outnumber humans and are far superior to them in intelligence. Unconsidered human actions can disturb the *jinnis* in their daily lives or even incur their wrath. For this reason, Maldivians in the past never threw anything away or spit on the ground without first warning any *jinni* who might have been in the area by uttering the words *Gaikolka gaigaa dhuru*, a sentence that translates "may this (object)

Right: Fanditha – healing through the spirit world and mysterious, if natural, substances.

not hit any being of high esteem." You can still hear this phrase spoken today, sometimes, too, at night, in which case it is called out particularly loudly. *Jinnis* normally remain invisible to the human eye, but they sometimes assume a shape that makes them visible to mortals. Since they are not bound to the laws of space and time, they can, with the wink of an eye, suddenly vanish and travel over colossal distances. They can conjure up past events, or bring future ones to life. In fact, *jinnis* can do just about anything conceivable. They reward positive thinking, and punish those who harbor negative attitudes. *Jinnis* are not spirits in the Christian sense, however; Maldivians in no way associate them with the souls of the dead.

Budhevi, the ruler of all the spirits, is omnipresent. A bringer of ill-fortune, he prefers to materialize after rainshowers, generally taking the form of a cat or an exceptionally strong man. *Vigani*, the spirit of death, lives in the sea and can appear on the water or on the horizon. With his elephantine trunk, he is said to drink the blood of the dead out of their graves at night. *Odivaru ressi*, the evil spirit of the fishermen, threatens fishermen in their boats.

Omens, both good and bad, are regarded as being of great significance in Maldivian society. Seeing a snake in the garden, for example, an occasional if infrequent event, augurs health and good fortune. White spots under one's fingernails are a sign that something bad is brewing. If a man's right eyelid twitches, it is a good omen; if his left one does, it's a very bad sign. With women, such twitching is read the other way round. A total of 189 of these traditional superstitions and omens have been recorded.

Another interesting aspect of Maldivian superstition is the belief in the evil powers of a so-called *ravaabeenaa*, a person who can bring ill-fortune down upon others with his or her wicked

tongue. Promises made by such people negate themselves immediately. If a *ravaabeenaa* says that a house is particularly well-built, for example, you can rest assured that the edifice will soon collapse. If somebody acquires the reputation of being a *ravaabeenaa*, others will do everything they can to avoid speaking to him or her. Mothers try to protect their children from *ravaabeenaas* and pregnant women get out of the way as soon as they spot one. One reported case was that of a *ravaabeenaa* man called Dhon Maniku, who lived in Male in the 1930s and 40s and supposedly drove many people to their deaths with his ostensibly friendly manner. To this day, *ravaabeenaas* are often held responsible for inexplicable illnesses among children.

Another form of superstition, or simply of traditional beliefs, is the form of occult medical teaching called *fanditha*, which combines elements of animism and exorcism with knowledge of natural homeopathic and herbal remedies. The widespread confidence in and respect for *fanditha* medicine men and women is even reflected in the charter of the country's regional health authorities, which issue *fandithas* with official licenses to practice their form of medicine. These traditional healers offer not only relief of headache, setting of broken bones, and the like, but can also successfully treat heartache and lovesickness, no mean feat.

In their practices the *fanditha* healers often have recourse to a mysterious spirit medium, through which they can contact the *jinnis*. In the past, the healers had no need for such mediums, as it went without saying that they were naturally endowed with the necessary supernatural abilities themselves. Today, *jinnis* may be summoned directly when necessary, invoked with the aid of trance-like, hypnotic singing. As the *fandithas* are also in contact with the stars, they practice astrology, and also carry out exorcisms.

Knowledge of occult practices recorded in old Arabic documents has survived to this day.

AMBERGRIS: THE FLOATING GOLD OF THE MALDIVES

Ambergris (from the Arabic *anbar*) is a waxy gray-black substance that's actually an excretion from the intestines of the sperm whale. It is believed to be a by-product of the remains of deep-sea giant squid, difficult to digest, but which are among the whales' favorite prey. However, it may also form in the disgestive tract as a result of illness. Once the whale has excreted it, it rises to the surface and floats on the water or is washed up on coasts. People may occasionally happen upon it in these places; nevertheless, whaling remains the main source of ambergris.

This valuable product of ocean life at first smells unpleasant, but then later takes on a pleasant, sweetish fragrance. The oxidation process of a triterpene alcohol, called ambrein, contained within this organic substance creates chemical bonds; their pleasant aromatic qualities are processed in alcohol solutions and later used in the manufacture of perfume.

Arab seafarers were already acquainted with the substance as early as the 9th century. They found it mostly in Maldivian waters and on the beaches of the islands. Suleiman described the plesant fragrance of ambergris, but was unable to explain its origin. He believed that large plants of it grew on the floor of the ocean. When they died, he hypothesized, they floated up to the surface, and the sea then cast large lumps of ambergris up on the beaches.

In the 10th century, Chinese writers gave a picturesque description of ambergris as the "spittle of dragons." They obtained it mainly from the "Mountains of Liu," which was their designation for Maldives at that time. In a fable, a Chinese scholar named Sheng Tseng wrote that many dragons dwelt among the rock faces of the Mountains of Liu, and spit up their saliva every spring. From this substance, at first truly disgusting, liquids could later be created which put people, as it were, in a better odor.

A Portuguese soldier named Barbosa, who was stationed on Maldives between 1501 and 1517, writes that he asked Arab merchants about the origin of this puzzling and precious substance. The Moors, as the seafarers and traders from Arab countries were known at the time, believed that ambergris consisted of bird droppings from the remote, uninhabited islands of the Maldivian archipelago. Their theory was that birds sitting on cliffs and rocks in the sea excreted it. Softened by sun, wind and rain, it was then loosened from the rocks in the ocean storms, and washed into the sea. There, lumps of it floated until they were netted or washed up on beaches.

Even before 1501, however, an anonymous but more realistic Portuguese writer had already recognized the true story. He reported that dead whales were often stranded on the beaches of the Dyve islands, as the Maldives were then called. The local inhabitants cut up these animals in order to extract oil from their meat. Some of the whales had lumps of ambergris, shaped like pine cones and of varying sizes, within their huge bodies. Usually there were between 20 and 40 of them, but sometimes the natives found as many as 200, clumped together in sticky masses. However, the author wrote, all such finds had to be handed over to the Sultan, in return for a reward; failure to do so could mean the death penalty. In those days, noble aromas were exclusively for noble bodies.

Right: Sperm whales egest a waxy mass from their intestinal tract – ambergris is then used in the perfume industry.

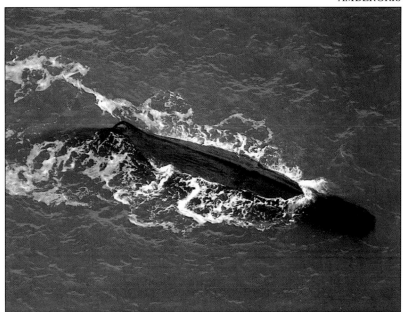

In a document by the English navigator John Davies, the author writes that in 1599 he was received by a "gentleman and his wife" in Male, the Maldivian capital. The lady's basket was filled with jewels and several roundish pieces of ambergris exuded a pleasant aroma. The man wore loose Turkish-style clothes and precious jeweled rings sparkled on his fingers. From this description of his wealth, we may suppose that the "gentleman" the English navigator encountered was none other than Sultan Ibrahim III himself.

In 1754, the Maldivians were even able to buy part of their independence with this precious substance. As a reward for defeating a fleet of Malabar pirate, who were, at that time, the scourge of the islands, they ceremoniously and gratefully presented the French with a piece of ambergris that weighed in at no less than 152.8 kilos.

In Europe, ambergris was known to the Spanish Moors. In the Middle Ages, it was used as an aphrodisiac and for medical purposes, in particular as a disinfectant and a protection against epidemics. The first detailed German description of ambergris appeared in 1673.

Anyone who wants to retrieve floating ambergris from the water has to act quickly and deftly. You have to grasp the precious lump firmly on the first attempt. If you accidentally touch the floating lump before you've got a hold on it, it will immediately sink to the floor of the ocean and remain there for several days before resurfacing.

In 1980, a massive lump weighing 214 kilos landed on one of the Maldives' islands. In March, 1995, local fishermen pulled up 187 kilos off the island of Kelaa in the North Thiladhunmathee Atoll. Ambergris finds, which have been known to weigh as much as 400 kilos, often mean sudden wealth for the lucky finder. A single gram can cost around $2.50. The government of Maldives saddles exporters of ambergris with an export tax of 100% on the precious substance.

METRIC CONVERSION

Metric Unit	US Equivalent
Meter (m)	39.37 in.
Kilometer (km)	0.6241 mi.
Square Meter (sq m)	10.76 sq. ft.
Hectare (ha)	2.471 acres
Square Kilometer (sq km)	0.386 sq. mi.
Kilogram (kg)	2.2 lbs.
Liter (l)	1.05 qt.

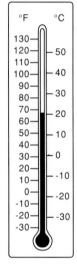

PREPARING FOR YOUR TRIP

Climate

As it is throughout Southeast Asia, Maldives' climate is largely determined by the monsoon winds. In summer (April to October), these blow from the southwest with gentle or moderate force; in winter (December to March), they come from the northeast. Storms are generally a rare occurrence. Rainfall is more common at night than by day, and comes in short, powerful showers; longer periods of rain are, fortunately for visitors, an exception rather than the rule. The average number of rainy days a month between May and December is 16; from January to April, only 7. Temperatures tend to remain at a summery 30°C all year round, falling only slightly at night, to around 26 °C. By day, the sun shines for 7 to 9 hours on Maldives; even on cloudy days, its rays are particularly intense thanks to the region's proximity to the Equator, and there's always a danger of sunburn. Water temperatures are generally between 27°C and 30°C.

When to Go

Because the Maldivian climate is basically the same all year round, thanks to the Equator, there's no real "season" on the islands; you can visit these archipelagos any time. More European tourists, of course, seek out tropical climes during the winter months in their homelands, so the Maldivians call the period between November and March "high season," and prices are correspondingly higher. Statistically speaking, the lowest rainfall is between January and March.

What to Pack / Diving Equipment

Light, airy summer clothing is perfectly adequate for a stay on Maldives, and is even appropriate in hotel bars and restaurants. Bathing suits are required on the beach: topless and nude sunbathing are prohibited. It's also wise to wear some form of head covering and sunglasses as protection against the strong rays. In the lagoon, thongs or plastic shoes are a good precaution against cuts from sharp pieces of coral. Even men should avoid baring their upper bodies. When visting one of the inhabited islands, respect local religious strictures by wearing clothing that reaches the knee and covers the shoulders. Low-cut or see-through garments on women are taboo, as are body-hugging clothes that emphasize the contours of the female form. These guidelines also apply to dressing on Male, especially for anyone planning to visit the Islamic Center.

If you have room in your suitcase, it's a good idea to bring along your own diving or snorkeling equipment. Try to bring at least the ABC gear of fins, snorkel, and a diving mask: this is not only a guarantee that the gear will fit, but also saves you the costs of renting it out (US$5-7 a day for the three basic pieces of gear).

Traveling In and Out of the Country

All foreign visitors with valid passports are issued a 30-day visa when they arrive in Maldives, as long as the passport is valid for at least six months past the date of the holder's return ticket. Visas from Israel pose no problem, and there are no restrictions on Israeli citizens entering the country. You can extend your visa for up to 90 days, but only on Maldives, at the Department of Immigration in Male, Huravee Building, Ameeru Ahmed Magu, tel. 328358, and you'll need $30 and two passport photos. Foreigners who work on Maldives can get special visas for longer stays. If you want to explore the atoll world on your own, you'll need a special permit from the Ministry of Atoll Administration in Male, Faashanaa Building, Marine Drive, tel. 322826 and 323070. This permit, however, is only awarded to those staying in the country for purposes of journalistic or scientific research. Individual travelers who aren't here for specific research purposes will need a written invitation from a local "sponsor." As this sponsor acknowledges complete responsibility for his guest, and guarantees to see to his accommodation and board, it's rather difficult to find such sponsors, and it takes a lot of time and energy to get a permit for this kind of trip. Setting out to travel on your own through Maldives is therefore not such a great idea. Some resort islands offer guests the chance to visit a "desert island" or deserted island for a day. To do this, the hotel management needs a permit itself, as uninhabited islands are generally privately owned.

Children have to be entered in their parents' passports. If they're more than 6 years old, they need their own children's passport, complete with a picture.

Arriving visitors are stringently checked for alcohol, pork and pork products, and pornographic materials (see "Customs"). Any visitors arriving by boat have to come directly to Male, rather than stopping off at the outer atolls. There, the port authorities can carry out port clearance and inform travelers of any other necessary entry formalities.

Tourists leaving the country from the airport at Hulhule are subjected to a thorough baggage search. Taking out any souvenirs that are prohibited by the Washington Endangered Species Protection Agreement is punishable by fine: this includes products from the ocean, even in processed or handcrafted form, such as coral, shells, or tortoiseshell.

Return tickets have to be confirmed 72 to 48 hours before the flight. In general, the tour organizers will place this call for their group. It's a good idea to get to the airport some 2 to 3 hours early, as there are usually long lines at the check-in counters. There's an airport tax of $10, which is only payable in American dollars. Some airlines include this in the price of a ticket.

Airlines in Male – Information and Confirmation: Air Lanka, tel. 323459, **Air Maldives**, tel. 322438, **Condor**, tel. 323612, **Emirates**, tel. 314945, **Airport Information**, tel. 322211, 322073.

Money

Maldives's currency is the Maldivian rupee (Rufiyaa, Rf). One rufiyaa is subdivided into 100 laaris; there are 1, 5, 10, 25 and 50-laari coins, as well as coins of 1 rufiyaa. Banknotes come in denominations of 2, 5, 10, 20, 50, 100 and 500 rufiyaa. The exchange rate in mid-1998: Great Britain: £ 1 = Rf 19.93; USA: US$ 1 = Rf 11.97; Switzerland: SFR 1 = Rf 7.84; the Netherlands: HFL 1 = Rf 5.86.

American dollars are accepted currency throughout the country, and the resort islands also take travelers' checks, credit cards, and several other currencies. Exchanging money for rufiyaas when you enter the country is therefore not strictly necessary. Visitors will only need local currency on the native islands, and even there you can often pay with American dollars. The hotel staff is always happy for a few dollar bills (see "Tipping").

Banks in Male are open Sun-Thu 9:00 am-1:30 pm, Sat 9:00-11:00 am, closed Fridays. There's a currency exchange office at the airport. You don't need any cash on the resort islands; everything is put on the bill, which is then calculated the night before you leave.

There's no limit on the import and export of rufiyaas and other currency.

Health Precautions

Although there have been no reported cases of malaria on Maldives in recent years, according to information from the Maldivian Ministry of Health, it's still a good idea to consult with a tropical disease specialist about malaria prevention before you go. These specialists can also provide information about inoculations against typhus and hepatitis A and B. Everyone should have adequate protection against polio and tetanus in any case (even if he or she isn't traveling to Maldives!). Yellow fever and cholera shots are required if you're traveling in from somewhere where these diseases have recently appeared.

You can reduce the danger of being stung by mosquitos, which sometimes carry malaria, by wearing light-colored clothing, using mosquito netting, and applying insect repellent (your pharmacist can advise you before you go). Too, it's a good idea to bring disinfectant, as a scratched mosquito bite can easily get infected and heals slowly in the tropics. Therefore, cuts and scratches, too, should always be disinfected. When putting together your traveling medicine cabinet,

make sure to include something against diarrhea. Make sure you only eat peeled fruit, and avoid drinks that are too cold, ice cubes, and ice cream. Don't use water from the tap or shower to brush your teeth, but use water from the containers that are always left in hotel rooms.

It's essential to bring adequate protection against the strong rays of the sun. Headgear of some kind helps guard against sunstroke, and good sunglasses will protect your eyes. You'll need sun lotion with a high SPF to prevent sunburn. People burn most easily in the water, especially when snorkeling, so make sure the sun lotion you bring is waterproof.

One common ailment is a viral infection known as "Maldives fever," which can suddenly descend upon a person, bringing fevers of 40°C and aching limbs. If you take fever medicine, however, it goes away again after a couple of days. Contact with ocean water often causes unpleasant ear infections in divers. Diving teachers usually have a supply of the most effective treatments on hand.

If you're bringing any antibiotics with you, you should note that tetracycline preparations can lose their efficacy if exposed to too much sun.

Medical Insurance

It's a good idea to get some kind of travel medical insurance before you leave on your trip. Any tour organizer can advise you on the best kind. As most health insurance doesn't cover diving accidents, decompression chamber treatments, helicopter transport or emergency flights home, divers should probably take out insurance with DAN (*Divers Alert Network*).

DAN's European headquarters are based in Italy: **DAN Europe Headquarters**, PO Box DAN, I-64026 Roseto (TE), tel. (085) 8930333, fax (085) 8930050, E-Mail: mail@daneurope.org.

TRAVELING TO MALDIVES

International Flights

All international flights land at the Male International Airport, 2 kilometers from the capital on the airport island of Hulhule. The flight from Frankfurt to Male takes about 9 or 10 hours. From the United States, Singapore Airlines and Malaysian Airlines offer some of the most direct connections. There are charter flights from all over Europe, including Great Britain. A huge number of tourists to Maldives come from Germany, and there are excellent air connections from that country's airports: LTU has daily flights from most major German cities; Condor runs two flights a week from Frankfurt and München; Air Lanka has three flights a week from Frankfurt via Colombo; and Emirates operates four times weekly from Frankfurt to Male by way of Dubai. From Zürich, Balair, Emirates, Air Lanka, and Pakistan International Airlines (PIA) all have service to Male. Lauda Air flies from Vienna every week, as do Austrian Airlines and Air Lanka. A total of 21 different airlines land at Male International Airport.

TRAVELING IN MALDIVES

Air Links Between Atolls

For several years now, Maldives has had great air links between individual atolls and islands. The companies *Hummingbird* and *Maldive Air Taxi* operate helicopter and modern single- and twin-engine seaplanes, which cut down considerable on travel time. On Hulhule, there's a special "water airport" for these craft. Many resort islands have set up landing space within their lagoons. Because of their popularity, air taxis are gaining the upper hand over the helicopters; excess baggage travels more slowly, by boat.

The national airline Air Maldives operates domestic flights to four local airstrips: to the south, 260 km from Male, Kadhdhoo Airport in the Haddumati Atoll; Kaadedhdhoo Airport in the Gaaf-Dhaal Atoll, 416 km away; and Gan's airport, 545 km away in the Addhoo Atoll, as well as Hannimadu Airport in the northerly Tiladummati Atoll, 287 km from Male.

Boat Safaris (see p. 228)

Organized water safaris are available for diving, sailing, and simple sightseeing trips. Safaris last from five to ten days; regions of preference are the North and South Male Atolls and the Baa, Ari, Faadhippolu, and Felidhoo Atolls. The current trend is leading to larger and larger cruise ships, which lumber through the atolls like floating hotels ("Floatel"). The average normal safari boat has some 8 to 10 cabins to accommodate 20 guests; but the new generation of cruise ships takes 100 (*Ocean Paradise*) to 156 (*Island Explorer*) passengers. As of May, 1998, there were 46 licensed safari ships plying Maldivian waters.

PRACTICAL TIPS FROM A TO Z

Accommodations

Sojourns on Maldives are generally booked as package deals: a two-week stay, including flight, hotel transfer, and full board, for a fixed price. At Christmas and Easter, prices are somewhat higher. Difference in individual prices is contingent on the price class of a bungalow (depending on size and comfort level) and the resort's amenities (swimming pool, tennis court, etc.). All accommodations on Maldives can be classified as between an average three- and five-star hotel. The best way to arrange a trip to Maldives is to book a package tour with your local travel agent. Individual bookings are to be avoided at all costs; even if you have a written confirmation of your reservation in hand from the island's management, they may well disregard it if they're booked out with a package tour when you arrive. Some hotels even offer all-inclusive packages, though in most cases there are considerable surcharges for beverages and sports activities. A PADI Open Water course, including test and certificate, costs around US$475; a single dive runs about $35. A bottle of mineral water (1.5 l) costs between $3 and $5. Nonetheless, you need to keep drinking as much as you can; it's very important in this hot climate, in the salt air.

In Male there are three leading hotels and some 30 guest houses. An acceptable single or double room generally costs between $20/$30 and $70/80. You don't need a special permit to stay in the capital, unlike other native inhabited islands.

Alcohol

In the Moslem Republic of Maldives alcohol is simply not for sale. The exception, of course, are the resort islands, where you can get a complete range of beverages; but they're extremely expensive. Safari boats with a special license are allowed to serve "soft alcohol," which is to say beer and wine. Even tourists aren't allowed to bring alcohol into the country.

Atolls

Usually, atolls in Maldives are known by their traditional names, which are generally very long and difficult for foreigners to pronounce. Increasingly, however, you encounter the simpler, official administrative designation. Each of the 20 administrative districts has been assigned a letter of the Roman alphabet, which you can see, for example, on the prows of local dhonis, where it has to be clearly visible so that the boat's provenance is easy to identify. The following listing of the atolls gives first the geographic name, then the administrative name and the letter in parentheses.

North Tiladummati (Haa Alifu, A)
South Tiladummati (Haa Dhaal, B)
North Miladummadulu (Shaviyani, C)
South Miladummadulu (Noonu, D)
North Maalhosmadulu (Raa, E)
South Maalhosmadulu (Baa, F)
Faddhippolhu (Lhaviyani, G)
Male (Kaafu, H)
North Ari (Alifu Utturu, I)
South Ari (Alifu Dekuno, I)
Felidhoo (Vaavu, J)
Mulaku (Meemu, K)
North Nilandu (Faaf, L)
South Nilandu (Dhaal, M)
Kolumadulu (Thaa, N)
Haddummati (Laamu, O)
North Huvadhu (Gaaf Alifu, P)
South Huvadhu (Gaaf Dhaal, Q)
Fua Mulaku (Gnaviyani, R)
Addhoo (Seenu, S)

Bookstores

On Male there are a number of small bookstores that stock a limited selection of picture books in a number of languages. The best selection can be found at the venerable Novelty Bookshop in Male and the Airport Shop. The resort islands also generally carry a number of books about Maldives.

Customs Regulations

Bringing alcohol, pork products, any kind of pornographic media or literature (incl. magazines like *Playboy*), weapons, explosives, drugs, harpoons, and condoms into Maldives is strictly prohibited. If you have used video cassettes with you, they'll be tested in Male, although empty cassettes for your own video camera, in their original packaging, can come through with no problem. Anything with a value of more than Rf 150,000 (about $ 14,000) as to be declared upon entering the country. Be careful when bringing in a strikingly large amount of any medication; a doctor's prescription with the name of the medication will help facilitate proceedings.

There is a strict ban on exporting any products that fall under the Washington Endangered Species Protection Agreement, although such articles are still sold all over Maldives. Don't buy them.

Dining

As the restaurants on the resort islands generally cater to tourists, they're geared to European palates and vary their menus every day. There are a number of rice dishes with tasty, fresh-caught fish and a wide selection of mild curries.

The local Maldivian cuisine is excellent, and well worth sampling. You can only find "home cooking," if at all, in the a la carte restaurants on some of the resort islands.

Drugs

Any kind of drug possession, including that of seeds for drug plants, is strictly prohibited on Maldives. Even tourists who violate this law are threatened with drastic punishment, including lifelong imprisonment.

Electricity

The current on Maldives is 220 V / 50 Hz; plugs are the three-pronged variety used in England. An adapter will enable you to use European appliances, but for American ones, you'll need a transformer or converter, as well. Some hotels have adapters available for the use of guests.

Emergency

In an emergency, the first place to go is the reception area of your hotel, where all of the necessary measures will be taken. Important emergency numbers on Male: **Ambulance** 102, **Fire Department** 118, **Police** 119. As few of the police speak English, a translator is advisable.

For divers, Bandos, in the North Male Atoll, has a **decompression chamber**, staffed round the clock with a diving doctor and qualified personnel. Tel. 440088.

Festivals and Holidays

The weekly day off is Friday, which is the Islamic equivalent of Sunday. In ad-

dition, there are 10 to 13 flexible holidays a year. These religious holidays follow the Islamic calendar, which began in the year AD 622 with the *hedshra*, Mohammed's emigration from Mecca to Medina (the year 1999 is therefore the Moslem year 1420). This calendar is calculated according to the lunar year, which is eleven days shorter than the solar year. As a result, religious holidays and the start of Ramadan move backwards through our calendar; they're eleven days earlier every year. The most important dates in 1998: Islamic New Year: April 27; the birthday of the prophet Mohammed: July 6; Huravee Day, celebrating independence from the Portuguese: September 24; Martyrs' Day or Maulid: November 20; start of the fasting month of Ramadan: December 20. In addition, there are fixed holidays on the Christian calendar, such as New Year's Day on January 1, Independence Day on July 26 and 27, Day of Victory on November 3, and National Day on December 11 and 12.

In the fasting month of Ramadan, Muslims (except for children, sick people, and pregnant women) are not supposed to eat or drink from sunrise to sunset. Any tourists visiting the native islands at such times have to observe this restriction as well. On the resort islands, of course, visitors can eat and drink normally, and the restaurants are all open.

Fishing

Nearly all the resort islands offer deep-sea fishing excursions as well as day and night fishing trips. You can also fish from a dhoni with rod and reel. Fishing from the island landing stage, however, is not allowed; and bringing nets and harpoons into the country, or using them at all, is strictly prohibited.

Hours of Business

Friday is the day of rest in the Muslim week, comparable to Sunday in Europe.

In Male, everything is closed on Fridays; only a few shops, which are open on other days from 8 am-noon and 12:30-10 pm, open for business at 2 pm on Friday afternoons. Many shops also close during daily prayers. Administrative offices are open daily, except Friday and Saturday, from 7:30 am-1:30 pm. Banks are open daily from 9 am-1 pm. Business hours may be irregular and unpredictable during the "fasting month" of Ramadan.

Medical Facilities

In case of illness or emergency, local diving schools can provide first aid. Only a few islands have the luxury of a permanent "island doctor." Acute cases are transported to Male, where there's a modern hospital, Indira Gandhi Hospital (tel. 316647), as well as two private clinics (AMDC Hospital, tel. 325979, and ADK Private Hospital, tel. 324331). Although examinations are free of charge, foreign patients have to pay for any more extensive procedures in advance, and settle up with their insurance providers when they get back to their own countries. In case of serious illness, contact your consular representative (see "Addresses") or appeal to the representative of your tour organizer on the island you're staying on.

Media

Maldives has its own radio station, *Voice of Maldives*, which broadcasts, in Dhivehi, from 5:30 am-10:45 pm. There is an English news broadcast every day at 6:30 pm. The national TV station often broadcasts prayers from the Koran as well as Indian film epics and news in the local language, or sometimes, in English.

The daily papers "Haveeru," "Aufathis" and "Miradhu," published in in Thaana, the writtten variant of the local language, all have one to two pages of current information in English. You can get English magazines on Male or on many of the resort islands.

Museum

The only museum in Maldives is the National Museum in Male. Located in the old Sultans' Park, it displays a true cross-section of various objects from the country's history in 10 galleries. Administered by directors who are German researchers from the Roman-Germanic Museum in Cologne, the museum is presently going through a phase of restructuring. It is open daily except Fridays and holidays 9 am-noon and 3-6 pm. The Sultans' Park is open daily (including Friday) from 4-6:30 pm.

Nude Bathing

Nude, or even topless, bathing is punishable on Maldives by a fine of US$ 1,000 or even deportation.

Pharmacies

To supplement your own traveling medicine cabinet, the hotels generally stock the most common medications. If you need any kind of special medication, make sure to bring an adequate supply with you. If you're bringing in large numbers of tablets, a doctor's prescription will facilitate matters with the customs officials. In Male, there's a pharmacy with a large selection of international medications right next door to the Indira Gandhi Hospital.

Photography

When taking pictures, photographers should take into account the shy restraint that typifies the local mentality and always ask permission first. Older individuals will often say no, and their wishes should be respected. Younger residents, especially children, will ask the photographer for a "small present," generally meaning one or two dollar bills.

The secret of capturing a postcard-blue sky and turquoise lagoon is to use filters that cut down on extraneous reflection and light. Sunsets are best photographed from a tripod, without use of flash.

Photographing government buildings or any facilities of the National Security Service is not allowed.

It's a good idea to bring adequate film along with you. In the bright light of the islands, the best film is not too sensitive, with an ASA of 50 to 100. Always try to keep your camera and film equpment out of direct sunlight, and store film in cool, shady places. The quality of film and developing of slides and prints on Maldives is questionable at best. The safest way to transport film is in lead bags that guard against damage from the x-ray equipment at the airport.

Post Office

Male's post office is located on Chandani Magu. Postcards from Maldives to Europe take stamps of Rf 3; air mail letters, Rf 10. It takes anywhere from ten days to three weeks for a letter to reach its destination. Maldives's stamps, appreciated by philatelists around the globe, are sold in souvenir shops on the resort islands or at the postcard stands in Male. The post office is open Sat-Thu from 7:30 am-1:30 pm and 4-5:30 pm.

Souvenirs

Popular souvenirs from Maldives include fine raffia mats with attractive patterns made of rushes (cadjan mats) or palm fronds (suvadiva mats) and gorgeous lacquerware on ornate wooden boxes and vases, manufactured on Thuladhoo in the South Maalhosmadulu Atoll. Also popular are hand-carved models of the traditional dhonis, made of palm wood without glue, assembled by means of careful joins.

Unfortunately, many shops still sell objects made of natural ocean products, such as sharks' teeth, coral necklaces, tortoiseshell, or prepared fish, all of which violate the Washington Endangered Species Protection Agreement. Don't buy any of these tasteless and wasteful items! In Male, fortunately, you can buy wonderful, colorful, handmade tropical fish carved of wood, attractive souvenirs that slide easily through customs. Another distinctive Maldives souvenir are *bodu badhis*, two-level vessels made of coconut shells bound together with coconut fiber to collect the sap of the palm blossoms. Shops on the resort islands and at the airport offer a small selection of distinctive souvenirs.

Taxis

In 1996, the city of Male, though less than 3 square kilometers in area, has an incredible 271 registered taxis. However, you can generally get to wherever you want to go faster on foot; it's only worth taking a taxi if you have a lot of luggage. None of the taxis has a meter, so you have to negotiate the price beforehand; the basic fare, regardless of where you're going or how long the trip, is about $1.

Telephone

If you're calling from abroad, the country code for Maldives is +960, after which you dial the six-digit phone number. There are no local area codes for the individual atolls or islands. If you're calling from Maldives, you simply dial 00 plus the country code (that is, 001 for the U.S. and Canada, 0044 for Great Britain) plus area code plus number to place an international direct dial call. Many hotel rooms have IDD (International Direct Dial) phones for their guests, enabling them to call all over the world. Be warned, however, that from a resort island the first three minutes of a call can cost US$20 to $25, with $8 for every additional minute. Calls are slightly cheaper from the Communication Office Dhiraagu in Male. There, you can buy telephone cards which you can use in some of Male's telephone booths, and even on some inhabited islands, to place international calls.

Information/Operator: for Maldives 110, international 190.

Time Difference

The time difference between Greenwich Mean Time (London) and Maldives is six hours in winter, five in summer. There's eleven hours' time difference between Eastern Standard Time (Washington, DC) and Maldives (when it's 7 am in New York, it's 6 pm on Male); while Pacific Standard Time (Los Angeles) is 14 hours off. Some islands keep a so-called "island time" which creates another half hour's difference.

Tipping

Tipping is generally expected everwhere. On the resort islands, $5 a week for the chamberboy and waiter are a noble sum. Bellboys should get $1 for every piece of luggage. Keep in mind the relative value of money in terms of the locals' low income. If someone does you a small favor, he'll probably appreciate a cigarette or a Coke.

Towels

If you want "spring-fresh" towels, you'd be wise to bring your own. The hotels do lay out fresh towels every day, but because of the humidity of the climate, these don't always exude the freshness and odor one might desire.

Valuables

All of the resort islands have safes in the reception area as a repository for guests' valuables, even though theft is highly uncommon on Maldives. Some hotels have even equipped all of their bungalows with mini-safes, where guests can store documents and valuables. In any case, no one should take expensive jewelry along when they travel.

Water

Drinking water on Maldives is in short supply. Hotels often use desalination equipment and rainwater cisterns for fresh water. Some islands even have a well, but the water is often slightly salty and brackish, and should only be used for showers: don't drink it by any means, since it may contain germs. For drinking and brushing your teeth, hotels often place a thermos of fresh water in the room, which is a better option.

Weights and Measures

Maldives has gone over completely to the metric system. Temperatures are sometimes still given in Fahrenheit (°F); for conversion table, see page 240.

GLOSSARY

Dhivehi, the local language, is a member of the Indo-Iranian language family, with roots in Singhalese and Tamil. In its written form, the language is called Thaana; it's written from right to left. In Male and in the Addhoo Atoll, many of the locals speak English.

Good day! . . . . *Salaam aleku*
How are you? . . . . . *Haalu kihineh?*
Good, fine . . . . *Rangalu*
Thank you . . . . *Shukriyya*
Yes . . . . *Aanh*
No . . . . *Noon*
What is that? . . . . *E korche?*
How much does that cost? . . . .
. . . . *Mi kihavaraka?*
expensive . . . . *Agu bodu*
cheap . . . . *Agu heo*
What is there to eat? . . *Kong kaa-etche huri?*
left . . . . *kanai*
right . . . . *wai*

ADDRESSES

Information

Maldives: Ministry of Tourism, Boduthakurufaanu Magu, Male, Republic of Maldives, tel. 323224, fax 322512, E-Mail: info@visitmaldives.com, Internet: http://www.visitmaldives.com.
Note: This website, in English, is a good source of information on all aspects of

Maldives travel, including resorts, prices, photographs, etc.

Sri Lanka: High Commission of The Republic of Maldives in Sri Lanka, 25 Melbourne Avenue, Colombo, Sri Lanka, tel. (01)586762, fax (01)581200.

You can also get information from local consular offices (see below).

Consulates / Embassies on Maldives and in the Vicinity

U.K.: The Honorary Consular Correspondent of the U.K. on Maldives is Mr. Bob Ure, M. Ocean Land 2, Mageedhee Magu, Male, c/o Dhiraagu Pvt., Ltd., P.O. Box 2080, Male, tel. 311205.

U.S.: There used to be an American Consulate in Male, but it's closed. The nearest consular representation is the U.S. Embassy on Sri Lanka at 210 Galle Road, Colombo 3, tel. 448007.

Diplomatic Representation of the Republic of Maldives Abroad

U.K.: High Commissioner of Maldives, 22 Nottingham Place, London W1M 3FB, tel. +44 171 2242135.

U.S.: Permanent Mission of Maldives to the United Nations, 800 2nd Avenue, Suite 400E, New York, NY, 10017, tel. (212) 599 6194.

AUTHORS

Christian Mietz, born in 1959, went to Maldives in 1985 and ran the diving bases on Little Huraa (Kuda Huraa) and Ellaidhoo. He works as a freelance journalist for diving and travel magazines, and has written a number of books on diving. His underwater photography has captured several awards.

Claus-Peter Stoll, born in 1952, is a diving and travel journalist and co-author of a number of books on dive sites in the tropics. He's been traveling to Maldives regularly for many years.

Special thanks to **Dr. Klaus Becker**, who collected the information for the features on "Flora" and "Fauna," as well as to **Mr. Adil** and **Mrs. Lahr** of the **Maldives Government Tourist Information Office** for their help and countless useful tips.

PHOTOGRAPHERS

Explore the World

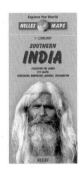

AVAILABLE TITLES

Afghanistan 1 : 1 500 000
Australia 1 : 4 000 000
Bangkok - *and Greater Bangkok*
1 : 75 000 / 1 : 15 000
Burma → *Myanmar*
Caribbean - *Bermuda, Bahamas,
Greater Antilles* 1 : 2 500 000
Caribbean - *Lesser Antilles*
1 : 2 500 000
Central America 1 : 1 750 000
Central Asia 1 : 1 750 000
China - *Northeastern*
1 : 1 500 000
China - *Northern* 1 : 1 500 000
China - *Central* 1 : 1 500 000
China - *Southern* 1 : 1 500 000
Colombia - *Ecuador* 1 : 2 500 000
Crete - Kreta 1 : 200 000
Dominican Republic - **Haiti**
1 : 600 000
Egypt 1 : 2 500 000 / 1 : 750 000
Hawaiian Islands
1 : 330 000 / 1 : 125 000
Hawaiian Islands – **Kaua'i**
1 : 150 000 / 1 : 35 000
Hawaiian Islands – **Honolulu**
- **O'ahu** 1 : 35 000 / 1 : 150 000

Hawaiian Islands – **Maui - Moloka'i
- Lāna'i** 1 : 150 000 / 1 : 35 000
Hawaiian Islands – **Hawai'i, The Big
Island** 1 : 330 000 / 1 : 125 000
Himalaya 1 : 1 500 000
Hong Kong 1 : 22 500
Indian Subcontinent 1 : 4 000 000
India - *Northern* 1 : 1 500 000
India - *Western* 1 : 1 500 000
India - *Eastern* 1 : 1 500 000
India - *Southern* 1 : 1 500 000
India - *Northeastern - Bangladesh*
1 : 1 500 000
Indonesia 1 : 4 000 000
Indonesia *Sumatra* 1 : 1 500 000
Indonesia *Java - Nusa Tenggara*
1 : 1 500 000
Indonesia *Bali - Lombok*
1 : 180 000
Indonesia *Kalimantan*
1 : 1 500 000
Indonesia *Java - Bali* 1 : 650 000
Indonesia *Sulawesi* 1 : 1 500 000
Indonesia *Irian Jaya - Maluku*
1 : 1 500 000
Jakarta 1 : 22 500
Japan 1 : 1 500 000

Kenya 1 : 1 100 000
Korea 1 : 1 500 000
Malaysia 1 : 1 500 000
West Malaysia 1 : 650 000
Manila 1 : 17 500
Mexico 1 : 2 500 000
Myanmar (Burma) 1 : 1 500 000
Nepal 1 : 500 000 / 1 : 1 500 000
Trekking Map *Khumbu Himal -
Solu Khumbu* 1 : 75 000
New Zealand 1 : 1 250 000
Pakistan 1 : 1 500 000
Peru - *Ecuador* 1 : 2 500 000
Philippines 1 : 1 500 000
Singapore 1 : 22 500
Southeast Asia 1 : 4 000 000
South Pacific Islands 1 : 13 000 000
Sri Lanka 1 : 450 000
Taiwan 1 : 400 000
Tanzania - *Rwanda, Burundi*
1 : 1 500 000
Thailand 1 : 1 500 000
Uganda 1 : 700 000
Venezuela - *Guyana, Suriname,
French Guiana* 1 : 2 500 000
Vietnam, Laos, Cambodia
1 : 1 500 000

*Nelles Maps are top quality!
Relief mapping, kilometer charts and tourist attractions.
Always up-to-date!*

Explore the World

AVAILABLE TITLES

Australia
Bali / Lombok
Berlin and Potsdam
Brazil
Brittany
Burma → Myanmar
California
  Las Vegas, Reno,
  Baja California
Cambodia / Laos
Canada
  Ontario, Québec,
  Atlantic Provinces
Canada
  Pacific Coast, the Rockies,
  Prairie Provinces, and
  the Territories
Caribbean
  The Greater Antilles,
  Bermuda, Bahamas
Caribbean
  The Lesser Antilles
China – Hong Kong
Corsica
Costa Rica
Crete
Croatia – *Adriatic Coast*
Cyprus
Egypt
Florida
Greece – *The Mainland*

Hawai'i
Hungary
India
  Northern, Northeastern
  and Central India
India – *Southern India*
Indonesia
  Sumatra, Java, Bali,
  Lombok, Sulawesi
Ireland
Israel - *with Excursions*
  to Jordan
Kenya
London, England and
  Wales
Malaysia - Singapore
  - Brunei
Maldives
Mexico
Morocco
Moscow / St. Petersburg
Munich
  Excursions to Castles,
  Lakes & Mountains
Myanmar (Burma)
Nepal
New York – *City and State*
New Zealand
Paris
Philippines
Portugal

Prague / Czech Republic
Provence
Rome
Scotland
South Africa
South Pacific Islands
Spain – *Pyrenees, Atlantic*
  Coast, Central Spain
Spain
  Mediterranean Coast,
  Southern Spain,
  Balearic Islands
Sri Lanka
Syria – Lebanon
Tanzania
Thailand
Turkey
Tuscany
U.S.A.
  The East, Midwest and South
U.S.A.
  The West, Rockies and Texas
Vietnam

FORTHCOMING

Canary Islands
Greek Islands
Norway
Poland
Sweden

Nelles Guides – authoritative, informed and informative.
Always up-to-date, extensively illustrated, and with first-rate relief maps.
256 pages, approx. 150 color photos, approx. 25 maps.